UNDERSTANDING RESEARCH IN EDUCATION

This text provides a solid introduction to the foundations of research methods, with the goal of enabling students and professionals in various fields of education to not simply become casual consumers of research who passively read bits and pieces of research articles, but *discerning* consumers able to effectively use published research for practical purposes in educational settings. All issues important for understanding and using published research for these purposes are covered. Key principles are illustrated with research studies published in refereed journals across a wide spectrum of education. Exercises distributed throughout the text encourage readers to engage interactively with what they are reading at the point when the information is fresh in their minds. This text is designed for higher level undergraduate and graduate programs. Course instructors will find that it provides a solid framework in which to promote student interaction and discussion on important issues in research methodology.

Fred L. Perry, Jr. is Professor Emeritus at the American University in Cairo, Egypt and an independent contractor with Grand Canyon Education, Inc., Grand Canyon University.

Joe D. Nichols taught middle and high school mathematics for 15 years and is now a Professor in the Department of Educational Studies at Indiana University – Purdue University, Fort Wayne.

UNDERSTANDING RESEARCH IN EDUCATION

Becoming a Discerning Consumer

Fred L. Perry, Jr. and Joe D. Nichols

Routledge
Taylor & Francis Group

NEW YORK AND LONDON

First published 2015
by Routledge
711 Third Avenue, New York, NY 10017

and by Routledge
2 Park Square, Milton Park, Abingdon, Oxon, OX14 4RN

Routledge is an imprint of the Taylor & Francis Group, an informa business

Library of Congress Cataloging in Publication Data
Perry, Fred L. (Fred Lehman), 1943–
Understanding research in education: becoming a discerning consumer /
Fred L. Perry Jr., Joe D. Nichols.
pages cm
1. Education—Research. I. Title.
LB1028.P347 2014
370.72—dc23
2014004332

ISBN: 978-1-138-77641-8 (hbk)
ISBN: 978-1-138-77642-5 (pbk)
ISBN: 978-1-315-77318-6 (ebk)

Typeset in Bembo
by Book Now Ltd, London

DEDICATION

We dedicate this book to our wives, who always give us their unconditional support and help us to stay practical at the applied level, and to all those discerning consumers of research.

CONTENTS

Preface   xi
Acknowledgments   xvii

PART I
Fundamentals for Discerning Consumers   **1**

1   Understanding the Nature of Research   3
     Introduction   3
         What Is All This Research About?   3
         Who Is All This Research for?   3
         Is All of This Research Really That Important?   4
         If Educational Research Is so Important, How Can
             We Understand it Better?   4
         Overview   4
     Who Is a Discerning Consumer of Research?   5
     Why Be a Consumer of Research?   5
     The Motivation Behind Research   6
         Demythologizing Research   6
         The Meaning of True Research   7
         Identifying Important Questions   8
         Where Are the Answers?   11
     Key Terms and Concepts   17
     Note   18
     References   18

2   How to Locate Research   20
    Chapter Overview   20
    Where to Look and What to Look for?   20
        Preliminary Sources   21
        Secondary Sources   25
        Tables of References/Bibliographies   28
    Is All Primary Research of Equal Weight?   28
    Differentiating Primary From Secondary   31
    How to Obtain Research Articles   33
    What Journals Are Related to the Field of Education?   34
    Key Terms and Concepts   35
    Additional Recommended Reading   35
    References   35

PART II
The Major Components of Published Research   **37**

3   Understanding the Framework of a Primary Research Article   39
    Chapter Overview   39
    The Framework of a Research Article   39
        The Title   39
        The Abstract   41
        The Introduction of a Study   43
        Method   46
        Results   52
        Discussion/Conclusion   52
    Key Terms and Concepts   53
    Notes   53
    References   53

4   Understanding Where Data Come From: The Sample   55
    Chapter Overview   55
    Sampling Terminology   55
    Sampling Paradigms   56
        The Representative Sampling Paradigm   58
        The Purposeful Sampling Paradigm: Sample Strategies for
        Maximizing Information   64
    Ethics in Sampling Human Participants   69
    Key Terms and Concepts   70
    Additional Recommended Reading   71
    Notes   71
    References   72

5   Understanding Research Designs   74
    Chapter Overview   74
    Classifying Research Designs   75
        The Basic–Applied Continuum   75
        The Qualitative–Quantitative Continuum   77
        The Exploratory–Confirmatory Continuum   82
    Questions and Designs   84
        The WHAT Questions   85
        The WHY Questions   88
    Internal Validity   92
    Key Terms and Concepts   107
    Additional Recommended Reading   108
    Notes   108
    References   108

6   Understanding Data Gathering   112
    Chapter Overview   112
    Collecting and Evaluating Verbal Data   113
        Observational Procedures   113
        Evaluating the Dependability of Verbal Data Procedures   121
    Collecting and Evaluating Numerical Data   126
        Procedures for Gathering Numerical Data   127
        Evaluating the Qualities of Numerical Data-Gathering Procedures 135
    Key Terms and Concepts   149
    Additional Recommended Reading   149
    Notes   150
    References   150

7   Understanding Research Results   152
    Chapter Overview   152
    Introduction to Data Analysis   152
        Numerical Versus Verbal Data   152
        Common Procedure   153
    Analysis of Verbal Data   153
        Evaluating Patterns and Themes   155
        Evaluating Explanations and Conclusions   158
    Analysis of Numerical Data   163
        Overview of Statistics   164
        Understanding Descriptive Statistics   165
        Understanding Inferential Statistics   166
        Inferential Statistical Procedures   170
    Key Terms and Concepts   188
    Additional Recommended Reading   189

Notes   189
References   189

8   Discerning Discussions and Conclusions: Completing
   the Picture   192
   Chapter Overview   192
   The Needed Ingredients   193
   Questions Every Consumer Should Ask   193
   References   199

Appendix A: Constructing a Literature Review   200
   Why Do a Review of Research?   200
   Where to Begin   202
   Abstracting Primary Literature   203
   Writing a Review of Research   205
   Meta-Analysis   206
   References   208

Appendix B: Going to the Next Level of Statistics   209
   More About Descriptive Statistics   209
      Types of Scales   209
      Shape of the Data Distribution   211
      The Average   214
      Data Variance   217
   More About Inferential Statistics   218
      Univariate Versus Multivariate Procedures   218
      More on Univariate ANOVAs   218
      Multivariate ANOVAs   220
      Degrees of Freedom   222
      Type II Error and Power   223
      Effect Size   224
   Key Terms and Concepts   225
   Notes   225
   References   225

Glossary   227
Index   236

PREFACE

This book is based on a previous book written by Prof. Fred L. Perry, Jr. (*Research in Applied Linguistics: Becoming a Discerning Consumer*, 2011, Routledge). The focus of that book was toward applied linguistics. However, the research principles in that book can be generalized to many disciplines. Several professionals in the field of education have expressed the need for a book like this for the wide area of education. Prof. Perry has used his first book as a template to develop this book. Prof. Joe D. Nichols agreed to join him in adjusting the first book for the area of education. Prof. Nichols took on the huge task to find appropriate examples and illustrations from various areas of education for this purpose.

This book is specifically written for those who want and need to be consumers of research—administrators, teachers, students, parents of students, but especially for MA students in various branches of education. These students tend to be thrown into the deep end of the pool of research from the first day they enter their programs, and find it necessary to become consumers of research overnight to fulfill the assignments given by their instructors. This text is designed to assist them in getting up to speed. The goal is not to develop just casual consumers who passively read bits and pieces of a research article, but discerning consumers who will read research reports from beginning to end with a level of understanding that can be used to address both theoretical and practical issues. Once this stage is reached, consumers will no longer look upon research journals as forbidding, boring documents that only university professors find interesting. Rather, they will regard them as important sources of evidence or counter evidence that can be used in arguing the pros and/or cons of implementing new ideas and methodologies in educational settings.

Organization of the Text

This book is organized in two parts. Part I introduces the reader to the fundamentals required for becoming a discerning consumer. Chapter 1 distinguishes between common conceptions of the meaning of research and how it is understood among professional researchers. It also discusses the driving force behind the entire research process: the research question(s)—the question(s) that guides the choices researchers make when planning and carrying out their studies.

Chapter 2 is intended to help students get a jump start on how to find research articles, through both traditional and electronic methods. Basic information accompanied by several walk-through examples is provided. Appendix A features detailed instructions on how to write a review of research. However, we have also included other ways to summarize research including meta-analysis. These instructions are put in an appendix at the end of the book, rather than in Chapter 2, so that readers can complete a review of research after they have become discerning consumers. Putting this material in an appendix also allows an instructor to assign reading this material at any time felt appropriate.

Part II is structured around the order in which each component appears in a typical research report used by most research journals. Chapter 3, the first chapter of this section, maps out these components along with brief explanations, and then examines the functions of the Title, the Abstract, and the Introduction in a typical study, along with descriptions of criteria used for evaluating these components. Here, and throughout the text, we aim at helping readers integrate the many aspects of research methodology by synthesizing them into graphic illustrations. This may appear to be somewhat reductionistic—that is, to leave out details some instructors might consider important—but our experience continues to lead us to understand that up-and-coming discerning consumers of research need to first develop a big picture schematic view of research before dealing with too many details. Once this overall framework is in place, the consumer will be able to accommodate whatever additional information considered important as time progresses.

In this regard, Chapter 4 focuses on sampling by introducing special terminology and then uses two broad sampling paradigms to encompass more detailed sampling techniques. It closes by looking at the ethics that need to be observed with using human participants in research.

Chapter 5, which deals with research designs, is in three sections. The first summarizes three related dimensions for classifying research, taking the reader beyond the somewhat limiting quantitative–qualitative debate, to provide a more realistic picture of research. The second section examines different research designs that answer the main research questions of what and why. The final section elaborates the principle of internal validity which is essential to evaluating the design used in a study.

Chapter 6 provides a conceptual framework to help the reader understand the numerous ways data are collected. It is divided into two sections. The first addresses how verbal data are collected and evaluated. The second looks at how numerical data are gathered and examined. In both sections, issues related to the quality and stability of the data are discussed.

Chapter 7 naturally follows by looking at how data are analyzed—whether verbal or numerical. Our intent is for readers to be able to look into the Results section of a research article with enough confidence to critically evaluate whether appropriate procedures have been used and correct interpretations have been made. This chapter is divided into two main sections. Section "Analysis of Verbal Data" relates to how verbal data are analyzed and interpreted. Over recent years, there have been important strides made in how to evaluate these procedures. We provide an overview abstracted from the leading authorities in this area. Section "Analysis of Numerical Data" focuses on numerical data. Here we discuss statistical issues without using formulas. Our goal is to not inundate the reader with more information than a consumer of research needs. We have approached this topic in layers according to frequency of use in the literature and relevance to the reader. The first layer is presented in this chapter. The next layer is presented in Appendix B containing important information but less common and a little more complex. In both layers, statistics are approached conceptually. Our contention is that consumers of research do not need to know math formulas to understand statistical concepts, but they do need to know why certain procedures are followed, how to interpret them, and whether they are appropriately used.

Chapter 8, the final chapter, provides a set of criteria by which to appraise the Discussion and Conclusion section of the typical research report. Here readers are drawn to examine the logical thinking researchers engage in when interpreting results, formulating answers to the research questions, generalizing to target populations, and discussing how results are applied to practical problems.

Selection and Use of Studies for Illustrations

We have illustrated each major point in the book with at least one research study published in a refereed journal where possible. When choosing these studies, we tried to follow five criteria. (1) The study should provide a clear example of the point being made. (2) It should be as recent as possible at the time of writing this book. (3) The topics of the research studies should vary to expose the reader to some of the breadth of the issues being researched in education. (4) The studies should come from a wide a variety of journals to familiarize readers with a good sample of the type of journals available. (5) Studies should look at the teaching and learning in different subject areas. After applying all five criteria, the possibilities were narrowed down considerably.

Though most of the studies used point out how certain criteria were met, on several occasions we identify where studies might have weaknesses in relation to the evaluative criteria being discussed. Our rationale is that readers' critical skills need to be sharpened to help them develop into discerning consumers of research. It is not enough to simply state that some published studies have certain weaknesses; the reader needs to see actual examples where such weaknesses did occur or could have occurred. The key word here is discernment, which does not mean fault finding. We do not want readers to become cynics who delight in slamming researchers on every little perceived weakness, but rather to develop a healthy skepticism. The objective is for readers to gain confidence in their own ability to assess research so that they will be able to evaluate the influence any one study should have on practical issues of concern. (Any researcher who has published one of the studies we used for this purpose should not take offense. No study is perfect, including our own.) On occasion, we tried to use some subtle humor to lighten up the reading, especially when dealing with heavy issues. This is risky, we know, because humor, like beauty, varies in the eye of the beholder and is very cultural. However, we have taken some risk because we think research should not be perceived as a dry, boring affair. Our goal is that every once in a while the reader might crack a smile even when reading difficult material.

The exercises distributed throughout the chapters play an important role. Our students come to class with questions generated from their work on these exercises. This leads to a very lively Q and A during the class period. They are expected to share their work with the rest of the class and respond to questions based on their assignments. Not only does this help individual students apply the criteria being learned on research studies, which match their own interest, it also exposes the entire class to a variety of studies and journals. By the end of the class session, students' exposure to how these criteria have been applied to recent research studies in different journals has grown exponentially.

The strategy that we use for interspersing exercises throughout the chapters, rather than placing them at the end, is based on the notion of the effects of adjunct aids. Based on research Prof. Perry and others did some years ago (e.g., Cunningham, Snowman, Miller, & Perry, 1982; Perry, 1982), they found that interspersed questions and exercises create strategic pauses for students to digest and apply what they have been reading. This creates an atmosphere which encourages readers to engage interactively with the text at the time of reading, when information is still fresh in their minds.

Rather than use a lock-step strategy of assigning readers the same article, the exercises allow students to select research articles on topics related to their own interest. Although using a lock-step strategy would make things simpler for us as instructors, in that everyone would have to respond to the same research articles, we have found that many students, especially graduate students, are not interested in topics that we think are interesting (can you believe it)! Our experience is that giving students the freedom to follow their own interests increases student motivation and appreciation for the course. It also enhances their confidence in their ability to find and work with published research. Finally, it encourages autonomous thinking.

Our hope is that this book is useful for achieving the goal of helping readers who work with education issues to become discerning consumers of research. Whether it is used as a textbook or independently studied, we believe that anyone wanting to improve his or her ability to understand research will find this book instrumental for achieving this goal. However, it is also important to keep in mind that this is just an introduction with the intention of providing a framework with which to begin one's search for answers to research questions related to educational matter.

References

Cunningham, D. J., Snowman, J., Miller, R. B., & Perry, F. L. (1982). Verbal and nonverbal adjunct aids to concrete and abstract prose memory. *Journal of Experimental Education*, 51, 8–13.

Perry, F. L. (1982). Test-like events: An aid to learning. *Singapore Journal of Education, 4*, 44–47.

ACKNOWLEDGMENTS

Like a small snowball that we make and then roll it on the snow to make a very big snowball to build a snowman, this book has developed in a very similar way. First, there was a first edition of a research book for people in applied linguistics, then a second edition, and now it has morphed into a research book for those in education. The number of people who have contributed to helping us build this book is beyond listing here. However, both of us clearly acknowledge the students who have provided us a sounding board for honing our thinking through continual engagement. We also want to thank Rebecca Novick and Trevor Gori at Routledge for their tireless assistance and professional advice to bring this book to completion.

PART I
Fundamentals for Discerning Consumers

1

UNDERSTANDING THE NATURE OF RESEARCH

Introduction

The amount of research in education pouring off of the presses today is staggering. Over 4,100 people presented papers in 296 areas of educational research at the 2013 American Educational Research Association (AERA) annual meeting. The authors of many of these papers will try to publish them in various research journals. The number of journals that publish research related to the many areas of education is beyond listing. Can you imagine how many research studies are published just this last year?

So what is all this research about? Who is it for? Is it important, and if so, how can we understand it better? Briefly, we will answer these questions, but the main purpose of this book is to answer the last question—how can we comprehend it all?

What Is All This Research About?

A quick answer is that research tries to provide answers to massive numbers of research questions that are being generated around the world in the areas of education. As mentioned above, there were 296 subject areas covered in the 2013 AERA annual meeting. The list is too long to present here, but you can get this at http://www.aera.net. Suffice it to say that research in the field of education covers topics that deal with just about anything related to education in society.

Who Is All This Research for?

It is for you, the person who, for whatever reason, wants or needs to gain a better understanding about educational issues that are important to you. This includes the following:

- Students working on their Masters or PhDs.
- Teachers in the classroom or working on advanced certificates.
- Administrators in the school systems.
- Parents of students who want to know more about what is impacting their children in the school systems.

Is All of This Research Really That Important?

Needless to say, education is the major way of maintaining society. Without it we would not know the world as we know it today. Literally everything that humanity has achieved would not have taken place without some form of education. Consequently, to study all that is involved in education is one of the major challenges that we believe we continually have before us today. Educational research has aided us in the improvement of teaching and learning of many studies throughout the world. Mankind's main hope is that this will contribute to humanity's understanding of one another and our environment to improve the quality of life and work toward an atmosphere of world peace.

If Educational Research Is so Important, How Can We Understand it Better?

This book is specifically designed to answer this question. We have divided it into two parts. The first consists of this chapter and Chapter 2, which will provide you with a foundation for working with the remaining chapters. This chapter introduces the concept of the *discerning consumer* and the meaning of research. The second chapter gives tools for finding research reports based on your own interests. Quickly mastering these simple guidelines will make accessible a wealth of information that can have a major impact on your career.

The chapters in Part II of the book are structured around the typical format used in published research. In them you will be given a set of criteria to evaluate each component of a research study. For each criterion, you are given excerpts from published research to illustrate how it is used for evaluation. By the end of the book, you should be able to approach any published study in education with confidence to not only understand it, but to evaluate its value for practical applications.

Overview

This chapter attempts to lay a foundation in building a framework for understanding a typical research study. We begin by defining the term *discerning consumer* and then argue for the importance of becoming one. This is followed by an attempt to demythologize how research is perceived by many people and then describe what it typically means to the educational community. In this description, a schematic understanding of the driving force behind research, the research question, is provided. With this perspective, you will be ready for the following chapters.

Who Is a Discerning Consumer of Research?

The term *consumer* in the business world means a customer—someone who buys and uses a product. In a similar fashion, readers of research are consumers in that they use research for specific purposes. To some degree, the readers of research might *buy into* the research product, if not actually pay money to obtain access to the research study.

There are two basic types of consumers: *casual* and *discerning*. *Casual* consumers are ones who passively read selective pieces of a research article out of curiosity. In the business world, they are the window shoppers who look, but do not buy. However, discerning consumers do more than window-shop. They want to use research for practical purposes; they want to read research reports from beginning to end with a level of understanding that can be used to address both theoretical and practical issues. We use the word discerning in two senses: penetrating and discriminating. In the first sense, discerning consumers are given the necessary tools to penetrate beyond the surface of the text to analyze the rationale behind the procedures used and the interpretations made. In the second sense, discerning consumers are able to discriminate between strong and weak research studies by applying the criteria that they will study in this book to make value judgments.

However, by discerning consumers, we do not mean *hypercritical consumers*. The key word here is *discernment,* not fault finding. We do not want readers to become cynics who delight in slamming researchers on every little perceived weakness and group all research as worthless. Rather, discerning consumers are ones who have self-confidence in their own ability to gauge research so that they can evaluate the influence that a study should have on practical issues of concern. When this objective is reached, research journals will no longer be looked upon as forbidding, boring documents that only university professors dare to read. Rather, they will be regarded as important sources of evidence or counter evidence that can be used in arguing the pros and/or cons of implementing new ideas and methodologies in our schools and classrooms.

Why Be a Consumer of Research?

Many students, teachers, and administrators are looking for practical information that will help them in their studies, teaching, or program development, respectively. They want immediate and practical information that they can use. They want to know how to teach various subject areas. They want to know what materials to use, what method works best.

However, there is no one way to teach. There is no one set of materials that can be used in every situation. We must make decisions, and these decisions must have some rationale for support. We must decide what, how, and when to teach based on the needs of the learner. We need to know how the learner thinks and feels, and what the best time is for teaching certain material via a certain methodology. To make these decisions, we must gather information, and this information is obtained through reading and doing research.

Unfortunately, we have seen many people in education over the years jump on various bandwagons regarding what to teach, how to teach, and how the learner acquires information and behavior. We have seen various charismatic experts sway audiences to accept their viewpoint as if it were the absolute truth. However, when the content of what was said was examined, little solid evidence was provided to back up the conjectures. Yet the audience pours out of the conference doors, back to their institutions, heralding the latest jargon, thinking that they have come on the most revolutionary thing they have ever heard. Programs are changed, new curricula are developed, and training sessions in new methodologies are imposed on the faculty. Yet have we really advanced in our discipline?

To avoid wasting time, money, human energy, and to prevent being led down the garden path, we argue that we must attend to what is happening in research. Yes, this will slow things down. People will become frustrated that they must wait for answers. They want quick solutions to their problems. An answer might never be forthcoming. What then? My response is that if we are unable to see some results based on careful research to guide us, we had better not take this route. Money in education is too limited to go out on wild goose chases to find out 5 years down the road that the latest fad was a waste of time.

Or maybe one wants to prepare a summary of research on a given topic in order to get a better picture of the state of affairs. Decisions must be made as to which set of research studies best fit the purposes of their endeavor.

In either of the above scenarios, we must learn to read research in education with a discerning eye. The purpose of this book is to help do exactly this: guide you in becoming a discerning consumer.

The Motivation Behind Research

To become a discerning consumer, we need to have a clear understanding of the driving force behind the research process. However, we require a working definition of the meaning of research first. Today it has many meanings, but much of what is called *research* would not be considered so by the scientific community. The purpose of this section is to explain how most professional researchers understand research by making contrasts with more commonly used definitions of research.

Demythologizing Research

Research Does Not Mean Searching for Articles to Write Papers

Probably the most common misconception about research is confusing it with papers we were asked to write back in secondary school or during our undergraduate days at the university—projects often referred to as research papers. Typically, such assignments mean that students go to the library and (re)search for a number of articles from a variety of sources. Then, they integrate the gathered information from these articles through summarizing and paraphrasing into papers addressing issues of importance with correct footnoting and referencing. However, the skills used in writing such papers, although important to research, should not be regarded as research.

The fact is consumers of research will spend most of their time in this searching activity. Even researchers have to spend a lot of time on the Internet and/or in the library looking up research articles. Both consumer and researcher have to summarize and paraphrase research articles and then integrate them into logical arguments. Both have to document everything and take care in referencing. However, these skills are especially needed at the preliminary stage of information gathering.

Working Only in Laboratories with Artificial Experiments

A second common misconception about research is to think that it only involves people in white coats working in spotless, white-walled laboratories running experimental tests on helpless rats or people. Included with this stereotype are graduate students sitting at computers analyzing statistical data with the hope of graduating one day.

These caricatures discourage many people from either reading research or doing it. Fortunately, it is not a true representation of what research is all about. Research is done in many different environments, such as classrooms, homes, schools, and even on the street. Few people wear white coats anymore except in chemical and animal laboratories. Most researchers whom we know would not look any different from many people we see on the street on any given day. As for computers, many people have them in their homes for their children to do their homework or play games. Computers have become so user-friendly that anyone can use them for all sorts of everyday applications. As for practicality, research results have been applied to help solve some important problems in the classroom and for developing new theoretical models.

Related to this is the misconception that you have to have a PhD (or at least be a PhD candidate) to understand published research. There is no mystery to research. It does not hide behind a veil that only those given the secret keys can unlock. Published research can be understood by anyone who is willing to take the time to understand the basic, and may we say simple, principles that are involved. This book provides these principles.

The Meaning of True Research

Research is the process whereby questions are raised and answers are sought by carefully gathering, analyzing, and interpreting data. In some cases, answers

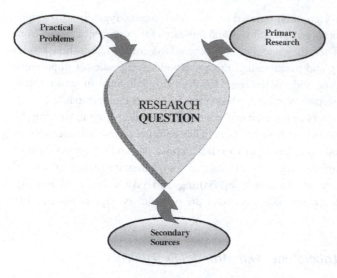

FIGURE 1.1 Sources for Research Questions

are hypothesized, predictions made, and data collected to support or discredit hypothesized answers. Figures 1.1 and 1.2 combined provide a general framework that encompasses the entire research process. Figure 1.1 illustrates the first phase, how research questions are formulated, and Figure 1.2 summarizes the second phase, finding the answers.

The *heart* of both figures is the research question. It is the beginning of the research process and the focus of both the consumer and the researcher. Any good research question asks, explicitly or implicitly, either what or why. Below are examples of how these two generic questions typically manifest themselves:

"What" questions:

> What phenomena are of importance?
> In what context do these phenomena occur (e.g., when, where)?
> What important relationships exist between phenomena?

"Why" questions (Causation):

> Why do these phenomena occur?
> Why do people differ on certain traits?

Identifying Important Questions

The motivating force behind research is the inherent curiosity of human beings to solve problems. We see phenomena around us, and we begin to ask questions: What is something made of? How did it get here? How does one phenomenon relate to another? Does one phenomenon cause another one to exist, decrease, or increase?

Our questions usually arise from several sources. Probably one of the most common sources is from observing *practical problems* (see Figure 1.1) in the classroom. Every day, teachers and administrators are confronted with issues that require informed answers. For example, Cooper, Robinson, and Patall (2006) were interested in determining whether the completion of school homework actually results in improved academic achievement for students. For years, teachers have traditionally assigned homework with the assumption that practicing math problems or spelling words would naturally result in improved grades and achievement. Was this an important question for these researchers to explore? Absolutely, since so much of traditional schooling revolves around the assignment, completion and grading of homework. Finding the answer to this question begins to help administrators and teachers determine whether their current practices should be continued, or whether better methods might be available to encourage deeper critical thinking and learning.

The second place where important research questions are often identified is *secondary sources*. We discuss these in more detail in Chapter 2, but for now textbooks and theoretical papers presented at conferences are examples. These sources are referred to as *secondary* because they summarize other people's research rather than provide firsthand reports by the original researchers. For this reason, they are very fruitful places for finding current research questions being asked by the educational community.

A good example of an application of this type of source in research comes from an article by McMaster and Espin (2007) where they explored the technical features of curriculum-based measurement in written expression. For their purposes, 28 technical reports and published articles were included in their review of the literature. They also summarized multiple measures of written expression and the differences in technical features of writing tasks, sample durations, and scoring procedures employed within and across elementary and secondary levels. In concluding their literature review, McMaster and Espin highlighted gaps in the research on this topic and suggested implications for future research. These are important questions for school administrators and teachers to ask to insure that current practices are effective and that all students are encouraged toward improving their skills.

The third resource for identifying important questions is *primary research*.[1] This is one of the most rewarding locations for discovering current questions being asked by the educational community. The better versed we are in the research literature, the more aware we become of the missing pieces in our framework of knowledge. For instance, we might notice that most of the research addressing a particular question has used a small number of people as participants. This is not unusual because it is common practice for researchers to use small groups of available students from their own programs as research participants. On careful examination, we begin to realize that important characteristics of the group of students we teach are not represented in the samples used in previous studies. This raises the question of how to generalize the findings to answer questions related to our students. We might have a suspicion that our group would behave differently. Such reasoning should lead us to be cautious toward making any practical recommendations based on such research. We would need to look for other studies using samples that are more similar to our students to see whether the same results occur.

Issues other than sampling might also lead us to raise important questions from previous research. The type of material used in a treatment, the method for administering a treatment, and the way in which the data were analyzed are often places where gaps might be found. Future research is needed to help complete the bigger picture before our own questions can be answered.

Besides looking for incongruities in research studies, the next best place to look for research questions is in the Discussion/Conclusion section of a study, usually identified by the terms *limitations* and *recommendations for further research*. Bursuck, Munk, Nelson, and Curran (2002), for example, described in their discussion section several limitations on the effects of reading problems for kindergarten and first grade students. Their study explored kindergarten and first grade teacher attitudes toward the knowledge of, and beginning reading practices that have been shown to prevent reading failure. One limitation suggested the survey they used, to examine teacher attitudes measured constructs such as knowledge and attitudes but that these responses might not measure actual teacher practices. The second limitation was that some of the teachers had prior advanced literacy training while others did not. The third limitation was that the survey that was used generated a return rate of only 30%. These limitations suggest that although the results are acceptable, there might be problems if we try to extend the findings to a broader population. Based on these limitations and recommendations, the next step would be to find whether there were any answers to these questions—which leads us to the following section.

At this point, we suggest that you complete the following exercise to apply what you have just read.

EXERCISE 1.1

1 Identify a question you have in the area of concern related to your area of interest.

2 Identify where you think this question came from:

    a   Your own experience.

    b   Your reading of books.

    c   The discussion section of a research article.

3 Why do you think this question is important for others beside yourself?

Where Are the Answers?

The purpose of research is not only to raise questions, but to provide answers to our questions. Unfortunately, most people look for answers in the opinions of famous people before going to primary research. Such opinions are found in textbooks, published papers, and public presentations. However, before expert opinions can have any weight, they must be supported by research. Regrettably, some opinions are given without supporting research and would be recognized for what they are: educated guesses and no more. They should not be given the same status as statements that are supported by research no matter how famous the person is. However, such opinions can be used as potential answers and subjected to research, as indicated by the arrow going to the Proposed Answers oval in Figure 1.2. To draw a direct arrow from Expert Opinion to Research Question is not allowed, although some people, either intentionally or unintentionally, try to make this leap of faith.

Theories are developed to generate proposed answers, as Figure 1.2 exhibits. A theory is an attempt to interrelate large sets of observed phenomena and/or constructs into meaningful pictures. In the field of education and social science research, there are a number of theories that attempt to describe how children and adolescents learn and develop. We do not necessarily have one all-encompassing theory that can provide explanations for all the phenomena that we might observe in a classroom. We do, however, use a variety of mini-theories, also

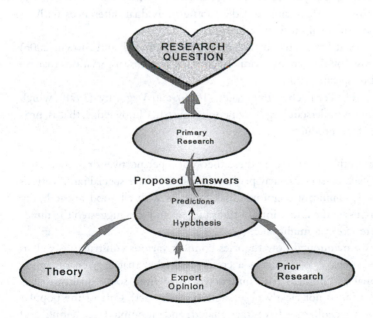

FIGURE 1.2 Sources for Answers to Research Questions

known as theoretical models, to help us make sense of what we observe and what might impact students' learning and behavior. Piaget's original theory of cognitive development (1929) tried to describe children's early cognitive and language development and also predicted what cognitive tasks we could expect children to be able to accomplish at specific age levels. Vygotsky (1978) not only acknowledged biological factors in early human development, but also focused on the role of children's social and cultural environment as an influence on early development. Other theoretical models like Bronfenbrenner's ecological systems theory (1989) suggested that multiple overlapping layers of a child's social environment could significantly influence children's development. These models as well as those that explore physical, moral, and social development help to give meaning to the many observed phenomena that we encounter in schools and social institutions.

Occasionally, you will come across studies that compare and contrast various theoretical perspectives or models. The article by Kleinert, Browder, and Towles-Reeves (2009) is a good example of this type of comparison. Kleinert and his colleagues looked at multiple examples of five theoretical models, specifically with a focus on the implications for students with cognitive disabilities. The examples they chose to explore focused on not only students with significant cognitive disabilities, but also on the implications for assessment. Three of the perspectives are listed below for illustration:

- The Differential Perspective by Pellegrino, Chudowsky, and Glaser (2001) which focuses on measuring and describing individual differences with an emphasis on the final product of learning.
- The Behaviorist Perspective by Skinner (1938) and Snell and Brown (2006) which focuses on the accumulation of stimulus–response associations that are translated to specific skills.
- The Cognitive Perspective by Piaget (1929) and Vygotsky (1978) which focus more on understanding how people construct knowledge, that is, process rather than product.

On the basis of their overview of these theoretical perspectives or models, they suggested that each perspective may play a role and may have special ramifications for students with significant cognitive disabilities. As with all good research, the authors also discussed the limitations of their project and also suggested the directions that future research might take.

Previously, we mentioned how theories connect various constructs as well as observed phenomena. A construct is a conceptual label that a given discipline (e.g., educational psychology) has constructed to identify some quality that is thought to exist but is not clearly observable (i.e., abstract). One of the popular constructs that psychologists have formulated and attempted to define and explore is the concept of motivation.

Constructs are defined in two different ways: either constitutively (Gall, Borg, & Gall, 2002) by using other constructs or operationally in behavioral terms. Although we know that in general, motivation is something that energizes, directs, and sustains behavior, it is not always easy to define, recognize, or measure. Many researchers have constitutively defined motivation with different constructs. Elliot and Dweck (2005) focused on a student's perceived competency toward a task. Dweck (2000) defined it as effort and persistence, and Urdan and Midgley (2001) used failure avoidance. This examination of multiple constructs begins to shed some light on how motivation can be defined and how it might be measured. Before a construct like motivation can be of any use in research, it (or its constructural components) must be defined operationally. An operational definition is one that defines a construct in observable terms. In the early 1900s, the construct of motivation was defined as specific innate or inherited tendencies, which were the essential springs or motive powers of all thought and action (McDougall, 1908). As simple as this definition may sound, motivational theorists began to deconstruct the concept of motivation into more specific components that could be observed and measured. Wijnia, Loyens, and Derous (2011) recently explored the effects of problem-based versus lecture-based learning environments on student motivation where they defined motivation as how students rated themselves on several motivational instruments. Using these behaviorally defined motivation constructs, the researchers were able to determine that students in problem-based learning environments, where they experienced collaborative learning, were perceived as more motivated than students receiving traditional lecture-based instruction.

Going back to Figure 1.2, when theory generates a potential answers to research questions, answers are in the form of a theoretical hypotheses. These are theoretical explanations that propose how several constructs or phenomenon relate to one another. For example, Johnson and Johnson (2009) argued that one factor influencing the success of cooperative group instruction was the positive motivational impact of peer support for learning. Building on their earlier work, they made the argument for the positive outcomes of cooperative learning and the relationship among theory, research, and practice. From the cooperative learning theory, they hypothesized that children are more motivated to learn if cooperative group learning is a component of instruction. Based on this they predicted that children who receive cooperative group instruction and work with their peers on learning activities would have greater learning and achievement gains than those students who work independently and receive traditional teacher-lead instruction.

As Figure 1.2 illustrates, hypotheses can also come out of previous research. Often larger theoretical models are not yet available from which to generate hypotheses. However, this does not stop researchers from trying to hypothesize why phenomena occur. When results repeat themselves over a number of studies, hypotheses can be formulated in an attempt to explain them.

A study that illustrates the previous point is Shechtman and Yaman (2012) who investigated the effect of social and emotional learning (SEL) integrated in a literature class (defined in their study as "affective teaching") as compared with conventional teaching. They attempted to measure student relationships, behavior, motivation to learn, and content knowledge. Their first hypothesis was that more favorable outcomes on each of the dependent variables would be found for children in the affective teaching condition when compared with students in the conventional teaching condition. This hypothesis was developed from the work of Zins, Elias, and Greenberg (2007) that explored associations among emotional abilities, social climate, and academic achievement. Their second hypothesis was that classroom and instructional climate as well as cohesion and behavior would predict outcomes (content knowledge and motivation to learn) so that more positive behavior and less negative behavior would be related to these gains. This hypothesis was drawn from the work of Durlak, Weissberg, Dymnicki, Taylor, and Schellinger (2011) who examined how discipline problems, poor interpersonal relationships, and poor academic achievement were interrelated.

All hypotheses are some type of relationship as illustrated in Figure 1.3. There are two basic types depending on the nature of the research question. One type is *simple relational*, which states that one construct relates to another. However, the simple relational hypothesis can be further divided into either *descriptive* or *predictive*. The *simple–descriptive–relational* hypothesis stipulates only that a relationship exists, such as "Anxiety negatively relates to learning." In effect, this means that as one construct changes (or varies), there is some degree of change in the other construct, but without concluding that one causes the change in the other.

An example of research on simple relationships is found in Gregory, Cornell, and Fan's (2011) study where they examined the relationship between structure and support in the high school climate and suspension rates of students using a large sample of 199 schools. The question of differential treatment of Black and White students was their central concern. They tested the hypothesis that an

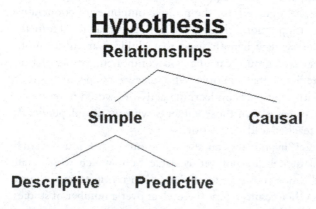

FIGURE 1.3 Types of Hypotheses

authoritative school environment would be associated with positive outcomes (less school suspensions) for both Black and White students. The second hypothesis tested was that there is a relationship between school environment, income level, ethnicity, lower school suspension rates, and academic outcomes.

The *simple-predictive-relational* hypothesis states that by knowing one or more constructs, performance on another construct can be predicted with some degree of accuracy. For example, Grissom and Anderson (2012) examined the high incidence of school superintendent turnover rates by conceptually defining superintendent turnover and operationally defining the results of school board survey data and administrative data. Among 215 of superintendents that were studied, 45% exited the superintendency within 3 years. Factors like how the school board rated its own functioning and the superintendent's performance and whether the superintendent was hired internally were both strong predictors of non-retirement exits. Interestingly enough, short-term school district test score growth was not a significant predictor of superintendent turnover.

The second type of relational hypothesis is *causal*, in that it states that one construct *causes* change in a second construct. A study that illustrates this was completed by Bong and Skaalvik (2003), who examined the effects of academic self-concept on school performance. In essence, children who view themselves as capable of academic success set higher goals, presumably work harder, and therefore *cause* an increase in their performance. As an additional note, causal hypotheses can be easily identified by the use of such verbs as *affect, influence, determine, impact, change*, and so on when connecting multiple constructs.

Both simple relational and causal hypotheses are either *directional* or *nondirectional*. These terms are used to specify the precise nature of the relationship between two constructs. In the case of a relational hypothesis, a directional hypothesis designates whether there is a positive or negative relationship. A *positive relationship* simply means that as one construct increases or decreases the other construct moves in the same direction. A *negative relationship* means that as one construct increases, the other decreases. If a relational hypothesis does not state clearly whether the relation is positive or negative, then it is nondirectional, meaning that the researchers are not sure which direction the relationship will take. The study by Bong and Skaalvik (2003) mentioned previously, clearly had directional hypotheses. They predicted that the more positive a child viewed themselves as a learner (academic self-concept) the more motivated they would be and, therefore, would experience greater academic achievement.

Causal hypotheses can also be directional or nondirectional. If a hypothesis proposes that one construct will cause change in a second construct in a certain direction, then it is directional. However, if it only poses that there will be a change without stating which direction the change will take place, it is nondirectional.

On what bases, you might ask, do some researchers make directional hypotheses and others do not? The answer lies in whether there is a theory or enough previous research to warrant the assertion that the results of the study will show a specific direction.

Hypotheses are usually stated in terms of abstract constructs. Yet as mentioned previously, unless the constructs are defined *operationally*, the hypotheses are difficult to test. When the constructs are transformed into operational definitions, the hypotheses become *predictions* (see Figure 1.2). In this form, the hypotheses can be tested. For example, the earlier study that was cited by Lepper, Corpus, and Iyengar (2005) defined the constructs of intrinsic and extrinsic motivation and used non-directional hypotheses to determine the relationship between both of these constructs and student academic outcomes. Once these relationships were established by examining the correlational relationships, it allowed the authors to begin to predict academic achievement based on motivation, and to additionally explore these effects based on grade level and student ethnicity.

Once predictions like Lepper's and his colleagues (2005) are determined, their hypothesis can be tested in additional primary research (see Figure 1.2) to confirm their findings and support the predictive nature of these relationships. Notice here that we use the phrase *primary research* rather than *published research* in contrast to Figure 1.1. Primary research is research reported firsthand by the researcher(s). Not all primary research is published; some research is presented orally at conferences, and some never see the light of day.

As you can see in Figure 1.2, all roads eventually lead to primary research for answering our questions. The results either *support* the hypothesis or *refute* it. Note that we did not say *prove* the hypothesis. *No theory or hypothesis has ever been proved*; although you would not get this impression after hearing some people talk about their pet theory. At best, a hypothesis may be supported, in which case we have a tentative answer to our question, not a conclusive one. If the results fail to support a hypothesis, the hypothesis is then *refuted*, meaning that it can be rejected as a possible answer. For those of you who want to get into this more deeply, we strongly recommend you reading Bhaskar's book *A realist theory of science* (2008).

We need to warn you that Figure 1.2 could be misleading if we are not careful. You might get the impression that one needs all of the elements in this figure before we can answer our questions. In fact all of the ovals in the figure, except the ones for primary research and the research questions, are not necessary. There are cases where researchers tackle questions without any previous theories or hypotheses. They go in with open minds, trying to uncover new information without having their perceptions biased by expectations imposed on them by any given theory. This research is exploratory and usually is seeking answers to *What* type questions. Do not be mistaken, however, just because there is no theory or hypothesis attached, this does not make the study inferior. In fact, you will find that there is much more exploratory research published than there is research testing hypotheses. More is said about research designs in Chapter 5.

In conclusion, the emphasis we want to make here is that there is no other place to find support for possible answers to our questions than from reading primary research. After a thorough search, we might find that sufficient evidence has been presented in answer to our questions. Yet if we find that our questions have not been answered adequately by previous research, we still benefit greatly by knowing that there remains the need for more research. In preparation for your own search for studies, the next chapter shows how you can access primary research for yourself. We think you will be surprised when you discover how much is readily available for your perusal.

Before you move on to the next chapter, however, we suggest you work through this next exercise to help you apply the information you have just covered.

EXERCISE 1.2

1   Define the following constructs each in two ways: 1) constitutively by using other constructs and 2) operationally in some behavioral terms.

    a   Motivation
    b   Anxiety
    c   Creative thinking
    d   Attitude

2   In each of the following hypotheses, do three things.

    a   Underline the construct(s) in each hypothesis.
    b   Identify whether each hypotheses is *relational* or *causal* and explain your reasoning.
    c   Determine whether each is *directional* or *nondirectional* and explain your reasoning. If directional, is it in a *negative* or *positive* direction (explain)?

Hypotheses

- The level of motivation will determine a learner's choice of extra-curricular activities.
- The more homework that is assigned, the greater the learner's score will be on the standardized exam.
- The more positive learners feel about their teacher, the better their attendance will be in class.
- The more positive learners feel about the country of the language they are learning, the better they will perform in their foreign language class.

Key Terms and Concepts

    construct
        constitutively defined
        operational defined

discerning consumer

hypothesis

    causal

    directional versus nondirectional

    refuted

    relational

    supported

positive versus negative relationships prediction

primary research

secondary sources

research versus search

theory

Note

1 Primary research (also referred to as empirical research) is research reported by the person(s) who actually did the research.

References

Bhaskar, R. (2008). *A realist theory of science.* New York: Routledge.

Bong, M., & Skaalvik, E. M. (2003). Academic self-concept and self-efficacy: How different are they really? *Educational Psychology Review, 15*(1), 1–40.

Bronfenbrenner, U. (1989). Ecological systems theory. In R. Vasta (Ed.), *Annals of child development* (Vol. 6, pp. 187–251). Greenwich, CT: JAI Press.

Bursuck, W. D., Munk, D. D., Nelson, C., & Curran, M. (2002). Research on the prevention of reading problems: Are kindergarten and first grade teachers listening? *Preventing School Failure, 47*(1), 4–9.

Cooper, H., Robinson, J. C., & Patall, E. A. (2006). Does homework improve academic achievement? A synthesis of research, 1987–2003. *Review of Educational Research, 76,* 1–62.

Durlak, J. A., Weissberg, R. P., Dymnicki, A. B., Taylor, R. D., & Schellinger, K. B. (2011). The impact of enhanced students' social emotional learning: A metaanalysis of school-based universal interventions. *Child Development, 82,* 405–432.

Dweck, C. S. (2000). *Self-theories: Their role in motivation, personality, and development.* Philadelphia: Psychology Press.

Elliot, A. J., & Dweck, C. S. (Eds.). (2005). *Handbook of competence and motivation.* New York: Guilford.

Gall, M. D., Borg, W. R., & Gall, J. P. (2002). *Educational research: An introduction* (7th ed.). Upper Saddle River, NJ: Pearson Education.

Gregory, A., Cornell, D., & Fan, X. (2011). The relationship of school structure and support to suspension rates for Black and White high school students. *American Educational Research Journal, 48*(4), 904–934.

Grissom J. A., & Anderson, S. (2012). Why superintendents turn over. *American Educational Research Journal, 49*(6), 1146–1180.

Johnson, D. W., & Johnson, R. T. (2009). An educational psychology success story: Social interdependence theory and cooperative learning. *Educational Researcher, 38,* 365–379.

Kleinert, H. L., Browder, D. M., & Towles-Reeves, E. A. (2009). Models of cognition for students with significant disabilities: Implications for assessment. *Review of Educational Research, 79*(1), 301–326.

Lepper, M. R., Corpus, J. H., & Iyengar, S. S. (2005). Intrinsic and extrinsic motivational orientations in the classroom: Age differences and academic correlates. *Journal of Educational Psychology, 97*, 184–196.

McDougall, W. (1908). *An introduction to social psychology*. Methuen: London.

McMaster, K., & Espin, C. (2007). Technical features of curriculum-based measurement in writing: A literature review. *Journal of Special Education, 41*(2), 68–84.

Pellegrino, J., Chudowsky, N., & Glaser, R. (Eds.). (2001). *Knowing what students know: The science and design of educational assessment*. Washington, DC: Committee on the Foundations of Assessment, National Academies Press.

Piaget, J. (1929). *The child's conception of the world*. New York: Harcourt, Brace.

Shechtman, Z., & Yaman, M. A. (2012). SEL as a component of a literature class to improve relationships, behavior, motivation, and content knowledge. *American Educational Research Journal, 49*(3), 546–567.

Skinner, B. F. (1938). *The behavior of organisms: An experimental analysis*. Englewood Cliffs, NJ: Prentice-Hall.

Snell, M., & Brown, F. (Eds.). (2006). *Instruction of students with severe disabilities* (6th ed.). Upper Saddle River, NJ: Merrill/Prentice Hall.

Urdan, T. C., & Midgley, C. (2001). Academic self-handicapping: What we know, what more there is to learn. *Educational Psychology Review, 13*, 115–138.

Vygotsky, L. S. (1978). *Mind in society: The development of higher psychological processes*. Cambridge, MA: Harvard University Press.

Wijnia, L., Loyens, S. M. M., & Derous, E. (2011). Investigating effects of problem-based versus lecture-based learning environments on student motivation. *Contemporary Educational Psychology, 36*, 101–113.

Zins, J. E., Elias, M. J., & Greenberg, M. T. (2007). School practices to build social-emotional competence as the foundation of academic and life success. In R. Bar-On, J. G. Maree, & M. J. Elias (Eds.), *Educating people to be emotionally intelligent* (pp. 79–94). Westport, CT: Praeger.

2

HOW TO LOCATE RESEARCH

Chapter Overview

In Chapter 1, we talked about generating research questions and searching for answers by looking into previous research. This chapter shows how you can find research studies that might provide potential answers to your questions. We first identify some of the main sources where you can find such research along with examples that walk you through the necessary steps for using them. We then give you guidelines on how to distinguish between the different types of published articles and how to weigh their value for answering questions. Finally, we provide you with suggestions for obtaining the articles you need.

Where to Look and What to Look for?

Remember the main goal is to find primary research. As stated in Chapter 1, primary research is the only way we can test proposed answers to our research questions. As mentioned earlier, the amount of research currently published is overwhelming. New journals arrive on the scene practically every year, dedicated to new areas of interest in the research community. Accessing this research can be a real challenge.

Although the amount of research being published continues to increase, do not despair. Today is the day of personal computers and the Internet, which make the task of finding relevant research much easier. If you have not yet developed an appreciation for these two technological advances, we strongly recommend that you take advantage of any training you might be able to get. It is well worth the investment in time and money.

These days you can often sit at your computer at home and access the information you need. Not only are you able to find out what and where studies are published, but you can often download them into your computer for reading and printing. What used to take many hours of work can be done in a matter of minutes. No longer do you have to go to the library to page through gigantic indexes trying to read type so small that you need a magnifying glass. The only disadvantage is that you miss the physical exercise of going to and from the library, not to mention the running around within the library looking for material.

There are three places where you can locate primary research: preliminary sources, secondary sources, and tables of references or bibliographies.

Preliminary Sources

Fortunately, a number of people have gone to the trouble of preparing sources to help us find research. Publications that lead us to primary research are known as preliminary sources. Some of the more traditional ones that can be found in bound copies in most university libraries (although this format is quickly becoming obsolete) are Educational Index, Current Index to Journals in Education (CIJE), National Society for the Study of Education (NSSE), Review of Research in Education (RRE), Social Science Citation Index (SSCI), International Bibliography, Social Science Index, Psychological Abstracts, and Resources in Education (RIE). Both the CIJE and the RIE are produced by the Educational Resources Information Center (ERIC). All of these sources are organized by a set of keywords that reveal the focus of the study.

Keywords are very useful for locating research articles. If you have an idea about what you are interested in, you can use the substantive words contained in your research question to guide you in looking up related studies. For example, let us say that you have formulated the question: "What is the relationship between anxiety and learning?" The keywords in your question are anxiety and learning. You would then search the above sources using these two key terms to locate relevant studies.

However, thanks to the computer age, many of the bound preliminary sources have now been converted to electronic databases and put into Web sites on the Internet. ERIC, Education Research Complete, and many others, such as Academic Search Complete, PsycINFO, and Sociological Abstracts, are available on the Internet through your library. Another database, JSTOR, not only contains some valuable data, it goes back as far as the 1800s. Last but not least, do not forget to use Google Scholar, which also has an advanced research option. Our students have found this database very useful for finding research articles.

A Walk-Through Example

To familiarize you with the use of an electronic database in your search for studies, we chose ERIC as an example. Although there are many other useful databases, this is the most accessible one on the Internet from almost any location. Moreover, both the CIJE and RIE have been made available online through ERIC.

If you are near a computer and have access to the Internet, try following the steps as you read along.

1   Go to the Web site www.eric.ed.gov; you will be taken to the main Web page for ERIC. This screen welcomes you to the ERIC Database, which is the gateway to more research than you will ever be able to read in your lifetime! The database currently contains research from the 1990s onward and is updated often.

2   Put the cursor in the **Search educational sources box**.

This is the box in which you can type the keyword(s). If you type in a broadly defined word like *education*, over a million references will result. Therefore, choosing the correct words or phrases during your search is a key to narrowing your list of potential articles.

3   Obviously, there are many articles in this list that might not relate to your research question. To narrow the list down to articles pertinent to your question, look on the left hand column and you will see ways to limit your search.

4   The headings in this column open up a number of ways to limit your search. First we can limit what years we are interested in under **Publication Date**. Note that you can look at what has happened just this year or go back as far as 20 years. Also on the right you will see the number of articles referenced for this time period. Under the next heading **Descriptor** there is a list of areas that will further restrict what references you obtain. For example, if you want to limit your search to anxiety related to adolescents, you click on this choice. The other headings in this column provide other delimiters to narrow your search. The goal is to narrow your search as much as possible without missing some key articles that you may need for your reference.

5   A useful tool to aid us is a thesaurus, which most databases, such as ERIC provide. We clicked on ERIC's **Thesaurus** and typed in *anxiety* in the **Search For** box. Clicking the **Search** button opened another screen with five related *descriptors* about anxiety.

      Another way to do this is to choose the Browse button back at the **Thesaurus Search**. This displayed a series of alphabetical letter buttons that take you to keywords beginning with the letter you choose. We clicked on **A** and scrolled down until we came across descriptors beginning with the word *anxiety*. If we click on *anxiety*, the thesaurus generates one term to broaden the search, five to narrow, six possible alternatives, and 14 related terms. You can play with these different terms to help uncover important article of interest.

6   Making use of accurate descriptors of your research question, and the Thesaurus, by separating terms with the use of the operators *AND* and *OR* will help to narrow your search while focusing in on specific terms that will keep you from missing key articles.

Now let us put this in practice. If we are interested in searching for articles that explore *adolescent anxiety* toward *mathematics*, we might begin like this. If we type "adolescent anxiety" AND mathematics in the main search box, we get 4,708 hits. Note that ERIC automatically listed the articles for your perusal. Do not worry if you do not get the same number. By the time you read this, the number of articles will have changed. If we restrict this search to the last 5 years, we get 1,351 hits.

But to spread the net a little more, we searched for anxiety in the Thesaurus and then to the descriptors screen and found mathematics anxiety. This is more useful than anxiety because it identifies the type of anxiety we want to investigate. Remaining under the Thesaurus search, we then clicked on mathematics anxiety and found mathophobia and mathematics avoidance. So we used the search terms adolescence AND mathematics anxiety OR mathophobia OR mathematics avoidance to develop a clear and concise search. This produced 305 hits for the last 5 years. If we only want peer-reviewed articles, the search drops to 236 articles.

If you want to only find articles that ERIC will provide in their full-text version, just click the box under the Search box and only those references will be given to you. Box 2.1 below provides a summary of four searches using these terms with three different limiting conditions.

BOX 2.1 ERIC SEARCH SUMMARY

Search One

Input: "adolescent anxiety" (AND) mathematics
Results: 4,708 documents found with no delimiters.

   When limited to past 5 years, 1,351 docs.

Search Two

Input: adolescence AND mathematics anxiety OR mathophobia OR mathematics avoidance
Results: 305 documents found for last 5 years.

   When limited to peer-reviewed articles, 236 docs.

It is important to understand that you may not be successful the first time when you do your search and that you may need to continue to modify your search terms (more broad or less broad; more limitations or less limitations) so that you can capture the information that you need. You can also quickly recognize how powerful a tool, an electronic search engine like ERIC, can be when you can narrow more than 4,708 documents down to only 236 within just a few minutes as demonstrated above.

The output will provide you with a list of references. This makes it easy to quickly survey various related articles and select the ones you want to look at in greater detail. Note that on the right it tells you whether the article has been peer reviewed and also whether you can go to a direct link to the article. If you click on the title of the article, a screen will pop up that gives an abstract of the article followed by two columns of further information about the article. There is also a list of other Keywords that help in providing other words to use in your search. Note an ERIC number in the first column that begins with ED or EJ. The former means that it is a document not necessarily found in a journal, whereas EJ indicates that the paper is published in a journal. The other information provided in these columns will further help your search.

The next step is to obtain full copies of the articles that you have narrowed down. One way is to click on the Full text available on ERIC box and run your search. However, ERIC does not have all of your articles in a full-text form, so you need to go to the publication that has the full article. If you click on the Direct link on the right side of the article it will take you out of ERIC and to the publication you want. Some journals are open access, so you can download the article directly. However, others require membership that you either have to subscribe to or be a member of a library that has access to these journals. Most modern university libraries have these privileges.

Other online databases that we have mentioned previously, such as Academic Search Complete, The International Bibliography of the Social Sciences (IBSS), Ingenta Connect Complete, JSTOR, Linguistics and Language Behavior Abstracts (LLBA), Modern Language Association (MLA), and PsycINFO work similar to ERIC. However, these are not as accessible as ERIC. So far, we have only been able to access these databases through university Web sites, which require identification codes and passwords. If you are a student at an educational institution, you might have access to your own institution's Web site or gain access to an outside Web site to use these databases.

At one of our universities, we used the same keywords (adolescence, mathematics anxiety, mathophobia, and mathematics avoidance) and time frame with the Academic Search Premier database and received five references. Again, we repeated the same with the PsycINFO database and got 198 citations. The same search with Education Full Text turned up five articles. The nice thing about university databases is that you can often search multiple databases at one time to generate articles within your research search topic. It is always wise to search various databases to make sure that there is not any important study out there in cyberspace that would be essential for the purpose of your search.

The previous sample exercise helps you to realize that phrasing questions may need some imagination if you are to produce fruitful literature searches. We dare say that if a question is of any importance, there will be primary research to be found. By playing around with the Thesaurus and different search terms, you will be able to unleash a wealth of material out there in cyberspace. The following exercise gives you another opportunity to put the above procedures into practice.

EXERCISE 2.1

1 Write down a question you think important for teaching another language.
2 Underline the key phrases.
3 Do an initial search using ERIC or some other database.

    a   How many articles did it turn up? Too many, or too few?
    b   If too many, add delimiters to reduce them down to a manageable size. If too few, go to the next step.

4 Look into the ERIC Thesaurus, or the thesaurus of the database available to you and identify related terms to the ones you have chosen. Plug those into the Search boxes and repeat steps 1–3.
5 When satisfied with your search, print out your results with a report on how you obtained the final list.

Secondary Sources

Besides primary research, your search using preliminary sources will turn up another category of literature referred to as *secondary sources.* As mentioned in Chapter 1, secondary sources are ones that refer to or summarize primary research through the eyes of someone other than the person(s) who did the study. Therefore, they are valuable places to find references to primary research. These are commonly found in the form of literature reviews, position papers, and books.

Reviews of Research

One of the most useful secondary sources is a well-written review of research. This is a very important piece of work that summarizes a number of primary studies related to a particular research issue. A well-written review tries to make sense out of all of the research that has been done in a given area. It compares and contrasts various studies and identifies areas that still need more research. We advise people to look for reviews of research as the first thing they do when trying to find out what research has already been done on a topic and what research-ers have concluded so far.

    An example of a well-written research review is found in Binyan's article (2010) "Research on Mathematics Education in China in the Last Decade: A

Review of the Literature" in the journal *Frontiers of Education in China*. This author provided a useful overview of research for the last decade on mathematics education in China and concentrated on summarizing the essence of classroom instruction, student learning, teacher education, and curricular reforms. We found this article through an ERIC Advanced Search where we typed the keywords *mathematics education* AND *curriculum*.

Some journals only publish research reviews. The *Review of Educational Research* is dedicated for this purpose in educational research. It comes out monthly, and each volume contains reviews on many different areas. Research reviews are also published in journals that contain primary research.

Let us interject a warning here regarding working with secondary sources. There is no substitute for firsthand reading of primary research. This means, for instance, that we cannot rely on summaries of research studies in secondary sources such as a review of research. The reason is that the reviewers select information only relevant to their review and leave out the rest. The selection process might have a particular bias that influences the spin that reviewers put on the information they are summarizing. Using this material in our own work would perpetuate this bias and misrepresent the original study. We strongly recommend that you do not yield to any temptation to short-cut the process, but that you take the extra effort to track down the articles that you want to examine and read them for yourself.

Position Papers

Another type of secondary source commonly found is the position paper. Often, it resembles a literature review but with a much more focused purpose. In it, a writer argues his or her particular viewpoint, or position, on various issues. For example, one of the articles we found in the literature search we did previously as an exercise (without restricting our search to journal articles only) was Mandinach and Gummer's (2013) paper entitled "A Systematic View of Implementing Data Literacy in Educator Preparation." This was published in a research journal but was not primary research. Rather, they argued the position that since data-driven decision making has become increasingly important in K-12 education, university teacher education programs need to provide prospective teachers more opportunities for data literacy development. The authors cited a number of studies to warrant their viewpoint.

Because position papers are not primary research, researchers cannot use them as direct evidence to support answers to research questions. The reason is that they usually draw the proposed answers (i.e., formulated hypotheses) out of the research studies they cite (see Figure 2.1). However, the research they cite cannot then be turned around to support their proposed answers (represented by the dotted curve line). In other words, the same research cannot be used for both things: proposing answers and justifying answers. If we generate a hypothesis (i.e., possible answer) from existing data and then turn around (the dotted curve line) and use the same data to support my hypothesis, we have fallen into the trap of

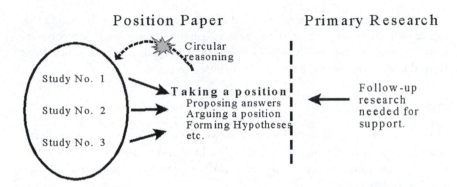

FIGURE 2.1 Relation Between a Position Paper and Primary Research

circular reasoning (Giere, 2004). There is nothing wrong with the first part (i.e., generating a hypothesis based on existing research), but we cannot use the same data to support the hypothesis from which it was derived. To test a hypothesis, we must do subsequent research to find support, as illustrated on the right side of the vertical dotted line in Figure 2.1.

Let us also reiterate here that we cannot use position papers to support a possible answer on the basis that the people giving the papers are famous or authorities in their field. Somewhere we seem to have picked up the notion that because people are famous, what they say must be true. Unfortunately, many people have been led down many a wrong path by relying on someone's fame or charisma. Therefore, unless these famous *someone's* back up what they say with solid research, they are just giving their own opinions, which cannot be used as evidence.

As with reviews of research, we cannot substitute position papers for personally reviewing primary research with our own eyes. In presenting their argument, Mandinach and Gummer (2013) summarized several primary research studies to generate their argument for improved data literacy skills. The temptation for us is to use their summaries rather than take the time to find the primary studies and summarize them ourselves. However, we cannot use such summaries as substitutes for summarizing primary research ourselves because it is not uncommon to only focus on information for the specific purposes of the position paper—important information critical for our purposes may have been left out.

Books

The third secondary source that can provide information about previous research consists of published books. Typically, books are used to provide people with foundations for the issues being considered in a given area. In the process of doing this, they cite and summarize large quantities of primary research. Yet again the discussion of such research has been run through the cognitive filter of the author(s) and cannot be relied upon as unbiased. Such material can help us become aware of existing research, but they cannot substitute for firsthand reading of such studies. However, there is one exception. Some books are compilations of primary research studies. As long as the research reported is first-hand from the researcher, it can be treated as primary research.

Other Places

Do not forget the Reference Librarian at your library. This person is a valuable source of information who can help you with ideas and locate other sources. Also, do not forget your professors and peers who can spur your thinking and advance your list of keywords.

Tables of References/Bibliographies

Other profitable places to find research studies, often overlooked, include tables of references or bibliographies of research articles that we already have found. Often we find benchmark (or seminal) studies this way. A benchmark study is one that either sparked interest in a particular issue or marked a pivotal directional change in the way research moved on a given subject. One tactic we use to identify a benchmark study is the frequency of citation. When you notice that just about every article you read cites a particular study, you can be sure that it is an important one in the history of the area you are investigating.

Is All Primary Research of Equal Weight?

We have stated that primary research is the only place where we can find evidence to answer our questions. However, not every piece of primary research that you find in your database search is of equal weight for supporting a proposed answer to a question. Figure 2.2 lists the various venues in which primary research can be found. The higher the venue is in Figure 2.2, the more weight it has. Two criteria are directly relevant to the weight: (a) whether the submissions for publication are refereed and (b) whether the referee is blind toward who wrote the study. A referee is usually someone who is either at the same academic level (thus the term *peer review*) as the person submitting the study for publication, or higher. They are considered by the journal publishers to have enough experience in research to give meaningful evaluations. A *blind* referee is one who does not know the researcher's identity when reviewing the article.

There are three general venues: published research, conference presentations, and databases. Under published research, there are three types of journals plus doctoral dissertations. Journals are divided into blind or nonblind refereed or nonrefereed. Most journals have editorial boards that review every manuscript that is submitted for consideration before being accepted for publication. Yet the rigor to which a manuscript is evaluated varies with the journal.

To add to the problem of weighing different sources, not all journals are equal in prestige, despite whether the referees are blind. Some journals are considered more important than others. Currently there are two ways to measure a journal's importance: the Institute for Science Information (ISI) Impact Factor and the PageRank procedures. The Impact Factor of a journal is a measure of the frequency with which the "average article" in a journal has been cited in a particular year while PageRank procedures use an influential algorithm that uses a model of Web use that is dominated by its link structure in order to rank pages by their estimated value to the Web community. Both consider the number of journal citations in relation to the number of articles published over a designated period of time; however, the latter uses a procedure that provides better information regarding the prestige of a particular journal.

There are several publications that provide lists of journals in the field of education that also include acceptance rates and impact factors of specific journals including *Cabell's Directory* and the *General Citation Report*. There are also various Internet sites that attempt to provide current rankings of journals although these are often subject to change based on the current research in the field. For example, you can complete a Google search using "ISI Impact Factor, education" to find the most recent ranking of the top 10 journals in this field based on the ISI Impact Factor approach. We are not aware of a ranking of specific education journals using current PageRank procedures but the research field is constantly changing and improving its techniques for ranking journals.

Consequently, more weight should be given to the studies that have been critiqued by qualified referees who are blind to the author of a study rather than giving weight to those which have not received this scrutiny. If you can also find the ranked position of a journal's prestige in the field, this adds to the weight of the research article. This type of information will be made more available as the discipline advances.

Notice in Figure 2.2 that we have placed Doctoral Dissertations higher than Nonrefereed journals. The reason we have done this is that doctoral dissertations typically go through rigorous screening by doctoral committees and are not accepted until everything is in a good order—at least that is what is supposed to happen. These dissertations are available, although not as readily as articles in research journals. They are also typically voluminous, which makes them much more difficult to work with. They can be ordered on microfiche, which saves on postage and storage but requires a microfiche reader. They are also becoming more accessible through Web sites (Google, doctoral dissertations). Eventually, some of these will be summarized and submitted for publication in research journals.

Primary research can also come in the form of papers read at conferences (see Figure 2.2). If you have ever attended any conference related to educational research (e.g., AERA), you will find many sessions where primary research is presented: At Paper Sessions, researchers present 15–20-min summaries about their research; at Round Tables, various researchers present short summaries of their research on a

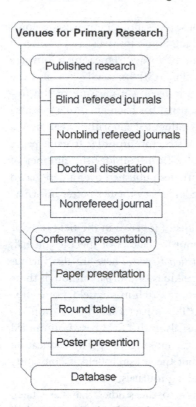

Venues for Primary Research
- Published research
  - Blind refereed journals
  - Nonblind refereed journals
  - Doctoral dissertation
  - Nonrefereed journal
- Conference presentation
  - Paper presentation
  - Round table
  - Poster presention
- Database

FIGURE 2.2 Levels of Weight Given to Research In Different Venues

common theme and are available for questions; and at Poster Sessions, researchers (often graduate students) exhibit their studies on poster boards and are available to explain their research to anyone interested. Notice in Figure 2.2 that we have put them in an order based on the degree to which they are critiqued. Although there is some degree of scrutiny applied before papers are accepted at conferences, research presented at this venue does not have the same weight as a study that has been published in a journal. The reason is that they have not gone through the same degree of rigorous evaluation prior to presentation. Yet some work presented at conferences is usually evaluated by discussants and certainly by those who hear the presentations. The problem for the consumer is that unless present at the time of the presentation these evaluations are not personally heard or read.

Least weight is given to any primary research that appears in a database which has neither been published in a journal nor presented at a conference. Some databases provide references for books, theses, dissertations, speeches, viewpoints, reports, conference papers, as well as primary research. They do not require any of these works to be published or presented at conferences. Therefore, some primary research referenced in them has been submitted by the researcher so that others might see what was done. For example, individuals can submit summaries of their research to ERIC, which references them for all to see and even provide full-text copies free of charge. A case in point is Tran's (2009) article on why older adult learners are unable to achieve native-like proficiency when learning a second language that is found in ERIC. From what we can see in the reference, it has not been published as of yet, nor presented at any conference. However, it is available through ERIC's Web site, www.eric.ed.gov, free on a Portable Document Format (PDF) file.

This is not to suggest that articles such as this are not useful research. There is a lot of important research that has not been published nor presented at conferences. However, because it has not gone through some form of peer review, it cannot carry the same weight as research that has.

A third criterion you want to keep in mind when gauging the usefulness of a research study for answering your question is *recency*. Studies that are 10 years old or older do not usually carry the same weight as more recent studies unless they are seminal studies. When searching, you will want to begin with the most recent and work your way back. The most recent research will bring you up to date on what is happening.

The order of recency usually goes like this: conference presentations, research journals, and secondary sources. The first is the most recent. If you are trying to get the latest research on a topic, the places to go are research conferences where people are reporting their own research, often still in progress. You can usually obtain complete research studies directly from the author(s) at these conferences. If authors do not have full reports or have run out of them, they are usually more than happy to send you a copy. Such conferences as American Psychological Association (APA), National Council on Measurement in Education (NCME), and AERA are full of sessions where the most recent research is presented. There are also a number of regional conferences where fresh research is presented.

Less recent are journal articles that may appear anywhere from 6 months or more from the time the research has been accepted for publication. Most journals take 6 months to a year before an article is published. Remember that the study itself may have been completed much earlier; therefore, the actual data could be 3–4 years old before you see the study in print.

The least recent research is material that is cited in secondary sources. Under this classification, literature reviews and position papers are less dated than books. The review of high stakes testing and the implications for English language learners by Solorzano (2008) for example, reviewed studies as recent as 2007. In contrast, books have older references simply because it takes much longer to publish a book than to get a literature review or a position paper presented.

Differentiating Primary From Secondary

One problem our students complain about is the difficulty in identifying primary research from position papers and even literature reviews when searching preliminary sources. Our suggestion is to first examine the title of the article. For example, in the following reference from an ERIC search, Chang (2012) informed us that her article is primary research by using the term longitudinal study in her title.

> Academic Performance of Language-Minority Students and All-Day Kindergarten: A Longitudinal Study. (EJ956582)
> **Author:** *Chang, Mido*

However, we cannot detect whether the following ERIC reference is a primary research article from the title:

> Role Strain among Dual Position Physical Educators and Athletic Trainers Working in the High School. (EJ894312)
> **Author(s):** *Pitney, William; Stuart, Moria; Parker, Jenny*

Are the authors collecting data or presenting a case for a particular theory or opinion? To be clear, we need to go to the next step of reading the abstract usually provided by the preliminary source. In our example, we would click on the button, **Show Full Abstract**, which provides an unabbreviated abstract of the article as seen next. Here, we look for key phrases that will give us a clue regarding the nature of the article. An abbreviated version of the abstract is provided.

ABSTRACT: The purpose of the mixed methods study was to identify the extent to which role strain permeates the professional lives of dual position physical educators and athletic trainers working in the high school setting and to identify which components of role strain (i.e. role ambiguity, role conflict, role incompetence, etc.) are most prevalent and which of the variables predict role strain. A survey was sent to 1,863 individuals who were certified teachers and athletic trainers working in a high school setting. The survey had a 31% response rate. Results revealed that 13.6% had high role strain, 28.5% had moderate role strain, 33% had low role strain, and 24.9% had minimal role strain. The regression analysis revealed only hours worked per week as an athletic trainer as a predictor role strain.

There are several indicators in the abstract that show the article is a primary study and not a position paper or a review. The phrases "mixed methods study" and "a survey was sent to 1,863 individuals" are both indicators that data were collected and analyzed. Not every abstract uses these exact words or phrases, but something is said to the same effect to indicate a primary study was undertaken.

The next ERIC reference does not reveal what type of article it is, in the title either:

Aesthetic Teaching: Seeking a Balance between Teaching Arts and Teaching through Arts. (EJ983011)

Author: *Sotiropoulou-Zormpala, Marina*

ABSTRACT: This article aims to examine the teaching practices that correspond to various educational roles ascribed to the arts within school curricula. Three teaching approaches are analyzed: (1) "teaching the arts", in which the arts are treated as distinct cognitive teaching subjects; (2) "teaching through the arts", in which the arts are used as teaching tools in the curriculum; and (3) "aesthetic teaching", in which the arts are treated as alternative ways of approaching and processing other academic subjects. The first two approaches are used regularly in elementary education settings, while the third is a potential future development that could constitute the basis of a revitalized arts education policy.

We can gain information not only from the title of the journal in which Sotiropoulou-Zormpala's article appears, *Arts Education Policy Review*, indicating this might be a policy paper, but also from the abstract that clearly informs us that she is arguing for a revitalized arts education policy. She makes no reference to collecting data or stating any results. This is most likely a position paper.

The third ERIC reference cited next, that does not specifically reveal the nature of the paper, was by Pumpian (2013). This title is so general that it could be anything. However, the abstract indicates that the author is stating an opinion and makes an argument for schools to incorporate the concept of tolerance as a source for student growth and development.

Tolerance: Woven into the Fabric of the School, or Not? (EJ1004187)

Author: *Pumpian, Ian*

ABSTRACT: The author posits that dealing with diversity is a 21st century skill set and that tolerance of difference is a rudimentary element of that set. The author argues that school leaders must purposefully and democratically create an inclusive school wide culture that welcomes and embraces its diversity. The capacity to tolerate others and their differences can become foundational to empathy, growth, and interdependence. The author urges schools to become models of democracy that teach students that our differences can be constructively explored and challenged and may be the source of positive collaborations, developments, and change.

How to Obtain Research Articles

Although finding references to research articles has now become much easier, there continues to be the major challenge of getting access to the actual journal articles. Databases, such as ERIC, usually provide information as to how to locate such material. Increasingly, this is the way most people are now accessing research.

If you cannot find a full-text version online, the next best place is your nearest university library. There, the article you want is either accessible in their collections or obtainable from another library through an interlibrary loan. Finding a good library that has helpful staff is like finding a gold mine.

If you do not have access to articles through a library, ERIC, JSTOR, or other databases give you an order number where you can order any article that they have in their database for a small charge. We recommend you order microfiche rather than a paper copy because they are cheaper, easier to post, and save trees. You can read the microfiche at your nearest library on their microfiche reader if available.

What Journals Are Related to the Field of Education?

There are many research journals that can be used for different areas of interest. The reason is that education is multidimensional, that is, many different disciplines are related to this broad field. You will find research related to education in journals dealing with anthropology, computer-assisted learning, psychology, sociology, and many more areas. We recommend that you check to see how many of these are easily accessible to you in an electronic format on the Internet and at your university campus library.

To apply what you have been reading, we recommend the following exercise. The objective is to train your eye to look for terminology that will speed up your ability to distinguish between the various types of literature you will encounter in your searches.

EXERCISE 2.2

1   Choose a topic related to education that interests you.
2   Go to one or more preliminary sources and select several references to articles related to your topic.
3   Examine the titles of these and try to determine whether they are primary studies, position papers, or literature reviews. What terminology helped you to decide?
4   Now look at the abstracts given by the preliminary source and try to confirm whether your decisions were correct. What statements provided you with further information regarding the nature of the study?
5   Lastly, decide from the title and the abstract whether each article you have listed is relevant to the topic you chose and defend your choice.

Key Terms and Concepts

delimiter
keyword
literature review
operator
position paper
preliminary sources
primary research
secondary sources

Additional Recommended Reading

Georgas, H. (2013). Google vs. the library: Student preferences and perceptions when doing research sign Google and a federated search tool. *Libraries and the Academy, 13*(2), 165–185.
Goldman, S. R. (2011). Choosing and using multiple information sources: Some new findings and emergent issues. *Learning and Instruction, 21*(2), 238–242.
Hock, R. (2004). *Extreme searcher's internet handbook.* Medford, NJ: Information Today.
O'Dochartaigh, N. (2001). *The internet research handbook: A practical guide for students and researchers in the social sciences.* Thousand Oaks, CA: Sage.
Walraven, A., Brand-Gruwel, S., & Boshuizen, H. P. A. (2009). How students evaluate information and sources when search the World Wide Web for information. *Computers and Education, 52*(1), 234–246.

References

Binyan, X. (2010). Research on mathematics education in China in the last decade: A review of journal articles. *Frontiers of Education in China, 5*(1), 130–155.
Chang, M. (2012). Academic performance of language-minority students and all-day kindergarten: A longitudinal study. *School Effectiveness and School Improvement, 23*(1), 21–48.
Giere, R. N. (2004). *Understanding scientific reasoning.* Graton, CA: Wadsworth.
Mandinach, E. B., & Gummer, E. S. (2013). A systematic review of implementing data literacy in educator preparation. *Educational Researcher, 42*(1), 30–37.
Pitney, W. A., Stuart, M. E., & Parker, J. (2008). Role strain among dual position physical educators and athletic trainers working in the high school setting. *Physical Educator, 65*(3), 157–168.
Pumpian, I. (2013). Tolerance: Woven into the fabric of the school, or not? *Voices from the Middle, 20*(3), 10–14.
Solorzano, R. W. (2008). High stakes testing: Issues, implications, and remedies for English language learners. *Review of Educational Research, 78*(2), 260–329.
Sotiropoulou-Zormpala, M. (2012). Aesthetic teaching: Seeking a balance between teaching arts and teaching through the arts. *Arts Education Policy Review, 113*(4), 123–128.
Tran, T. H. (2009). The critical period and second language acquisition. Retrieved from ERIC database (ED507240).

PART II

The Major Components of Published Research

3

UNDERSTANDING THE FRAMEWORK OF A PRIMARY RESEARCH ARTICLE

Chapter Overview

Research articles typically follow a standard format for presentation in research journals. We have used this format to organize the following chapters.

The purpose of this chapter is to provide you with a framework as an introduction to the rest of the book. We begin by describing what a typical research study looks like with a brief explanation of each component. The first three parts—title, abstract, and introduction—are discussed more fully in this chapter, whereas separate chapters are dedicated to the remaining components. We provide you with examples of current research from different journals and have interspersed some exercises to help you develop an overall schema of the basic structure of a research article.

The Framework of a Research Article

Most research articles adhere to the following format:

1 Title
2 Author(s) and institution(s)
3 Abstract
4 Introduction
5 Method (Methodology)
6 Results
7 Discussion/Conclusions
8 References

The Title

Although many readers might not think the title is very important, it is in fact critical. Titles either attract potential readers or dissuade them from reading the article. A well-written title should give enough information to inform the consumer what the study is about. It might suggest what the research question is or even what hypothesis is being tested, but there should be no doubt what issue is being investigated.

The title should also indicate what type of article it is. There should be no necessary guessing as to whether it is primary research, a review of the literature, or a position paper. For example, there is little doubt what Nosek and Smyth's (2011) study is about, entitled "Implicit Social Cognitions Predict Sex Differences in Math Engagement and Achievement." It is a primary study that examines implicit math attitudes and stereotypes based on gender, among a large sample of over 5,000 participants. In contrast, West-Olatunji, Baker, and Brooks's (2006) paper entitled "African American Adolescent Males: Giving Voice to Their Educational Experience" is unclear as to whether it is primary research or a position paper. It could be either. The reader has to go to the abstract or the body of the introduction to find out which it is.

At the same time, the title should not require unnecessary reading. Some titles are short and succinct, clearly telling the readers what they want to know, such as Williamson and McLeskey's (2011) study titled "An Investigation Into the nature of Inclusion Problem Solving Teams." Others can be quite long and unnecessarily complex (in our opinion), such as the study entitled, "Tripartite Growth Trajectories of Reading and Math Achievement: Tracking National Academic Progress at Primary, Middle, and High School Levels" (Lee, 2010). Although this title clearly indicates what the study is addressing and that it is a primary study, it could probably have done without the final phrase, "at Primary, Middle, and High School Levels." This comes down to a stylistic preference but many times a short, clear title conveys the necessary information without overcomplicating the topic.

In summary, the three criteria to look for in a title are: focus of the study, type of article, and succinctness. The first two are the most important, because they quickly inform you whether the paper is what you are searching for. The third is more of a stylistic issue, which you should keep in mind if you ever have to entitle a paper of your own. Take time to do the following exercise to apply these criteria to some example titles that we have supplied, and then apply the criteria to other articles from your own search.

EXERCISE 3.1

Look at each of the following titles of real studies and answer the following:

1   What is the study's:

    a   focus?

    b   research question?

    c   hypothesis (if any)?

2   Can you tell whether the article is a primary study, a position paper, or a literature review? Explain your reasoning.

Titles

- What the U. S. could learn from South Africa about Education and Social Justice (Books & Ndlalane, 2011)
- Exploring sixth graders' selection of nonfiction trade books (Moss & Hendershot, 2002)
- Switching schools: Revisiting the relationship between school mobility and high school dropout (Gasper, DeLuca, & Estacion, 2012)

The Abstract

The abstract in a research article is written by the author(s) of the study. This is not always the case with the abstract written in preliminary sources, such as ERIC or another database. Therefore, the abstract in the article is usually much more reliable to identify the content of the study.

A well-written abstract should summarize five essential things to help the reader know what the study is about: (a) purpose of the study, (b) source(s) from where the data are obtained (usually referred to as participants), (c) the method(s) used for collecting data, (d) the general results, and (e) general interpretation and/or applications of the results. Some abstracts may contain more than these things, but unfortunately some abstracts do not contain some (if not all) of these essential elements.

With this information, the consumer will know from the abstract whether the article is of interest. To illustrate, we extracted the above five pieces of information from the abstract of a study by Strom, Thoresen, Wentzel-Larsen, and Dyb (2013), which looked at whether adolescents' exposure to violence, sexual abuse, and bullying would have a significant impact on their academic achievement in school. The following is a copy of the abstract from their study with the essential information summarized in Table 3.1. As you can see, this abstract provided enough information to decide the relevance of the study for the reader's purpose.

> The study investigated academic achievement among adolescents exposed to violence, sexual abuse, and bullying. Moreover, we sought to determine the individual and contextual influence of the adolescents' school environment in terms of bullying, classmate relationships, and teacher support on academic achievement. This is a cross-sectional study sample of 7,343 adolescents between the ages of 15 and 16 from 56 schools in Oslo, Norway. We investigated associations between violence, sexual abuse, bullying, classmate relationships, teacher support, and academic achievement. Linear regression was used to investigate associations on the individual level. Multilevel analyses were conducted to test for school level differences while controlling for both

individual and contextual factors. On an individual level, all combinations of violence and sexual abuse categories were significantly associated with lower grades. This was also true for bullying, while teacher support resulted in better grades. Each unit of increment in bullying in school corresponded to an average 0.98 point decrease in grades ($p < 0.01$) when we controlled for sociodemographic characteristics. Our results indicate that students attending schools with higher levels of bullying may show poorer school performance. This was true for all students regardless of their exposure to violence and sexual abuse. This emphasizes the need for preventive efforts that focus not only on vulnerable groups, but on all students and the school context. (p. 1)

There is nothing like firsthand experience to get a better grasp of the prior discussion. The following exercise provides you with a framework for analyzing and evaluating research abstracts.

Table 3.1 Analysis of an Example Abstract

Essentials	Content
Purpose of the study	This paper investigated academic achievement among adolescents exposed to violence, sexual abuse, and bullying.
Sample	7,343 adolescents between the ages of 15 and 16 from 56 schools in Oslo, Norway.
Method used for collecting data	Multilevel analyses were conducted to study school-level differences while controlling both individual and contextual factors.
Results	All combinations of violence and sexual abuse categories were significantly associated with lower grades.
Interpretation of results	The results indicated that students attending schools with higher levels of violence and bullying may show poorer school performance. The results also emphasize the need for preventive efforts.

EXERCISE 3.2

Find a recent research study of interest and examine the **abstract** carefully. Fill in the information using the headings in Table 3.1.

1   What other information is in the abstract? Summarize in your own words.
2   Was the abstract succinctly written?
3   Was it easy to understand?

The Introduction of a Study

The "Introduction" is the *brain* of the study. In it we should define the topic being investigated, why it is important enough to be studied, the research question(s), any theory being considered, any hypothesis being proposed, and any predictions made. In addition, constructs and special terminology that are used throughout the study should be defined.

Typically, the introduction should provide historical context to the issue being investigated and bring in any theory that may be relevant to the reader. Often this is referred to as the *literature review* of the study (although not necessarily referred to as such), in that it summarizes and references a number of articles to introduce the reader to the study (e.g., Levitt & Red Owl, 2013). However, this is not a review of research, such as referred to in Chapter 2, which is a complete document that provides a broad overview of research and thinking on a given area. Rather, a literature review within the introduction of a study is a highly orchestrated, logical argument consisting of a number of propositional statements to provide the reasoning behind the study. With each statement, a study is summarized and/or referenced for support of the statement. At the end of the argument, there should be a conclusion in the form of at least one research question and possibly a hypothesis or several hypotheses. Hypotheses, in turn, should be operationally defined and translated into predictions.

In logic (Giere, 2004), a statement is either true or false and is used in a logical argument as one of the premises of the argument (see Appendix B for a more detailed explanation). Each statement needs to be supported by findings from at least one study to warrant the statement as a premise of the argument. If no support is provided, then the statement is no more than a hypothesis itself and needs to be tested before it can be used as a premise in any argument. For example, if we want to make the statement "Males are better at learning geometry than females" as one of the premises of our argument, we should cite at least one study to back this statement up. If there is no primary research to back this statement up, it cannot be used as one of the premises of our argument. It becomes itself a hypothesis that needs to be tested in a study of its own.

The support for each statement will be in the form of at least one reference to a primary study that you can look up to see whether the statement has support. If there is no reference to a study after a statement, the statement should be treated with suspicion. Statements without support weaken the overall argument.

However, not every reference that follows a statement is a research study. Sometimes references only cite the opinion of someone else. For example, S. K. Silverman (2010) included the following statement in the introduction to her study that examined preservice teacher beliefs about various identities associated with terms such as diversity and multicultural to better understand what is meant by these terms. She uses this statement in the introduction to her study. "Over the past decade, scholars have addressed the growing need for educators to possess a greater awareness of and sensitivity to multiculturalism in the classroom" (p. 292) and cited

Delpit (1995), Ladson–Billings (1994), and Zeichner (1993) in her introduction. The three references that she cited are not studies supporting the statement but are articles or comments from books that made an argument for an opinion. She is very clear in her introduction to distinguish between citations that are support- ing studies and citations that reference opinion.

A well-written paper lets the reader know in the text whether the reference is a study or an opinion. If you are not sure, look at the title in the full reference section to see whether you can identify which one it is. If that does not work, and you are really curious, you need to look at the abstract of the study provided in one of the preliminary sources (e.g., ERIC), or the study.

To illustrate the argument process, an analysis of the introduction section of Nosek and Smyth's (2011) study is provided in Box 3.1. It provides a reasonable illustration of the points made above.

BOX 3.1 ANALYSIS OF THE ARGUMENT FOR A STUDY

The problem: Gender stereotypes in math and science.

The argument

Context: There is a controversy regarding what influences gender stereo- types in the engagement in classes and achievement in science, technology, engineering, and mathematics (STEM). A number of factors may contribute to this gender gap engagement in these types of courses that are implicit and available to conscious introspection.

First premise: The fact that women are less likely than men to pursue and persist in many STEM college majors is widely recognized. Halpern and his colleagues (2007) have explored this problem for decades and have deter- mined that the problem is complex.

Subpremises

1   Unconscious bias or implicit social cognition might affect the STEM gap (Strack & Deutsch, 2004).
2   One bias may be explicit, characterized by intention, awareness, and control (Gawronski & Bodenhausen, 2006).
3   One bias may be implicit, characterized by lack of intention, awareness, or control (Bargh, 1994; Greenwald & Banaji, 1995).

Second premise: Although explicit expressions are valuable indicators of respondents' explicit beliefs, it also not clear how conscious experience captures actual mental processing of experiences (Nosek, 2007).

Third premise: Implicit measures, such as the implicit association test (IAT) may be able to assess mental processes that the respondent may be unwilling or unable to report (Greenwald & Banaji, 1995; Greenwald, McGhee & Schwartz, 1998).

Fourth premise: Implicit stereotypes about math and science are widespread and are important indicators of math and science engagement and achievement (Nosek, Smyth et al., 2007).

The conclusion: A study needs to be done that examines implicit stereotypes and if they predict interest and self-identification in math and science.

Hypotheses: Based on the previous premises, this study will test the following hypotheses related to implicit cognitions:

1   Implicit stereotyping of math as male will result in favorability toward math among men and less toward women.
2   Women involved in STEM will show a greater favorability toward math and weaker implicit stereotyping.
3   Implicit measures may explain the variation of STEM engagement in women and men.

As can be seen in the above example, the authors built their argument so that the reader can understand why this particular study was needed. After every premise, they supplied references to studies that provided support. If they had not, the argument would have been flawed. This is very important when the goal of the argument is to lead the reader to a hypothesis that the researcher wants to propose.

A detailed analysis of the argument in the introduction is not something consumers will do every time they read an article. However, to help develop a mindset for reading introductions in this fashion, we suggest you do the following exercise. It is not an easy exercise, but you will find that it focuses your mind more than usual when you read an introduction to a study. After doing this several times, you will find that you will be doing this automatically.

EXERCISE 3.3

Task: Find a research study of interest and examine the introduction carefully. Perform the following tasks:

1   Identify the purpose of the study.
2   Outline the argument with the main points (see Box 3.1).

(Continued)

(Continued)

> a   List down the premises of the argument.
>
> b   Indicate what support is given for each premise by citing one reference to a primary research study. If there is no supporting reference, indicate this.
>
> c   State your opinion on how well you think the points are logically related to one another.
>
> d   Are there any gaps in the logic? If so, what are they?
>
> 3   Identify the conclusion of the argument that should be in the form of questions and/or hypotheses/predictions.
>
> 4   State your opinion on how well you think the conclusion logically relates to the preceding argument.

Method

The *method* (*or methodology*) section consists of the skeleton of the study. If it is well written, others should be able to replicate the study exactly. The ability to replicate the study is the principal criteria used for judging the quality of this component of a research report.

The method section tells us who were studied, what was studied, and how the information was collected and analyzed. The following outline lists the typical subsections that are under this heading. Studies vary in what subsections authors include under the method section, but the information contained in the following subsections should be presented in a similar manner. The following chapters discuss many of these subsections in detail, but we provide a brief definition for each in the following:

- Sample
- Research design
  - treatment(s) (optional)
    - techniques (optional)
    - materials (optional)
- Data-collection procedures
  - instruments (optional)
  - observational methods
- Procedures followed

Sample

This subsection of the method section describes the participants/subjects or the objects of the study from which the data were gathered. A well-written sample section should provide as much detail as needed about the participants/objects. It should also explain the rationale used for selecting the participants so that the reader may be able to assess whether the resulting data are valid for the purpose of the study.

For example, O'Connor, Mueller, Lewis, Rivas-Drake, and Rosenberg (2011) used participants and described them as 44 Black students in their 2012 and 2013 graduating classes that included the highest achieving Black students (eight for this study) and a subset of low achievers. They continued with their description by providing information about the time of year these students were interviewed (winter of 2001) and also information about the research team that included their race, age, and gender. With this information, the reader can decide whether the results of the study are applicable to the question under consideration.

However, there are studies that look at objects rather than participants, such as Vurdien's (2013) study, which explored the use of personal blogs in an advanced English class to enhance writing skills of students in Spain. The author argued that due to their asynchronous nature, blogs allow second language learner students to write and publish their thoughts and views at their own pace without space and time constraints. In this study, the class discussions observed by the researcher and students' personal blog entries were the data source that was analyzed. Chapter 4 expands more on a number of important issues regarding the sample subsection of which the consumer will want to be aware. Although this segment of the study, at face value, appears to be routine, extremely large or small sample sizes and whether or not participants or objects are generating the data, will either add to or distract credibility from the study's results.

Research Design

The research design subsection, often referred to as *design*, explains the overall structural design used in the study. There are a number of designs available, and each one has its appropriate use. Each has its strengths and weaknesses depending on how well the data answer the research question(s).

In a well-written design section, the *variables*[1] of the study are clearly identified and defined. In fact the term *construct* is usually replaced by the term *variable*. If something does not vary, then it is not a variable. For example, *motivational potential* is a construct that varies (i.e., people vary in their potential for motivation). Therefore, it is referred to as a variable when used in a study, regardless of whether the word *construct* is used. Variables can take four different forms or scales. They can vary by discrete categories, rank order, or continuous scores on some measure. Gender is an example of the first (e.g., male vs. female), rating one's writing ability from 1 to 5 illustrates the second, and scores on a math test is the third (see Appendix B for more detail).

Variables can have different classifications. A variable may be *descriptive, correlational, independent, dependent, moderating,* or *extraneous.* How a variable is classified depends on the role the variable plays in a study and the type of research design being used, which is determined by the research question(s). In other words, the same variable can be descriptive in one study, correlational in another, independent in a third, dependent in a fourth, moderating in a fifth, and extraneous in a sixth. To make things more challenging, research studies vary in how many of these different types of variables are present.

Although we explain more about variable classification within the context of our discussion of the different research designs in Chapter 5, let us give you a brief overview of these different types of variables. *Descriptive variables* are variables that are observed and described without looking at the effect of one variable on another. These variables are mostly used to answer the *What's out there?* question. The data recorded on these variables are usually in the form of detailed verbal descriptions and/or frequency of occurrence. A study by Ajayi (2011) provides a clear example of a study that examined descriptive variables. It is clear from the title that there were three variables of interest: (a) preservice teachers' understanding of the changes in literacy practices, (b) preservice teachers' perceptions of their readiness to teach new literacies, and (c) preservice teachers' anticipation of teaching multiliteracies. Her main goal was to identify how well preservice teachers were prepared to teach new literacies as new teachers in the field. Data were in the form of frequencies that were generated from responses to a questionnaire.

Correlational variables (CV) are collected for the purpose of finding relationships between two or more variables. The variables are typically measured by counting their frequencies of occurrence or by scores on instruments that measure the variables. To illustrate, Kelly and Price (2011) examined relationships between multiple variables including poverty variation, racial heterogeneity, selectivity, electivity, and school mean test scores to explore the extent to which schools implement academic tracking policies. They used an extensive analysis of curriculum guides and school policies to identify highly elaborate tracking systems that were in place in high schools. The researchers found that instead of linking high-track course enrollments to overall programs of study or gifted-and-talented designations, schools increase the scope of tracking with co-requisites. To come to their conclusions, they correlated multiple variables in different combinations as they analyzed the data.

An *independent variable* (IV) is regarded as a variable of influence—that is, it affects the variation (or change) in another variable. The variable being influenced (or changed) is labeled the *dependent variable* (DV) in that its variation depends on changes in the independent variable. These two variable labels are found in research designs that look at causation.[2] The way you can identify the two variables is to note which one is thought to affect (i.e., impact, change, cause, influence, etc.) the other. The one doing the affecting is the independent variable, and the one being affected is the dependent variable. Often you can spot them in the title of the study. For example, the title of R. Silverman's (2013) study is "Investigating Video as a Means to Promote Vocabulary for At-Risk Children."

The IV is something related to video presentation. In operational terms, the IV was using video presentations repeatedly to supplement normal vocabulary development. The DV was the accumulation of vocabulary growth. A study can have more than one independent variable and/or dependent variable as well. For instance, Herbers et al. (2012) study entitled "Early Reading Skills and Academic Achievement Trajectories of Students Facing Poverty, Homelessness, and High Residential Mobility" indicates three IVs, poverty, homelessness, and high residential mobility, and two DVs, reading skills and academic achievement.

Some research designs have what is referred to as a treatment or maybe even several treatments. This is usually done when the researcher(s) manipulates an independent variable and looks at its effect on a dependent variable. The treatment may involve some technique as demonstrated in Wirkala and Kuhn's (2011) study, where they explored the impact of problem-based learning (PBL) on students' comprehension and applications of material compared with traditional lecture-based classes. In this example, PBL was the treatment.

The treatment might also consist of some type of material. The material can be in the form of written, audio, or visual information presented to the participants. This is illustrated by Stein and Kaufman (2010), who examined the effects of different types of math curricular materials and the conditions under which they are most effective. They specifically explored two types of math curriculum, Everyday Mathematics and Investigations in two different school districts.

The *moderator variable* (MV), as the name suggests, works as a go-between from one variable to another; that is, it moderates the relationship between two CVs, or influences the degree to which an IV affects a DV. Figure 3.1 shows the mediating role the MV plays in a study involving an IV and a DV. An MV can be in any of its possible forms: categorical, ordinal, or continuous. For instance, in the study by Alivernini and Lucidi (2011), the independent variables were self-determined

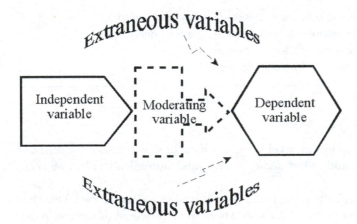

FIGURE 3.1 Relationship Between Some Variable Types

motivation, self-efficacy, and students' perceived support from parents. The DV was drop-out rates from high school. However, they used two MVs as well: academic performance and socioeconomic status, which were measured by course grades and level of income. In other words, they wanted to know whether the effect of the three IVs on the DV was different depending on academic accomplishment and the students' level of income.

Extraneous variables (EV) are any variables that the researcher does not want to influence the relation between two CVs or the variance of a DV other than by an IV. As shown in Figure 3.1, these variables are lurking around a study trying to creep in for distorting the results. In some studies, researchers may not want their data influenced by differences in such variables as gender, age, level of language proficiency, intellectual development, and so on. The design of the study, if planned appropriately, should keep the influence of these variables at bay. Chapter 5 provides a detailed description of many types of EVs that can mess up a study. A well-written study mentions what EVs threaten the results and states what was done to prevent their effects.

Identifying variables of a study is not a straightforward task. Therefore, we have included the following exercise to give you an opportunity to identify variables and classify their types in studies that you have found. We suggest that you use Figure 3.1 as a guideline for making your decisions.

EXERCISE 3.4

Use a recent journal related to education. Find a research study of interest and examine the introduction and the method sections carefully. Perform the following tasks:

1   Summarize the purpose of the study in your own words.
2   Classify the variables according to the previous definitions.
3   Identify the forms (scales) of the variables.
4   Provide a rationale for your classification.

Data-Collection Procedures

This subsection explains in detail how the information is collected for the purpose of a research study. Most studies involve either instruments and/or observational procedures.

Instruments specifically relate to the devices used to collect the data. These are usually in the form of surveys or tests. They can be presented in written, audio, or visual format. Responses can be gathered via paper-and-pencil tests, computer administered tests, video camera or audiotape recorder.

Other studies may not involve any data-gathering instruments but may involve personal observations of subjects or objects. These studies typically use video or audio recording to keep a record of the data in case there is need for validation, but the actual data collection is done by an observer or a group of observers.

In some studies, confusion between the instruments and the materials used in the treatment can occur if the reader is not careful. One might think of the material as the stimulus that elicits the behavior that is measured or observed by the instrument. For example, Kong (2010) examined student teachers' reflections on their teaching performance by using a web-enabled video system. The video system was not the instrument of the study, however, but rather the instrument used to elicit the student teachers' reflective comments on their student teaching practices. Using the web-enabled video of their student teaching was a secondary issue to the study. The data of interest were the participants' reflective responses. As with other sections of a study, more needs to be said about data gathering. Chapter 6 provides a more detailed discussion on this.

Procedures Followed

This subsection is a detailed explanation of how the complete study was executed. In some studies, the data-collection procedure subsection and this section are the same. The procedure subsection describes when and how the treatments (if any) were administered, when and how the instruments (if any) were given, and/or when and how observation methods were used. The main criterion for judging the quality of this subsection is whether we have enough information to replicate the study if need be. In Edens and McCormick's study (2000) they were interested in examining how adolescents process advertisements and were also interested in looking at the influence of ad characteristics, processing objective, and gender. In their procedures section, we are told that their subjects viewed six advertisements from recent magazines and then were asked specific questions about the advertisements. The subjects were given 20 s to view each advertisement and then a few minutes to respond to questions. The amount of time they gave the students to complete the task and the amount of time subjects were exposed to the advertisements were important to know. The reason is that if anyone wanted to replicate this study, they would also have to limit their participants to the same time constraints. To give you a feel for what has just been discussed, we recommend you doing the following exercise.

EXERCISE 3.5

Use the same research study that you used for Exercise 3.4. Examine the method section carefully. Complete the following tasks:

(Continued)

(Continued)

1 Briefly summarize the procedure that the researcher(s) went through to collect their data.
2 Estimate whether you could replicate this study if you had the facilities. If you could not, explain what pieces of information you would need to repeat this study.

Results

In this section, the results of any analysis of the data are given. Depending again on the nature of the research design, different methods are used to try to make sense out of the data. One common method is to use statistics. Often, many readers jump over this section, thinking it is only for the mathematically inclined. However, one of our goals in Chapter 7 is to help the consumer of research not to be intimidated by strange Greek symbols, tables full of numbers, and graphs full of lines.

Not all studies have results sections filled with statistics. In some studies, what we later refer to as *qualitative studies*, the results section contains verbal data consisting of detailed descriptions of what was observed. Researchers spend extended amounts of time gathering large quantities of verbal data with the main purpose of identifying patterns and trends that will guide in answering the research questions of the study. Occasionally, some descriptive statistics are used to help illustrate these patterns. More is said about the issues involved in this type of analysis in Chapter 7.

The results section of a study is important and should not be avoided. The strengths and weaknesses of a study can often be found in the choice of a data analysis procedure that affects the results. Conclusions based on faulty results cannot be used to answer our research questions. Chapter 7 expands the results section more. It compares how verbal and numerical data are treated and the criteria that need to be used when evaluating whether they have been properly used.

Discussion/Conclusion

The final section of a research study discusses the results and concludes the study. If the discussion is exceptionally lengthy, the conclusions may be separated from it. Here is where the results are interpreted in light of the research question(s) being asked and/or any hypothesis being tested. A well-written discussion/conclusion section also relates the findings of the study to previous research that has been done and to any theorizing that has been going on regarding the research topic. In addition, authors should evaluate their own study by pointing out its strengths and weaknesses. This section characteristically concludes with what further research needs to be done and suggestions on how it might be done. Chapter 8 spends more time describing what constitutes a well-written discussion section.

Key Terms and Concepts

abstract
data-collection procedures
instruments
material
method
observational methods
participants/objects
premise
research design
sample
treatment
variables
    correlational
    dependent
    descriptive
    extraneous
    independent
    moderating

Notes

1 A variable is something that varies, usually corresponding to one of the constructs in the study.
2 Studies that look at predictive relationships also distinguish between IVs and DVs, but cannot conclude causation.

References

Ajayi, L. (2011). Preservice teachers' knowledge, attitudes, and perception of their preparation to teach multiliteracies/multimodality. *The Teacher Educator, 46*, 6–31.

Alivernini, F., & Lucidi, F. (2011). Relationship between social context, self efficacy, motivation, academic achievement, and intention to drop out of high school: A longitudinal study. *Journal of Educational Research, 104*(4), 241–252.

Books, S., & Ndlalane, T. (2011). What the U. S. could learn from South Africa about education and social justice. *Educational Foundations, 25*(1–2), 83–102.

Delpit, L. (1995). *Other people's children: Cultural conflict in the classroom.* New York, NY: New Press.

Edens, K. M., & McCormick, C. B. (2000). How do adolescents process advertisements? The influence of ad characteristics, processing objective, and gender. *Contemporary Educational Psychology, 25*, 450–463.

Gasper, J., DeLuca, S., & Estacion, A. (2012). Switching schools: Revisiting the relationship between school mobility and high school dropout. *American Educational Research Journal, 49*(3), 487–519.

Giere, R. N. (2004). *Understanding scientific reasoning.* Graton, CA: Wadsworth.

Herbers, J. E., Cutuli, J. J., Supkoff, L. M., Heistad, D., Chan, C-K., Hinz, E., & Masten, A. S. (2012). Early reading skills and academic achievement trajectories of students facing poverty, homelessness, and high residential mobility. *Educational Researcher, 41*(9), 366–374.

Kelly, S., & Price, H. (2011). The correlates of tracking policy: Opportunity hoarding, status competition, or a technical-functional explanation? *American Educational Research Journal, 48*(3), 560–585.

Kong, S. C. (2010). Using a web-enabled video system to support student teachers' self-reflection in teaching practices. *Computers in Education, 55*(4), 1772–1782.

Ladson-Billings, G. (1994). *The Dreamkeepers: Successful teachers of African American children.* San Francisco, CA: Jossey-Bass.

Lee, J. (2010). Tripartite growth trajectories of reading and math achievement: Tracking national academic progress at primary, middle, and high school levels. *American Educational Research Journal, 47*(4), 800–832.

Levitt, R., & Red Owl, R. H. (2013). Effects of early literacy environments on the reading attitudes, behaviors, and values of veteran teachers. *Learning Environments Research, 16*(3), 387–409.

Moss, B., & Hendershot, J. (2002). Exploring sixth graders' selection of nonfiction trade books. *The Reading Teacher, 56*(1), 6–17.

Nosek, B. A., & Smyth, F. L. (2011). Implicit social cognitions predict sex differences in math engagement and achievement. *American Educational Research Journal, 48*(5), 1125–1156.

O'Connor, C., Mueller, J., Lewis, R. L., Rivas-Drake, D., & Rosenberg, S. (2011). "Being" Black and strategizing for excellence in a racially stratified academic hierarchy. *American Educational Research Journal, 48*(6), 1232–1257.

Silverman, R. (2013). Investigating video as a means to promote vocabulary for at-risk children. *Contemporary Educational Psychology, 38*(3), 170–179.

Silverman, S. K. (2010). What is diversity? An inquiry into preservice teacher beliefs. *American Educational Research Journal, 47*(2), 292–329.

Stein, M. K., & Kaufman, J. H. (2010). Selecting and supporting the use of mathematics curricula at scale. *American Educational Research Journal, 47*(3), 663–693.

Strom, I. F., Thoresen, S., Wentzel-Larsen, T., & Dyb, G. (2013). Violence, bullying, and academic achievement: A study of 15-year-old adolescents and their school environment. *Child Abuse and Neglect: The International Journal, 37*(4), 243–251.

Vurdien, R. (2013). Enhancing writing skills through blogging in an advanced English as a foreign language class in Spain. *Computer Assisted Learning, 26*(2), 126–143.

West-Olatunji, C., Baker, J. C., & Brooks, M. (2006). African American adolescent males: Giving voice to their educational experiences. *Multicultural Perspectives, 8*(4), 3–9.

Williamson, P., & McLeskey, J. (2011). An investigation into the nature of inclusion problem-solving teams. *The Teacher Educator, 46*(4), 316–334.

Wirkala, C., & Kuhn, D. (2011). Problem-based learning in K-12 education: Is it effective and how does it achieve its effects? *American Educational Research Journal, 48*(5), 1157–1186.

Zeichner, K. M. (1993). *Educating teachers for cultural diversity.* East Lansing, MI: National Center for Research on Teacher Learning.

4

UNDERSTANDING WHERE DATA COME FROM

The Sample

Chapter Overview

The first subsection in the methodology section of a study typically informs the reader where the data come from (i.e., the sample). You might ask, "What is so important about a sample of participants that we have to spend a whole chapter on the topic?" As we hope you see while reading this chapter, what initially appears to be an insignificant portion contained in the methodology section of a study proves to be one of the foundation stones upon which the study is evaluated regarding its usefulness.

The purpose of this chapter is to provide you, the consumer of research, with an overall understanding about the importance of and the thinking that goes on when choosing a sample. We first provide some initial definitions of terminology, which are essential for understanding the rest of the discussion. These definitions are followed by two segments that discuss the two major sampling paradigms found in educational research. The choice of paradigm, as you might suspect by now, is guided by the research question being asked by the researchers. The chapter ends with a discussion of the ethics of using human participants in a research study.

Sampling Terminology

The *sample* is the source from which data are drawn to answer the research question(s) and/or to test any hypothesis that might be made. The sample consists of one or more *cases*. In most studies, the cases are made up of human beings referred to as *subjects* or, more currently, *participants*. For example, Lopes, Mestre, Guil, Kremenitzer, and Salovey (2012) used 463 students from two Spanish high schools and one American university to examine students' abilities to evaluate emotionally challenging situations and to identify effective strategies for managing their emotions.

In other studies, the cases might be inanimate *objects* from which researchers extract their data. Examples are *corpora* of verbal discourse such as an accumulation of journals, blogs or twitter statements, or when researchers cull their data from transcriptions of taped dialogs. McGrail and Davis (2011), for instance, used the blogs of 16 elementary students and examined their writing in terms of content, voice, connections, relationships, and thinking. They examined samples of their writing as pre- and post-blog activity and compared the writing samples of students who participated in blogging with those who did not participate in blogging. Although the researchers mentioned that 16 students were involved, the real data source, or objects, from which the data were drawn was the pre- and post-blog writing samples and the actual blog records of the participants.

Sometimes the reader can be confused as to what makes up a sample, as seen in the McGrail and Davis (2011) study. However, one of our students found another study that was even more challenging. Lawson and Alameda-Lawson (2012) explored the social processes and outcomes associated with a school-linked, community-based program that successfully engaged Latino parents and children in a low-income school community. Although data were collected initially from 12 Latino parents, several of them eventually dropped out of the study and alternatively parents were then included to raise the total to 32 participants. A second study group of 20 participants was also selected from a list of 841 parents who had participated for at least a month in the preceding 2 years. The data sources included a parent questionnaire, a semistructured interview, focus groups, archival records, program activities, and participant observation. Now for the question: Who and/or what make up the sample? The answer is determined by which data source is used to answer the research question(s). So the answer is, all of the above. Data were drawn from multiple sources and multiple participant samples. For reasons outlined next, there were different uses that demanded different combinations of participants/objects to answer different questions.

Sampling Paradigms

There are a number of ways that a sample is chosen to do research. Table 4.1 provides a list of some of the most commonly used techniques along with the main purpose for using them and brief definitions. The two general paradigms are *Representative (probability)* and *Purposeful (nonprobability)*. The first consists of techniques that try to capture a sample that represents a defined *population* based on probability theory. The second attempts to identify samples that are rich in specific information. Representative sampling (more commonly referred to as probability sampling) has one aim: to find a sample that reflects salient characteristics of a specific population so that the results of the study can be generalized to that population. Purposeful sampling (also referred to as nonprobability or

Table 4.1 Sampling Terminology

Paradigm	Purpose	Sampling Strategy	Definition
Representative (Probability) Sampling			A sample representing the population.
	Generalizability		Inferring the results of the study from the sample to the population.
		Simple random	Everyone has an equal chance to be chosen.
		Systematic random	Cases are selected across the population in an orderly fashion.
		Stratified random	Cases selected within different strata in the population.
		Proportional	Selected to reflect the proportions of the strata in the population.
		Nonproportional	Selected to reflect the strata but not the proportions.
		Cluster	Intact groups are randomly selected. All cases within the selected groups are used.
		Multistage	A combination of cluster sampling combined with another random selection technique.
Purposeful (Nonprobability) Sampling			
	In-depth information gathering		Focus on the quality of the information.
		Convenience sampling	Cases selected because they are readily available.
		Extreme/deviant case	Cases that are atypical.

(Continued)

Table 4.1 (Continued)

Paradigm	Purpose	Sampling Strategy	Definition
		Intensity (expert, critical case)	Ones that contain high amounts of the characteristics being studied.
		Snowball/chain sampling	Rare cases are found via other rare cases.
		Criterion sampling	Cases used who meet specific criteria.
		Typical case (modal)	Ones that represent the average.
		Maximum variation sampling	A cross section of cases that represent a wide spectrum.
		Stratified purposeful sampling	A few cases from each stratum.
		Homogeneous sampling	Cases that are very similar.
		Volunteers	Individuals that offer to participate.

purposive sampling) is more concerned with the unique characteristics of the sample itself apart from any larger population—which is not to say that the results cannot be applied to other situations (more on this later).

The Representative Sampling Paradigm

As previously mentioned, in the representative sampling paradigm, the goal of the researcher is to generalize the findings and interpretations of the study to a larger population. The sample is a portion of a larger population. The word *population* usually means everyone in a country or a city. In research, this word has a more technical use; although similar, *population* means *all* the members of the group of participants/objects to which researchers want to generalize their research findings. This is referred to as the *target population*. In other words, the criterion for defining a target population is determined by the group of people to which researchers would like to generalize the interpretations of the study. For example, the population might be all middle school special education students or it might be a more limited group of all middle school special education students that have been diagnosed with attention deficit disorder who attend school in a specific school district. For another study, the target population may be entirely different.

Typically, having access to the entire target population to which researchers want to generalize their findings is impossible. For example, having access to all middle school special education students with attention deficit disorder throughout the world is, in practice, impossible. However, researchers may have access to a limited number of schools in their own county, state, or country. Whatever is available for use becomes the *experimentally accessible population* (Gall, Borg, & Gall, 1996). It is to this population the findings of a study can be directly generalized, not to the entire target population. The only time researchers could make inferences from the findings of their study to the target population is when they can show that the experimentally accessible population possesses similar characteristics as the larger target population. For the rest of the book, we use the phrase target population with the understanding that we are referring to the *experimentally accessible* population.

Selecting a representative sample is important for making use of the findings of a study outside of the confines of the study itself. This is because the degree to which the results of a study can be generalized to a target population is the degree to which the sample adequately represents the larger group—the degree to which a sample represents a population is determined by the degree to which the relevant attributes in the target population are found in the sample.

Figure 4.1 illustrates the relationship between the sample and the population. We have used different graphic symbols to represent different attributes of a population. These attributes could be gender, age, level of education, level of language proficiency, and so on. Notice that the attributes in the sample (A, B, C, D, F) almost match exactly the attributes in the population; however, attribute E is missing in the sample. In this case, the sample is not 100% representative of the population, but it is very close. Most likely we could conclude that the population was representative enough to make tentative generalizations. However, there would always remain caution due to the missing attribute E.

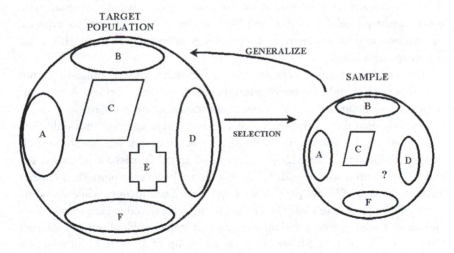

FIGURE 4.1 Illustration of a Sample Partially Representing a Target Population

The degree to which findings of a study can be generalized to a larger population or *transferred* to similar situations is referred to as *external validity* (or *transferability*; Miles & Huberman, 1994). To achieve this type of validity, researchers must demonstrate that the samples they use represent the groups to which they want to apply their findings. Otherwise, without this important quality, the findings are of little use outside of the study. The more representative the sample is to the population, the greater the external validity. In other terms, the more similar the characteristics of the sample are to other situations, the better the transfer of conclusions.

Identifying the target population is not always easy. For example, Hong-Nam and Leavell (2007) examined the language learning strategies of bilingual and monolingual students. The authors described the participants as 428 monolingual Korean university students (223 males and 205 females ages 18–28) and 420 bilingual Korean–Chinese university students (182 males and 238 females, ages 20–28). They also provided information about the bilingual participants that included the number of students using either Korean or Chinese at home, with friends and overall proficiency (beginning, intermediate, or advanced) in both languages. Then they compared the two groups on gender, English proficiency, years of study, years studying English, test taking experience, and travel abroad.

You can see rather quickly that the sample becomes more complex as the authors add more details about the participants. Without a careful read of the article, it can quickly become confusing about who the target population is? In this study, the target population is identified in their research questions as monolingual Korean and bilingual Korean–Chinese university students. All of this additional information is important to the study, but does it add to or distract from clarifying the target population? Is it all bilinguals who use more complex strategies to learn when compared to monolinguals or is it only bilinguals with more extensive English backgrounds? These questions are important to answer if the researchers want to generalize their findings to larger populations than these subgroups represent.

The problem of researchers not identifying their target populations is not uncommon in published research. However, without this information, the consumer cannot evaluate whether correct generalizations are being made.[1]

An additional note is that choosing a representative sample is not only used for quantitative research. Some qualitative studies also seek this quality in their samples. To illustrate, Maher (2007) interviewed 25 (12 females and 13 males) gay and lesbian alumni who attended Catholic high schools to explore their experiences in the area of family, peers, school, spirituality, and identity while attending school. These participants were "recruited through a gay and lesbian organization and through advertisement and through gay and lesbian publications and Internet bulletin boards" (p. 459). Maher expected this group of 25 to be a representative sample of students who attended Catholic schools who were also gay and lesbian.

Sampling Strategies for Making Generalizations

There are a number of strategies used to try to achieve a representative sample (see Table 4.1). Because the manner in which a sample is chosen is so important, published studies in education should inform the reader how the samples were selected. The following is a summary of the more common sampling strategies and the rationales used to warrant them. Note that all methods under this heading use the word *random*. This term technically means that the procedure used gives every member of the pool from which the sample is being taken an equal chance of being selected—it does not mean haphazard.

The ideal strategy for statistical purposes, yet rarely achieved in social research in general and educational research in particular, is *simple random* sampling. This method attempts to ensure that every member of the target population has an equal opportunity for being chosen. In addition to facilitating obtaining representative samples, this method can control unwanted influences from extraneous variables. As mentioned in Chapter 3, these are variables which could impact the variables being studied and produce spurious results. The reason simple random sampling controls the impact of these nuisance variables is that it disperses their effect throughout the sample. For example, if a researcher is not interested in whether males behave differently than females, yet gender could affect the dependent variable in some undesirable way, the researcher would want to ensure that the sample consisted of approximately half males and half females. One way to do this is to obtain a sample randomly. If the sample is randomly chosen (and large enough), there is a high probability that both genders will be equally represented, which would wash out any gender effect when the data from the two groups were combined.

However, as just alluded to, simple random selection on its own does not guarantee a representative sample; sample size is also a consideration. Obviously, a sample of one person would not represent a population of language students even though randomly selected. The target population might consist of males and females, but a sample of one is not representative because only one of the sexes is represented. Or, if the sample of one is a male, but the dependent variable does not behave with males as it does with females, then the findings would be misleading. To avoid these two problems, you need to use a larger sample. The maxim in research that aims to make generalizations is *the larger the sample, the better*. In Chapter 7, when we discuss some statistical issues, we show the relationship between size of sample and the risk of getting a nonrepresentative sample. But suffice it to say here that the larger the random sample, the greater the *probability* of getting a representative sample.

The negative impact of overall small sample size is exacerbated if there is any *attrition* (i.e., loss of participants).[2] An example of how this might work is Morgan, Fuchs, Compton, Cordray, and Fuchs' (2008) study, which explored early reading failure and its impact on children's motivation to read. The research design used a pretest–posttest control group design with random assignment of first-grade children to multiple subgroups for reading ability level to determine their different levels of interest in reading as a function of their relative success or failure in learning to read. The abstract states that sixty participants were used in the total sample. In the methods section, the authors state that they "recruited 75 first-grade students and identified 30 of these as highly skilled (HS), 30 students as low skilled nonresponders (LS), and 15 students as low skilled nonresponders who were tutored (LS–T)" (p. 389). Since this was a longitudinal study of more than 1 year, the relocation of some first-grade participants, especially the smaller group of 15, to other school districts during the study would make the different groups of children incomparable.[3]

In Table 4.1 *systematic random sampling* is listed. We will not elaborate on this one because it is so seldom used. If you are interested in knowing more, search the term on Google or some other search engine.

A procedure that you might see in the research literature is *stratified random sampling*. This method is especially useful when the population consists of subgroups such as males or females, various proficiency levels, and so on. In this scenario, one of two forms of *stratified random sampling* can be used: *proportional* or *nonproportional* (Gall et al., 1996).

Proportional stratified random sampling attempts to choose cases that represent the proportion of each of the subgroups in the population. For example, Odinko and Williams (2006) sought to investigate how preschool teachers and their pupils interact during instruction in numeracy lessons in Nigeria. They sampled 2,859 children from three different regions of Nigeria that represented a proportional representation of students from private, public, urban, and rural schools. If 45% of the students attended public schools, 5% private schools, 35% urban schools, and 15% rural schools, the sample should include students matching these proportions. The results can then be generalized to the whole population of preschool students in this region of Nigeria. Had the researchers used a simple random sampling procedure, they would most likely not have obtained these proportions.

On the other hand, if the main intent was to compare the subgroups with one another, the researchers need to have equal numbers of participants for each group. To do this they should use a *nonproportional stratified random sampling* strategy. That is, the researchers will randomly sample the same number of participants from each of the levels or categories that are represented.

The following study exemplifies the use of the nonproportional stratified sampling strategy. LaVergne, Larke, Elbert, and Jones (2011) explored the attitudes toward diversity inclusion in Texas secondary agricultural education programs. Their target population consisted of all Texas secondary agricultural teachers listed for the 2006–2007 academic year. Due to the unavailability of some personal information from the Texas Education Association, access to all 1,732 was not feasible. Working off of a list of 1,500 agricultural teachers, the researchers then used a nonproportional stratified random sampling process to ensure that all 10 administrative areas defined by the Texas Future Farmers of America (FFA) Association would be represented in the study. The researchers randomly selected 32 teachers from each area to complete their questionnaire. With these samples, they could make reasonable comparisons between the 10 administrative levels and their perceptions of diversity in secondary agricultural education.

A strategy used to help manage very large populations is *cluster sampling* (see Table 4.1). Rather than trying to randomly sample from every member of a population, researchers randomly sample groups from within the population, such as schools or programs. Once these clusters are chosen, all the members of the clusters are used as participants. A permutation of this method is the *multistage* method that initially selects clusters randomly followed by use of another random selection procedure. For example, Hossein, Asadzadeh, Shabani, Ahghar, Ahadi, and Shamir (2011) combined cluster sampling with random sampling of the effects of indirect and significant effects of Invitational Education on performance through inherent and incremental intelligence beliefs. The accessible population for the study included all high school students studying in the academic year of 2009–2010 in Kashmar, Iran. The research sample included a total of 540 students (270 males, 270 females), selected through multistage random sampling: the city was divided into three separate regions or clusters (north, center, and south), and then four schools in each region and three classes in each school were randomly selected. By using this type of sampling technique, the authors assumed that their sample adequately represented the high school student population in Kashmar.

The following exercise gives you the opportunity to find a study that used the representative sampling paradigm.

EXERCISE 4.1

Select a study of interest that used one of the representative sampling techniques previously discussed. Summarize the following:

1   The purpose and the research question(s) of the study.
2   Define:

    a   The target population to which findings were intended to be applied. You most likely have to infer this from the questions, hypothesis, or discussion section.
    b   The experimentally accessible population.
    c   How the sample was chosen (e.g., simple random method, stratified random method, etc.).
    d   The size of the sample.
    e   Characteristics of the sample.

3   Evaluate the sample whether it was a representative of the target population. Defend your answer.

The Purposeful Sampling Paradigm: Sample Strategies for Maximizing Information

The purposeful sampling paradigm focuses on the specific characteristics of whom or what is selected for the sample. The question that decides this is "Does the sample contain the needed information being sought?" This can range from one participant or object, as in a case study, to larger numbers. However, with this approach, the emphasis is more on the *quality* of the information taken from the sample. We discuss this approach more fully in the next chapter.

We are convinced that the purposeful sampling paradigm is more commonly used than representative sampling in educational research. Although one particular genre of research methodology, *qualitative research*, uses this type of sampling paradigm almost exclusively, researchers using *quantitative* designs in the field of education also use it the majority of the time. We base this on years of experiencing our students' searching for studies that use one of the representative sampling strategies to complete Exercise 4.1. Therefore, we want to spend more time on the various strategies used under this heading than is commonly found in textbooks on research methodology.

Rather than trying to find a sample to represent some population as with representative sampling, purposeful sampling stresses strategies for selecting samples for in-depth data gathering. Gall et al. (1996, pp. 231–236) summarized 15 *purposeful sampling strategies* (see Patton, 2002, pp. 230–246) for deliberately choosing a sample to supply the most information possible regarding the research question. While reviewing these, we found a fair amount of overlap among the 15 strategies. In Table 4.1, we have regrouped these to reduce the redundancy, and included two that are not normally included under purposeful sampling: convenience and volunteer sampling. In addition, you will see that these strategies are not mutually exclusive. They are often used in combination to select the best sample.

The first purposeful sampling strategy we discuss is *convenience sampling*—though sometimes associated with representative sampling. In practice, having access to all members of the entire population to obtain a representative sample is often impossible due to time or financial constraints. Instead, researchers access participants from those immediately available, but do not do this randomly. They select their conveniently available sample so that it fulfills the purpose of the study. For example, Isik-Ercan, Inan, Nowak, and Kim (2012) wanted to determine the impact of using 3D technology and visualization while urban second graders covered a solar system literacy unit. Their preference would have been to include all second-grade classrooms in the school district. However, they were only given access to two second-grade classrooms for a pilot project for a total of 35 students in the sample. In this case, the access to a sample of second-grade learners was smaller than anticipated and resulted in a sample of convenience. The authors' ability to draw broad conclusions about all second graders from this one project becomes limited due to the convenient sample. Therefore, we have placed this sampling strategy under the purposeful sampling paradigm because the sample is usually biased and is not representative of a larger population. In addition, it is purposeful in that the researcher determines that the sample is the right one for gathering the data needed for the study—this is not to be confused with haphazard.

Whether one can apply their findings from a convenience sample to a larger target population depends on how well one can show that the sample corresponds to the larger population on important characteristics. This is done by providing clear descriptions of how the sample shares these features. Often the researcher gathers this type of information through surveys and tests prior to the implementation of the study.

From many studies that our students and we have seen, our conclusion is that many studies use *convenience sampling* when selecting samples. Another such study that clearly used a convenience sample was done by Leston, Jessen, and Simons (2012) who investigated and compared Native Alaskan and non-Native Alaskan students' perceptions of sexually transmitted diseases, human immunodeficiency virus (HIV)/acquired immune deficiency syndrome or acquired immunodeficiency syndrome (AIDS), and unplanned pregnancies. They "used a convenience sample of 105 Alaska Native and non-Alaska Native rural youth from 5 communities in Alaska and then had them participate in 21 focus groups to address their knowledge, attitudes, and beliefs about sexual health" (p. 2). However, Leston et al. also stated that although their sample was one of *convenience*, an effort was made "to select a range of several small communities in the area." This being said, the authors also stated that since the youths volunteered and self-selected for the study, the results "might not be representative of all youth in the community" (p. 3).

Despite their limitations, we encourage you not to think that such studies have little value; but, rather, you need to take the findings from such studies with the understanding that they need to be replicated with different samples. We think it is safe to say that very few studies use samples that pass all of the criteria for a good sample. Therefore, the consumer needs to look for similar studies using different samples to see if the results are repeated. If so, you can have more confidence in the answers to your questions.

The second strategy in the list (see Table 4.1), *extreme/deviant case*, selects cases that stand out either above or below the average. The purpose is to look for characteristics in cases that are unusual and then contrast or compare these traits with average cases. For example, Greiner (2010) used interviews of an "ordinary" woman growing up and living in Appalachia to compare and contrast her experiences to other women from different environments. Greiner learned from her research experience that "ordinary" people like her participant, contribute uniquely to our understanding of the human experience.

The next strategy in Table 4.1 is *intensity* sampling within which we have included *expert* and *critical case* sampling. These share the goal of using cases that should concentrate the traits that are being studied. As an example, Zehr, Moss, and Nichols (2005) purposely chose only one teacher to study a teacher's personal perspective as to how his own life as an Amish school teacher influenced his family's life and his community. The researchers justified their choice of participant by stating:

> The teacher whose life and practice is discussed here was a middle school teacher in an Amish school in the community in which he was raised. While harvesting wheat at his father's place, in 1988, he overheard a discussion between his sister and her husband about the discipline problems in the Amish school that their children attended. He decided at that point that he felt like he could teach and the next night, the Amish school board came over to his house to ask if he would consider teaching. (p. 592)

In other words, this teacher, in the author's opinion, was an appropriate person to study to provide the information needed—this participant was *information-rich*. The value of using this type of sampling paradigm is seen in the participant's following discovery:

> This project has resulted in more conversations among some of us: Amish teachers and parents who want to provide our children with the education they need to be productive. While this project provided the kind of feedback we need, it also allowed more Amish to become aware of how English people think about us and how we think about what it means to be Amish. (p. 612)

Another strategy listed (see Table 4.1) is *snowball or chain* sampling. For those in climates that have not seen snow or made snowballs, let us try to explain. You first pack a little snow into a ball in your hand and then add more snow making the ball bigger. Once it gets big enough you roll it on the ground until you end up with a big snow ball. It is very similar to how a dung beetle builds up a ball of dung—maybe we should call it the *Dung Beetle sampling method* for those in warmer climates. This strategy is helpful for finding individuals who are normally difficult to find to use for a sample. Kupczynski, Mundy, and Maxwell (2012) studied faculty perceptions of cooperative learning and traditional discussion with a special focus on distance learning and virtual classrooms. Although in the end, only five participants were involved with the project, the initial first participant was asked to recommend someone else with comparable background and interest and then that person recommended another. This process continued until the desired sample size was finally achieved.

Following this sampling method listed in Table 4.1 is *criterion* sampling. This strategy uses a set of criteria to determine whether or not to select an individual as part of the sample. Akbas (2012), for example, used 87 students in his study that investigated high school students' reasons for mistrust of other people. He clearly stated that he used criterion sampling based on the "criteria of gender, grade level, socio-economic level, achievement, and willingness to participate" (p. 605). Although 104 students were in the original sample, only 87 met the initial criteria and only 10 students of this 87 replied "no" to the question of "can most people be trusted?" These 10 students then eventually constituted the number of participants that were interviewed by the researcher about the topic of mistrust.

If researchers want to select a sample that represented the average person or situation, they would use the *typical case (modal)*[4] strategy (see Table 4.1). Chaapel, Columna, Lytle, and Bailey (2012) purposefully selected 10 parents of children with disabilities with the intent to explore their opinions about adapted physical education services that were available for their children. The parents participated in one-on-one semistructured interviews with the researchers. Clearly, the researchers considered these parents typical examples of a growing number of parents with children who suffer from some type of learning disability and therefore, had the information they needed for their study.

Other studies use a *maximum variation* sampling strategy (see Table 4.1) to see what type of information might be collected over a wide variety of individuals. Guilloteaux and Dörnyei (2008) examined how teachers' strategies for motivating their students influence student motivation. They clearly stated their sampling strategy: "The main criterion for our specific sampling was to generate as much diversity as possible in terms of school location and the teachers' age, qualifications, experience, and level of English proficiency" (p. 60). They also employed the use of snowball sampling to obtain an adequate number of participants. The result was that their sample consisted of 20 schools, 27 teachers, and 1,381 students in 40 classes. Now one might think that the researchers are using a representative sampling paradigm with such large numbers. However, they were very explicit in stating that they were using a purposeful sampling paradigm with the goal to obtain information-rich date, for example, "we focused on examining the quality of the teachers' overall motivational teaching practice by generating a composite index of the rich observational data" (p. 60).

Another strategy that is similar to the maximum variation sampling strategy is the *stratified purposeful* sampling strategy. However, rather than trying to maximize the variation of the sample, its aim is to insure that there is at least one participant from each strata in a population. This sounds very much like stratified random sampling under the representative sampling paradigm (see Table 4.1), but it differs in that it does not select participants randomly from the different strata and does not necessarily have to use large samples. Chavez, Ke, and Herrera (2012) used this method in gathering their sample for investigating how face-to-face, online courses, learning at home, in extended families, and in tribal contexts affect Latino and Native American college students' learning and success. The researchers stated that "Our goal in sampling was to gain as diverse a group of students as possible with these cultural identities" (p. 785). They stated that they determined the minority student population of the university was 57.3% Latino or Native American and then used a demographic online survey to determine the ethnicity of potential participants. After this step 50 students who identified as Native American or Latino eventually agreed to participate in the study. The researchers did not specify that this was a randomly selected sample, so we classify this sample as a *stratified purposeful* sample.

On the opposite side of maximum variation sampling is the *homogeneous sampling* strategy. The aim of this strategy is to select participants that share the same attributes. Fugate, Zentall, and Gentry (2013) studied the capacity for creativity in students with attention deficit hyperactivity disorder (ADHD). The researchers assessed working memory and creativity in two groups of gifted students, those with ADHD characteristics ($n = 17$) and those without ($n = 20$). All of the participants were equivalent on fluid intelligence defined by the researchers as (a) an IQ score of 120 or above, (b) a score in the 90th percentile or above on a national or state achievement or aptitude test, and (c) a grade point average of 3.5 or greater in talent areas (e.g., mathematics, chemistry). Therefore, the researchers wanted participants who were different on their ADHD designation but homogeneous on the three criteria that they defined for the study.

Last, in Table 4.1 we have listed the use of *volunteers*. Many research methods textbooks list volunteers as a separate sampling strategy (see Table 4.1). However, we believe that this can no longer be used as a separate sampling strategy for the simple reason that all participants or their parents/guardians have to agree to participate in any study, that is, volunteer. This is due to laws that are now in place for the protection of human rights as outlined in the following section of this chapter on ethics. Regardless of which previously discussed sampling paradigm is used participants must in essence volunteer. Traditionally, volunteer samples were considered biased for reasons outlined in texts like Gall et al.'s (1996). However, what makes a sample biased depends on the sampling paradigm. Representative sampling should result in unbiased samples, and purposeful sampling will almost always produce biased samples.

In summary, whatever sampling paradigm researchers use, they should give attention to precision in describing why a sample was chosen and what steps were taken to ensure that the best sample was selected. The more precise the description the more credence can be given to the interpretation and application of the results. For further reading on sampling theory, we suggest you read Gall et al. (2008). You might also be interested in reviewing the article by Delice (2010) where she explores some general concerns for the generalizability and repeatability of educational research. She gives some special attention to sampling techniques and the poor attention that it is often given in quantitative research.

What about sample size and purposeful sampling? The rule *the more the better* also holds true for this paradigm—although for different reasons than for representative sampling. As stated previously, the purpose for using the purposeful paradigm is to do in-depth investigations which need information-rich samples. So, it is logical to conclude that larger samples should lead to more information-rich data.

The last point we want to make is that although researchers using the purposeful sampling paradigm are not generally concerned with *generalizing* their findings to larger populations, they are usually hoping that the interpretations of their data can be *transferred* to other situations. With a sample of one, for example, Zehr et al. (2005) did not try to generalize their findings to *all* Amish teachers; however, their findings were informative for similar situations and certainly opened the door for further conversations and future research. More is said about the issue of transference in Chapters 5 and 7.

We suggest that you do the following exercise so that you can get firsthand experience looking at a study which has used the purposeful sampling paradigm.

EXERCISE 4.2

Locate a study of interest that used the purposeful sampling paradigm and complete the following:

1 Summarize the research questions under investigation.
2 What purpose did the researcher(s) state for selecting the sample?
3 How was the sample selected?
4 Summarize the characteristics of the sample.
5 Explain how you think the sample was appropriate for the purpose of the study.

As we conclude this chapter, we trust you have gained a healthy appreciation regarding the need for researchers to provide a clear description of the sample they use in their studies. The Sample subsection should contain detailed characteristics of the sample and the conditions under which it was selected. The two main criteria are (1) whether you are able to identify the sampling paradigm that the researcher(s) used and the reason for its use and (2) whether you have enough information to decide whether the findings of the study can be generalized or transferred (see Figure 4.1) to the target population or similar situations. The choice researchers make will guide how you evaluate the conclusions and applications suggested from the findings of the study. In addition to these basic criteria is the need for researchers to point out what precautions were taken to ensure the safety and the confidentiality of any human participants. The final thought is, although the Sample subsection in a research article may consume little space, the implications have profound effects on the rest of the study.

Ethics in Sampling Human Participants

When using human participants in a study, there are a number of ethical issues that must be addressed. The main concern is that the rights and privacy of human participants are protected. This is such an important issue that the U.S. government set up a commission in 1974 which produced The Belmont Report in 1979. In 1991, a number of U.S. government agencies adopted a number of regulations to protect human participants (AERA, 2000). In fact, they established the Office for Protection from Research Risks inside the Department of Health and Human Services to monitor any misuse of participants.[5] Every research institution and university must have an Institutional Review Board that must examine and approve any research being done on humans.

In essence these guidelines can be summarized in the following statement. "The 'rights' of a research subject include reading and discussing the informed consent with study staff, answering any questions, voluntary participation, and a right to information about the study's procedures, risks, and benefits" (AERA, 2000, ¶ 5).

There are some situations where these rules do not have to apply. They are listed below (AERA, 2000, ¶ 5):

1   Research conducted in established or commonly accepted educational settings.
2   Research involving the use of educational tests, surveys, interviews, or observation of public behavior.
3   If the human participants are elected or appointed public officials or candidates for public office.
4   Research involving the collection or study of existing data, documents, or records.
5   Research and demonstration projects which are conducted by or subject to the approval of Department or Agency heads, and which are designed to study, evaluate, or otherwise examine public benefit or service programs.

As seen in these five exceptions to the rule, there is a lot of latitude that keeps researchers from being overly tied up in red tape. However, it is important that participants are protected from research that violates their rights to privacy.

Key Terms and Concepts

attrition
case
cluster sampling
convenience sampling
criterion sampling
experimentally accessible population
external validity
generalizability
information-rich
intensity (expert, critical case) sampling
maximum variation sampling
multistage sampling
objects

participants

proportional/nonproportional stratified random sampling

purposeful (nonprobability) sampling paradigm

representative (probability) sampling paradigm

sample

simple random sampling

stratified random sampling

systematic random sampling

target population

transferability

typical case (modal) sampling

volunteers

Additional Recommended Reading

Delice, A. (2010). The sampling issues in quantitative research. *Educational Sciences: Theory and Practice, 10*(4), 2001–2018.

Gall, M. D., Gall, J. P., & Borg, W. R. (2008). *Educational research: An introduction* (8th ed.). Upper Saddle River, NJ: Pearson.

Leedy, P. D., & Ormrod, J. E. (2013). *Practical research: Planning and design.* Upper Saddle River, NJ: Pearson Publishing.

Menhil, V. C. (2005). The importance of introductory statistics students understanding appropriate sampling techniques. *AMATYC Review, 26*(2), 38–52.

Onwuegbuzie, A., & Leech, N. L. (2007). Sampling designs in qualitative research: Making the sampling process more public. *The Qualitative Report, 12*(2), 238–254. Retrieved from http://www.nova.edu/ssss/QR/QR12-2/onwuegbuzie1.pdf

Sampling for quantitative research designs, see Lane, D. M. Retrieved from http://www.davidmlane.com/hyperstat/sampling_dist.html

Sampling for survey research designs see, National Center for Educational Statistics. Retrieved from http://nces.ed.gov/statprog/2002/std3_1.asp

Teddlie, C., & Yu, F. (2007). Mixed methods sampling: A typology with examples. *Journal of Mixed Methods Research, 1,* 77–100. doi:10.1177/2345678906292430

Trochim, W. M. *The research methods knowledge base* (2nd ed.). Retrieved from http://www.socialresearchmethods.net/kb/ (version current as of October 20, 2006).

Notes

1 We believe that all journals should add to their criteria for publication a clear statement by researchers that identify the target population if the researcher plans to generalize his or her findings.

2 For effects of small samples see www.unf.edu/dept/fie/sdfs/selecting_programs_2004. ppt (retrieved June 7, 2004).

3 For sample size and sampling error see www.davidmlane.com/hyperstat/sampling_dist.html (retrieved January 10, 2004).

4 Modal refers to the Mode, i.e., the average.

5 If you are interested in getting more details regarding this, I suggest that you go on the Internet to the site of the Department of Education, www.ed.gov/offices/OCFO/humansub.html. From there you will be able to locate a number of documents that will spell out clearly what these regulations are.

References

Akbas, O. (2012). Reasons for high school students to mistrust most people: A study in the context of values education. *Educational Sciences: Theory & Practice, 12*(2), 603–608.

Chaapel, H., Columna, L., Lytle, R., & Bailey, J. (2012). Parental expectations about adapted physical education services. *The Journal of Special Education, 47*(3), 186–196.

Chavez, A. F., Ke, F., & Herrera, F. A. (2012). Clan, sage, and sky: Indigenous, Hispano, and Mestizo narratives of learning in New Mexico context. *American Educational Research Journal, 49*(4), 775–806.

Delice, A. (2010). The sampling issues in quantitative research. *Educational Sciences: Theory and Practice, 10*(4), 2001–2018.

Fugate, C. M., Zentall, S. S., & Gentry, M. (2013). Creativity and working memory in gifted students with and without characteristics of attention deficit hyperactive disorder: Lifting the mask. *Gifted Child Quarterly, 57*(4), 234–246.

Gall, M. D., Borg, W. R., & Gall, J. P. (1996). *Educational research: An introduction* (6th ed.). White Plain, NY: Longman.

Greiner, K. P. (2010). Coming from the margin: Research practices, representation and the ordinary. *The Qualitative Report, 15*(5), 1191–1208.

Guilloteaux, M. J., & Dörnyei, Z. (2008). Motivating language learners: A class-room orientation investigation of the effects of motivational strategies on student motivation. *TESOL Quarterly, 42*, 55–77.

Hong-Nam, K., & Leavell, A. G. (2007). A comparative study of language learning strategy use in an EFL context: Monolingual Korean and bilingual Korean–Chinese university students. *Asia Pacific Education Review, 8*(1), 71–88.

Hossein, M., Asadzadeh, H., Shabani, H., Ahghar, G., Ahadi, H., & Shamir, A. S. (2011). The role of Invitational Education and intelligence beliefs in academic performance. *Journal of Invitational Theory and Practice, 17*, 3–10.

Isik-Ercan, Z., Inan, Z. H., Nowak, J., & Kim, B. (2012). "We put on the glasses and the moon comes closer!" Urban second graders exploring the earth, the sun and moon through 3D technologies in a science and literacy unit. *International Journal of Science Education, 36*(1), 1–28.

Kupczynski, L., Mundy, M., & Maxwell, G. (2012). Faculty perceptions of cooperative learning and traditional discussion strategies in online courses. *Turkish Online Journal of Distance Education, 13*(2), 84–95.

Lawson, M. A., & Alameda-Lawson, T. (2012). A case study of school-linked, collective parent engagement. *American Educational Research Journal, 49*(4), 651–684.

LaVergne, D. D., Larke, A., Elbert, C. D., & Jones, W. A. (2011). The benefits and barriers toward diversity inclusion regarding agricultural science teachers in Texas secondary agricultural education programs. *Journal of Agricultural Education, 52*(2), 140–150.

Leston, J. D., Jessen, C. M., & Simons, B. C. (2012). Alaska Native and rural youths' view s of sexual health: A focus group project on sexually transmitted diseases, HIV/AIDS, and unplanned pregnancy. *American Indian and Alaska Native Mental Health Research: The Journal of the National Center, 19*(1), 1–14.

Lopes, P. N., Mestre, J. M., Guil, R., Kremenitzer, J. P., & Salovey, P. (2012). The role of knowledge and skills for managing emotions in adaptation to school: Social behavior and misconduct in the classroom. *American Educational Research Journal, 49*(4), 710–742.

Maher, M. J. (2007). Gay and lesbian students in Catholic high schools: A qualitative study of alumni narratives. *Catholic Education: A Journal of Inquiry and Practice, 10*(4), 449–472.

McGrail, E., & Davis, A. (2011). The influence of classroom blogging on elementary student writing. *Journal of Research in Childhood Education, 25*, 415–437.

Miles, M. B., & Huberman, A. M. (1994). *Qualitative data analysis: An expanded sourcebook* (2nd ed.). Thousand Oaks, CA: Sage.

Morgan, P. L., Fuchs, D., Compton, D. L., Cordray, S. S., & Fuchs, L. S. (2008). Does early reading failure decrease children's reading motivation? *Journal of Learning Disabilities, 41*(5), 387–404.

Odinko, M., & Williams, J. (2006). Language of instruction and interaction patterns in pre-primary classrooms in Nigeria. *Journal of Classroom Interaction, 41*(1), 22–32.

Patton, M. Q. (2002). *Qualitative evaluation and research methods* (3rd ed.). Newbury Park, CA: Sage.

Zehr, H., Moss, G., & Nichols, J. D. (2005). Amish teacher dialogues with teacher educators: Research, cultural, and voices of critique. *The Qualitative Report, 10*(3), 592–619.

5

UNDERSTANDING RESEARCH DESIGNS

Chapter Overview

The research design is the overall plan for carrying out a research study. This design is like the blueprint for building a house. Its purpose is to guide researchers in constructing the strongest and most efficient structure to provide the most useful data to answer the research question(s). Just like a poorly designed blueprint, which results in a house full of problems and possible collapse, a poorly designed research study produces results containing many flaws, and consequently, has little practical use.

The goals of this chapter are to help you understand the technicalities of the design subsection of a study and be able to determine whether the appropriate design was used. There are a number of different research designs currently being used to answer a wide variety of questions. This is where things can get confusing, and remembering them all can be somewhat overwhelming. In addition, there might be several *best* research designs to answer the same question. Therefore, one needs to develop a discerning eye. As you will see, one should judge a design's suitability by whether it answers the research question.

To aid in accomplishing the previously stated goals, we have divided this chapter into three sections. Section "Classifying Research Designs" provides a conceptual framework for classifying various types of research designs to help reduce the confusion. Section "Questions and Designs" describes in more detail the various research designs used for finding answers to the two basic research questions: *what* and *why*. Section "Internal Validity" discusses the factors that can interfere with the results of a study under the heading of *internal validity*. Examples of published research are given to illustrate the main points of the discussion.

Classifying Research Designs

Life would be so simple if we had only one kind of everything, but it would also be very boring. In keeping up with the rest of life, research does not provide just one simple type, or even a choice between only two types. Rather, research can be classified, at least, by three intersecting continua: *Basic–Applied, Qualitative–Quantitative*, and *Exploratory–Confirmatory* (see Figure 5.1). Although these continua are independent from each other, any given study can be classified somewhere on an intersection of the three. This means that a study would appear at some point out in the three-dimensional (3D) space, represented by Figure 5.1. Each continuum is first defined with an explanation showing how a study can be located on it. Then an example will be given on how one study can be classified on all three continua simultaneously and what this might look like in the 3D space.

The Basic–Applied Continuum

This continuum represents research that ranges from the highly theoretical (basic) to the very practical (applied). At the basic end of the continuum, researchers focus on the theoretical, dealing mainly with highly abstract constructs. These studies are not, at first sight, very appealing to the classroom teachers who are looking for immediate ways to improve their students' learning. Nevertheless, these studies are very important for looking at the underlying cognitive, psychological, or sociological mechanisms that might be eventually applied in the classroom. In fact, one

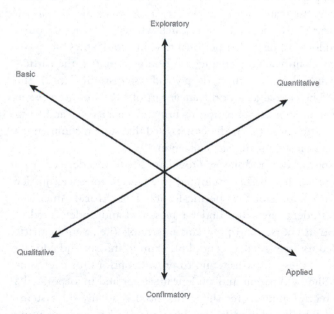

FIGURE 5.1 Design Continua for Classifying Research

might argue that this type of research reveals the theoretical foundations upon which all other research rests. For example, unless we have demonstrated in basic research that the brain processes information in a certain way, it would be difficult to promote a teaching method that elicits this type of brain processing.

Some studies can be identified immediately from their titles as basic research. For example, Nieto's (2013) study entitled "Language, Literacy, and Culture: Aha! Moments in Personal and Sociopolitical Understanding" appears to be at the end of the basic continuum and focuses on the theory of language, literacy, and culture and how these have influenced the author. This does not mean, of course, that this research is of little value. Her findings might be useful for conceptually thinking about diversity and language development in children can be used to inform practice and policy. Hence, in line with our first impressions, we placed it near the basic end of the continuum, as shown here.[1]

At the other end of the same continuum is applied research. As you would expect from the previous discussion, research that is directly applicable to the teaching or learning situation would be placed here. Studies that deal with teaching methods, or ones that try to address immediate problems in the classroom, would fit at this end of the continuum.

The research genre called *Action Research* (AR) which has received a lot of attention is one of the purest forms of applied research. There are journals dedicated solely to this type of research, for example, *Applied Research* and *Educational Action Research*. A. Burns (2010) defined it as research where "a teacher becomes an 'investigator' or 'explorer' of his or her personal teaching context... One of the main aims of AR is to identify a 'problematic' situation or issue that the participants ... consider worth looking into more deeply and systematically" (p. 2). She continued by saying, "The central idea of the *action* part of AR is to intervene in a deliberate way in the problematic situation to bring about changes and, even better, improvements in practice" (p. 2). She emphasized that such recommended improvements are based on systematic data collection.

A study that illustrates AR was done by Dowden (2010), was derived from the concerns of the researcher as she attempted to advocate for social justice as a high school guidance counselor. She specifically noted that African American, Hispanic, and Latino students are often under-represented and underserved in many valuable education courses and programs in schools (i.e., a problematic situation). She decided to form an after school program to inform and educate minority students about these disparities and to provide options for overcoming these disparities. She held parent and student meetings and incorporated a nearby university to recruit mentors for these students. Eventually, she systematically gathered data, which she used to develop a plan to bring about more opportunities to assist these students. This study clearly can be placed at the applied end of the continuum.

However, other studies might be fitted in between these two extremes. If a study is built on a heavy theoretical base, yet has clear practical implications, it would fall somewhere in the middle. For example, Jadallah et al. (2011) examined the effect of teacher's pedagogical scaffolding on children's performance in free-flowing child-led small-group discussions. The authors relied heavily on Vygotsky's sociocultural theory, defining the difference in actual versus potential levels of cognitive development. Within the Vygotskian framework and using the concepts of scaffolding and appropriation, the authors make the argument that this type of assistance is critical to the acquisition of children's cognitive and social skills. The authors concluded that the findings suggested that a teacher's scaffolding, even in a modest form, can have a significant impact on children's thinking. Based on this, we would place the study near the middle of the continuum.

The prior discussion illustrates that the consumer of research should read research along this continuum. One type is not more important than another. Therefore, journals contain research covering the entire spectrum of this continuum (cf. *Action Research* with *Teacher Education & Practice*).

The Qualitative–Quantitative Continuum

The qualitative–quantitative continuum has received a lot of attention over the past 30 years, usually accompanied with much controversy. When you read articles dealing with this debate, you might think that this is not a continuum, but two distinct armed camps. However, as you become more familiar with the research available, you will find that many studies are neither purely qualitative nor quantitative. This is in line with Leedy and Ormrod (2013), who recognize that qualitative and quantitative research are not exclusive of one another and can be thought of as existing on a continuum of research that can include a mixture or blend of both methodologies. Where a study lies on this research continuum is dependent on the research questions and the methodology used by the researcher. Our students' findings concur with this opinion, in that they have classified many studies somewhere between the two ends of this continuum.

The problem is that epistemological issues regarding the nature of reality have been wedded with these two methodologies, resulting in the polarization of a number of researchers into *camps*. We agree with Miles and Huberman (1994), however, who stated, "We believe that the quantitative-qualitative argument is essentially unproductive ... we see no reason to tie the distinction to epistemological preferences" (p. 41). Therefore, we are not going to address the related philosophical issues of positivism and postpositivism in this book because we do not believe that they are important for the consumer of research at this time. However, if you are interested in reading more about this, we recommend Chapter 1 in Tashakkori and Teddlie's book (1998).

We try to use the terms *qualitative* and *quantitative* in ways that separate them from this philosophical spat—getting into epistemology is not necessary. However, you should be aware of the designs and methodologies which are typically associated with quantitative and qualitative approaches. Familiarization with these methods will enable consumers of research to be eclectic and versatile—ready to digest whatever research method comes their way. Only then will the consumer be better able to find potential answers to research questions.

The two ends of this continuum mostly have their origins in different disciplines. Quantitative research has come mainly from the field of psychology where there has been heavy emphasis on the use of statistics to make generalizations from samples to populations, thus the label *quantitative methods*. However, most methods under qualitative research have originated with anthropologists and sociologists who rely heavily on verbal description rather than numbers. Consequently, quantitative research is characterized by the use of numbers to represent its data, and qualitative research is characterized by verbal descriptions as its data.

We would add, in light of the discussion in Chapter 4, that sampling paradigms also help distinguish between the two. Quantitative research frequently uses representative sampling strategies for generalizing findings to larger populations, whereas qualitative research works to uncover information from small purposeful samples.

Although some mistakenly think that qualitative research does not use any numbers or statistics, this is not necessarily so. A number of qualitative studies involve numbers in the form of frequencies of occurrence of certain phenomena and are analyzed by such statistical methods as *chi-square*. In fact, a number of books have been written (e.g., Coladarci, Cobb, Minium & Clarke, 2004; Leonard, 2000) describing statistical procedures for qualitative research.

Another misunderstanding regarding the differences between qualitative and quantitative approaches is that the former is atheoretical, whereas the latter is not. Although most qualitative research studies do not begin with theoretical hypotheses, developing theory (or, to be more precise, a theoretical hypothesis) is often their goal. For instance, an approach referred to as *grounded theory*, which arose out of anthropology, has become a part of the qualitative research repertoire in applied linguistics. The express goal of this method is to develop a theoretical hypothesis from descriptive data as the data accumulate from the ground up. A good example of how such a theory is developed is Peine and Coleman's (2010) qualitative study, which looked at the activity of sitting and waiting in classrooms as a universal predictor of being gifted. The goal was to develop a *grounded theory*—one that is inductively based on the data rather than deductively derived from a predetermined hypothesis. In this case, "the children's voices tell educators much of what it is like to be gifted in the general education classroom" (p. 220).

So what is *qualitative research*? Miles and Huberman (1994, pp. 5–8) defined what they thought common features across different manifestations of qualitative research are. We have extracted and summarized them in the following list. Data are gathered:

- in natural settings,
- through concentrated contact over time,
- holistically—"systematic, encompassing, integrated",
- from deep inside the situation trying to hold preconceived notions in check,
- by the researcher who is the "main 'measurement device'",
- to analyze for patterns, comparisons, and contrasts,
- with interpretations constrained by theoretical interests and/or "internal consistency",
- consisting mainly of verbal data.

In other words, any study that is done in a real-life setting, involving intensive holistic data collection through observation at a very close personal level without the influence of prior theory and contains mostly verbal analysis, could be classified as a qualitative study.

However, there are differing opinions as to what constitutes qualitative research. Gall, Borg, and Gall (1996) list under their section on qualitative research such things as case studies, along with a list of 16 research traditions that are typically referred to as *qualitative research*. Among these are methods such as ethnography, protocol analysis, and discourse analysis—all commonly used methods in educational research. Wolcott illustrated over 20 strategies in his famous tree diagram (Miles & Huberman, 1994, p. 6). Tesch organized 27 strategies into a flowchart under four general categories (Miles & Huberman, 1994, p. 7).

Consequently, it is difficult to provide a simple overview of all of these qualitative research strategies for the up-and-coming consumer. Other texts are better designed to do this (e.g., Denzin & Lincoln, 2000; LeCompte, Millroy, & Preissle, 1992).

Case Studies

These types of studies are frequently found in research. Gall et al. (1996) define a *case study* as

> the in-depth study of instances of a phenomenon in its natural context and from the perspective of the participants involved in the phenomenon. A case study is done to shed light on a phenomenon, which is the processes, events, persons, or things of interest to the researcher. Examples of phenomena are programs, curricula, roles, and events. Once the phenomenon of interest is clarified, the researcher can select a case for intensive study. A case is a particular instance of the phenomena. (p. 545)

Notice that the focus of a case study is on a specific phenomenon. Margiotta (2011), for example, did a case study that focused on "the influence of parental support and interactions on their children's learning outcomes during piano lessons" (p. 17), as the phenomena in three different locations (private studio, private school, and music conservatorium). The data were gathered from the observations of 34 parent and 34 piano students in these locations and information from a completed questionnaire. Being a case study, the researcher recognized the limitations of the results from this small sample. However, she believed that her findings were valid to transfer important implications for young musicians and their parents.

Ethnography

The term originally comes out of anthropology and means the study of human societies and culture. An ethnographic study is characterized by the researcher(s) getting as close as possible to the culture under study over an extended period. Data are gathered from a number of sources (e.g., notes from observations, interviews, transcriptions of video and audio recordings, etc.), resulting in large quantities of verbal information. For example, Hickey (2013) completed an ethnographic study over 5 years investigating female immigrants' oral history narratives in an attempt to explore family acculturation issues from a U.S. and Muslim perspective. She described how she interviewed 11 self-identified Muslim female immigrants and transcribed these interviews for later thematic analysis. She focused much of her interviews on family and child rearing practices in Muslim and U.S. Muslim families.

Discourse and Conversational Analysis

These two methods are related in that they analyze connected discourse. However, they differ in the scope of the discourse they analyze. In fact, some argue that conversational analysis (CA) is a restricted form of discourse analysis (DA) (see Paltridge, 2006 for an excellent summary). DA is more an umbrella label that subsumes a number of ways to study connected discourse, whether written, spoken, or sign language. Whereas, CA is a specific fine-grain analysis of limited spoken discourse. Both aim at identifying patterns in discourse that provide new insights into relationships within the discourse.

An example of DA is the study by Singh (2013) that used it to analyze student use of Facebook Groups. He specifically wanted to explore the difference in instructor-guided, assessed Facebook Groups versus student-led, nonassessed Facebook Groups that supported a form of open discourse. His stated goal was to study the online discourse and to compare these interactions in both structured and unstructured configurations (p. 38). More is said in Chapter 6 about the gathering of these types of verbal data. Needless to say, this would fall on the qualitative end of the continuum.

Qualitative ← → Quantitative

Protocol Analysis

Another qualitative approach mentioned by Gall et al. (1996) has its origin in the field of cognitive psychology. Gall et al. define it as "asking individuals to state all their thoughts as they carry out a challenging task, so that the researcher can obtain a holistic overview of their cognitive activity as recorded in their verbal reports" (p. 596). This is commonly known as the *think-aloud* approach. Similar to other qualitative procedures, audiotapes are made as participants think aloud. The tapes are transcribed and analyzed.

An example of a study that used protocol analysis was done by Blumberg and Randall (2013), who investigated the problem-solving behaviors of fifth, sixth, and seventh graders used to negotiate a novel recreational video game. The researchers' goal was to illustrate children and adolescents' approaches to game play by asking participants to think aloud while playing over a sustained period. Participants were actively encouraged to continually vocalize their thoughts about how to solve the problem through a series of prompts of the form, "What are you doing now?" provided by the experimenter after 8 s. of nonvocalization. This technique was maintained throughout the playing of the subsequent video game. Audiotapes and eventually transcripts were made of all participants' comments during video game play and were verified by an independent reader using the original audiotapes.

At the other end of this continuum is the *quantitative approach*. As you would expect from the label, the data for this approach are some type of numbers. These numbers can be frequencies, percentages, proportions, rankings, and/or scores on some type of test or survey. Furthermore, the method for analyzing the data is some form of statistical procedure. Finally, quantitative studies ideally use large representative samples. However, realistically many studies use smaller purposeful samples—often convenient samples. Studies located toward this end might test hypotheses or only gather information to answer questions.

An example that we place toward the quantitative end of the continuum is Turney and Kao's (2009) study, which compared the school involvement of immigrant and nonimmigrant parents and the impact it may have on their students' achievement. The first indicator is apparent in the title, "Barriers to School Involvement: Are Immigrant Parents Disadvantaged?" (p. 257). This title suggests that the study will try to generalize the findings to immigrant parents. The next indicator is found in the *Participants* section (i.e., the *Sample*) where the authors used a large survey gathered from the Early Childhood Longitudinal Study from

1,000 schools and 12,954 parents of kindergartners. The authors state that they gathered data in a multistage sampling process from parents and also collected student standardized test scores. The third indicator is that they used inferential statistics to analyze their data. Below, we illustrate our placement.

Qualitative ⟷ Quantitative

Often you will find studies that fall somewhere in the middle of the continuum. They land in between the two extremes, depending on how much each methodology is used. These are referred to as *mixed-method* approaches (Creswell, 2002; Tashakkori & Teddlie, 1998, 2003) which combine both qualitative and quantitative methodologies in one study. The following study illustrates this point.

McCrudden and Sparks (2014) clearly stated in their title "Exploring the Effect of Task Instructions on Topic Beliefs and Topic Belief Justifications: A Mixed Methods Study" that this is a mixed methods study. The authors stated that they "used embedded sequential mixed methods design, which enabled us to examine both quantitative and qualitative aspects of topic beliefs" (p. 2). They investigated whether the task instructions that asked adolescents to evaluate the merit of both sides of a controversial issue would affect their topic beliefs and topic belief justifications after they read belief-consistent and belief-inconsistent information. In the quantitative phase, participants were assigned to one of four conditions and asked to indicate their beliefs about the controversial topic. In the qualitative phase, participants were asked to explain their responses in the quantitative phase. Similarly, in the *Findings* (i.e., *Results*) section, they reported on both quantitative and qualitative findings. As you would expect, we place this study right in the middle of the continuum.

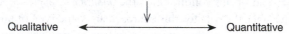

Qualitative ⟷ Quantitative

The Exploratory–Confirmatory Continuum

The third independent continuum is labeled *Exploratory–Confirmatory* (Figure 5.1). The main characteristic of this continuum is whether a study is trying to find information to answer research questions without any hypothesis or to find evidence to support (i.e., confirm) a hypothesis.

On the confirmatory side of this continuum, Boon's (2008) study sought to test two hypotheses. The first was that challenging behavior (i.e., school suspension) predicts low academic student achievement or at-risk status; and second, challenging behavior more predicts low achievement than socioeconomic or additional family structure variables. The results confirmed both hypotheses in that for both indigenous and nonindigenous students, suspensions were a strong predictor of low achievement and suspensions were stronger predictors of low achievement when compared with SES or family structure variables. Boon's study can easily be plotted near the confirmatory end of the continuum, as shown here.

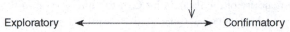

Several of the other studies cited in this chapter so far (i.e., Blumberg and Randall, 2013; Dowden, 2010; Hickey, 2013; Peine and Coleman, 2010; Turney and Kao, 2009) did not test any hypotheses. They were exploratory. They attempted to find out what was happening without trying to support any particular hypothesis. They should all be located toward the exploratory end of the continuum. However, just an additional note, there are studies that can be placed more in the middle of this continuum if they have more questions than they have hypotheses to answer them.

As shown in Figure 5.1, the three continua intersect. This means that any given study can be plotted along all three continua at the same time. We have tried to show in Figure 5.2 how this might be done with Blumberg & Randall's (2013) which we discussed earlier. Point A shows where the study represents the point of intersection between the Basic–Applied and the Exploratory–Confirmatory continua. It is an exploratory study that is relatively basic, trying to determine what children and adolescents think about when playing video games. Point B at the

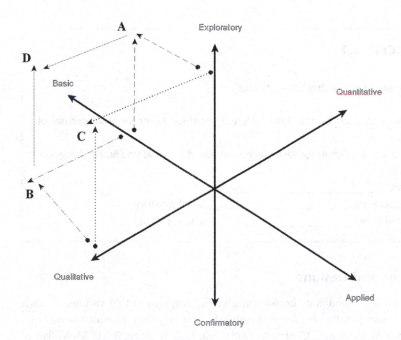

FIGURE 5.2 Example of Classifying a Study (Blumberg & Randall, 2013) on Three Design Continua

intersection of the Basic–Applied and Qualitative–Quantitative continua points out that the study is qualitative and relatively basic (verbal responses from students generated the majority of the data). Point C at the intersection of the Exploratory–Confirmatory and Qualitative–Quantitative continua means that the study is qualitative or exploratory. You will have to use your imagination a little to see where a study intersects when all three continua are considered. Point D attempts to show this, although it is difficult to display a 3D graph on a 2D piece of paper. The study is qualitative, exploratory, and relatively basic.

After all of this discussion, we hope you understand that using *only* one of these continua is somewhat simplistic for describing research. The picture is even more complicated than this. We can think of three other continua: Authenticity (natural–contrived), Focus (unrestricted–restricted), Behavior (external–mental); but for the moment, we have used the three continua discussed to illustrate that there is more to a research study than what we might first be led to believe.

You might ask why this information is important for consumers to know. The importance lies in the fact that researchers' system for choosing procedures and an interpretative framework for their study is based on how their study is designed. For consumers, knowing where a study intersects on these continua provides an overall framework for understanding the remainder of a study.

To help you become more familiar with the classification system we have just outlined, do the following exercise.

EXERCISE 5.1

Find a recent study that interests you.

1   Plot the study on the three different continua based on your perusal of the study.
2   Provide a rationale for each placement based on what you find in the study.

Basic_____ Applied
Exploratory_____Confirmatory
Qualitative_____ Quantitative

Questions and Designs

Most research methodology books can give the impression that various research designs are independent from one another by the way they present them (i.e., a chapter per method; e.g., Creswell, 2008; Gall, Gall & Borg, 2010; McMillan & Schumacher, 2010; Mertler & Charles, 2011;). However, in our opinion, a more useful way to understand research designs is by organizing them around the type of research question under investigation.

As outlined in Chapter 1, the two generic questions found in research literature center around *What* and *Why*. Section "Questions and Designs" of this chapter is structured around these generic questions and their subquestions. For each question type, we present the most common research designs found in educational research.

The WHAT Questions

What Phenomena Are Important?

To answer this question, researchers use designs that are usually classified as either Qualitative/Exploratory or Quantitative/Exploratory. These combinations can be placed anywhere on the Applied–Basic continuum. In such studies, there are no hypotheses to test. Rather the researcher is trying to gather information not known previously. The purpose might be to develop a hypothesis during the investigation as in grounded theory ethnography or fill in missing information, but it is not to confirm an existing hypothesis.

To illustrate, Blakesley (2011) conducted a (qualitative/exploratory/applied) study using interviews of four school principals in Canada's Yukon Territory. In the abstract, the author suggests that his methodology for the project uses a critical ethnographic approach. His interest was to explore how these administrators defined educational leadership "despite the inability on the part of universities, the extant body of literature, or education systems to articulate a definition of leadership" (p. 4). Extensive interviews, observations, and document reviews were part of the data that was collected over 6 months. The principal interviews were recorded and eventually transcribed to text that was eventually analyzed for themes using a qualitative data analysis program. The author summarized his findings by suggesting that these principals see their positions as similar to teachers in an expanded role as they constantly juggle the continuous ambiguity of school leadership. *Note:* Because of the overwhelming amount of material that is often collected in ethnographic projects, authors will often reported a fraction of their data due to restrictions and space limitations imposed by journals that publish this type of work (see the *Findings* section of Blakesley's study).

However, quantitative designs are also used to answer *What* questions. Turney and Kao's (2009) study, as you might remember, examined the school involvement of immigrant parents and the impact that it may have on their children's academic achievement. Although they were specifically looking at parent involvement in schools, they gathered numerical data on a number of variables including demographic information (i.e., ethnicity, English proficiency), standardized student achievement scores, and parent interviews. By collecting this type of information, they hoped to eliminate the effects as extraneous variables on the variables of interest. A quick glance at the *Results* section confirms the quantitative nature of this study. The fact that the study did not have any specific hypothesis shows that Turney and Kao were exploring for information not confirming anything.

Before moving on, do the following exercise to provide a firsthand experience to apply the principles in the prior discussion.

EXERCISE 5.2

Find a recent study that tries to answer the following question: What phenomena are of importance (i.e., **NOT** correlational, nor cause/effect)?

1   Classify it on the three continua.
2   State the research question(s).
3   Identify the variables in the study.
4   Summarize the methodology of the study by explaining in your own words how the researcher(s) designed the study to answer the research question(s).

What Simple Relationships Exist Between Phenomena?

Except for research that only wants to identify and describe phenomena, all other research is in one way or other looking at relationships between phenomena (see Figure 1.3 and related discussion). Some researchers want to know if there are any *simple relationships* between constructs. However, by *simple*, we do not mean the relationships are unimportant or lack complexity. Here the term means a relationship between two variables. Many simple relationships have profound implications for the educational environment and classroom.

A synonym commonly used for a simple relationship is *correlation*. This is not to be confused with the term *correlation coefficient*, which is a specific statistic used to indicate a correlation (i.e., a type of simple relationship).

Research on this question can be classified anywhere on all three of the classification continua. It can be confirmatory or exploratory, qualitative or quantitative, or basic or applied. Different from the previous *What* question, researchers might have a hypothesis to test for answering the question. Following the research question "What relationships exist?," for instance, they may hypothesize that a relationship between certain variables does exist. The researchers could do this based on theory or the findings of previous research.

The most common design used to examine simple relationships gathers data on two or more variables and then correlates each pair of variables using various statistical procedures. Skiba, Poloni-Staudinger, Simmons, Feggins-Azziz, and Chung (2005) examined the relationship among race, poverty, and special education identification to arrive at a more precise estimate of the contribution of poverty to racial disparities. To answer their research question, they gathered district-level data on general and special education enrollment in disability category by race, socioeconomic level, local resources, and academic and social outcomes. They examined the relationship of each pair of five variables illustrating the use of the *shot-gun* method. That is, all of the data for all of the variables are processed in one correlational analysis. The resulting matrix of correlation coefficients revealed that there were some significant relationships between some pairs of variables. The advantage of this method is that a lot of relationships can be explored simultaneously.

Another type of simple relationship study as mentioned back in Chapter 1 (see Figure 1.3) is *predictive*. On the basis of simple pairwise relationships between variables, a researcher can explore what variables can be used to predict behavior on another variable. For example, Silverman (2010) examined preservice teacher beliefs about diversity and multiculturalism and explored this within the context of the classroom, including efficacy for multicultural instruction, sense of responsibility for teaching about diverse people, and sense of advocacy for oppressed groups. To answer her research question, she gathered survey data and demographic information about the participants and analyzed the relationships. She began by producing a matrix of correlation coefficients to determine which potential predictor variables should be used for the second phase of the study. The next step was to use a statistical procedure called *multiple regression* (more about this in Chapter 7) to identify the best set of predictors. You can see from this that *simple* can mean complex as we previously mentioned.

Regarding the above correlational studies, however, we want to reiterate a very important principle here. *Finding a relationship between two variables is not enough to conclude that one variable causes the other to change.* Skiba et al. (2005) could not (and did not) conclude from their data that poverty actually *caused* the differences in the ethnic disproportionality in special education classrooms. The reason for this is that correlations are symmetrical, meaning that variable A correlates with variable B in the same direction and magnitude as variable B correlates with variable A. But now we are getting into issues that we discuss more fully in Chapter 7.

For a similar reason prediction studies do not show cause and effect relationships. Silverman (2010) based her predictions on simple relationships which are symmetrical. Although intuitively one might think that demographic variables such as race, faith, sexual orientation, gender, and so forth, might make an impact on (i.e., cause) beliefs about diversity and multiculturalism, such conclusions cannot be based on these data. Silverman was careful to not make this type of error in her study.

We recommend that you take this opportunity to do the following exercise to give you another example of a study looking for simple relationships. To help locate one more quickly, we suggest you look for the keyword, *relation(ship)*, or *predict* in the title.

EXERCISE 5.3

Find a recent study that investigates the following question: Are there any important simple relationships between phenomena?

1   Classify the study on the three continua.
2   What relationships were being examined?
3   State any hypothesis and/or prediction made (if any).
4   Identify the variables in the study.
5   Summarize the methodology of the study by explaining in your own words how the researcher(s) designed the study to answer the research question(s).

The WHY Questions

Once we begin to understand what phenomena are out there, or what relationships that exist between variables, we begin to ask *why*. Why do people vary in the phenomena we observe to be important to a particular issue? Why do certain variables relate with one another? The essence of this type of question is *causation*. Causation indicates a more specific type of relationship between variables than only a *simple* relationship. Causal relations delineate how variables (i.e., constructs) affect other variables. Why do some people learn languages better than others? What makes people good readers? Does using computers affect the way people write? If only we could discover why, we might be able to help improve desirable abilities and discourage undesirable ones in learning various subjects.

To refresh your memory from Chapter 3, the variable(s) that is suspected of causing variation in another variable(s) is the *independent variable(s)* (IV). The variable(s) that is being influenced by the independent variable(s) is the *dependent variable*(s) (DV). Sometimes the intent of researcher is made clear in the title of a study where variables are easily identified. Xu and Wu (2013) suggest in their title "Self-Regulation of Homework Behavior: Homework Management at the Secondary Level," that they are exploring a causal relationship. They inform the reader that they are exploring factors that may impact the management of school homework. Other researchers might use terms in their titles such as *impact, influence, improve, change, role of,* and so on when they are investigating whether variables cause changes in other variables. But they are all referring to causation.

Such studies have at least one independent variable and at least one dependent variable. The study just mentioned, Xu and Wu (2013), has multiple independent variables (learning-oriented reasons, affective attitude, self-reported grade, family homework assistance, and teacher feedback) and one dependent variable (self-regulation of homework management). Some studies might even have more than one dependent variable (see Appendix B).

Research into causal relationships is not restricted to any one end of the three continua discussed in section "Classifying Research Designs" of this chapter. Causal studies can be placed anywhere on the Basic–Applied, Exploratory– Confirmatory, or Qualitative–Quantitative continua. The key characteristic of this type of study is that it is looking for one or more causal relationships.

Causal Qualitative Studies

Some mistakenly believe that causal relationships can only be studied using quantitative approaches. However, Miles and Huberman (1994) have clearly described how causal relationships are studied using qualitative research designs. A study that illustrates this is one by A. B. Burns (2010) who examined how preservice teachers view the role of the history of mathematics in the high school curriculum. The independent variable in this project was the use of enhanced learning activities throughout the semester that focused on the history of mathematics. The dependent variables were preservice teacher views on integrating the history of mathematics and being prepared to incorporate this history of mathematics in their own teaching after their exposure to this series of assignments. By analyzing the verbal output of each of the preservice teacher participants, Burns suggested a causative effect from being exposed to these learning activities. We classified this study as *qualitative/exploratory/applied* on our three intersecting continua.

Causal-Comparative Designs

On the more quantitative side, one common research design that is used to examine causal relationships is the *causal-comparative* design. However, as is made apparent below, the findings from this design might suggest cause or effect, but researchers cannot answer for sure whether the variation in the dependent variable is caused by the independent variable.

Let us first illustrate this method with a study. Holmes (2012) studied whether gender or age influenced elementary children's preferences for the outdoor activities and size of play groups. Gender and age (defined by the grade level) were the IVs and preference and group size the DVs. The two IVs are already established and cannot be manipulated, so this qualifies as a causal-comparative study. On the basis of frequency data, they found that gender did make a difference as well as age.

Why is it important to understand this intricate mixture of independent, and dependent variables when you are looking for causal comparisons? The reason is that by not being able to control or manipulate the independent variables, other variables might be the real cause behind any variation in the dependent variable rather than the independent variable itself.

Take *gender* or *age* for example. Holmes (2012) found differences in preferences for activities but could they conclude that gender or age *caused* these? In their limitations, Holmes recognized that "The playground consisted of an asphalt surface with little playground equipment except for a portable basketball court. The setting clearly drove the behavior that occurred in it, and comparisons among different types of playgrounds would be interesting to pursue." (p. 347). This suggests that there might be other causes behind the outcomes other than gender and age, though they most likely play a part.

For practical or ethical reasons, many independent variables cannot be manipulated. If researchers want to know whether economic status influences the use of reading strategies for example, they cannot manipulate the economic status of the participants. In other words, they cannot choose random groups of people who have no economic status and then randomly assign each group where they manipulate participants' economic level. Participants already come from different economic levels when they participate in the study. So, researchers take random samples from each economic group and then examine whether the participants differ on what reading strategies they choose (i.e., the dependent variable). As with gender and age, the difficulty is that economic groups differ in a number of other ways that might influence how they choose reading strategies.

The validity of any causal conclusions based on results from a causal-comparative study increases with the amount of care the researcher takes when designing the study. Therefore, you need to attend carefully to how the researcher tries to control for any competing alternative explanations for the potential results.

Now let us see if you can find a causal-comparative study for your own by doing the following exercise. The keywords to look for in the title, abstract, or research questions in the introduction of the studies you peruse are: *effect*, *impact*, *influence*, and so on, along with variables that cannot be manipulated, such as gender, age, language level, nationality, and so on.

EXERCISE 5.4

Identify a recent study from a research journal that answers a WHY question using a causal-comparative design.

1   State the research question.
2   Identify the independent variable(s) and the dependent variable(s).
3   State any hypotheses and/or predictions made (if any).
4   Study the *introduction* and *methodology* section. In your own words, explain why you think this is a causal-comparative study.
5   Identify any strategies used for controlling for any alternative explanations of the results.
6   How strong were the conclusions in your opinion? Were they justified?

Experimental and Quasi-Experimental Designs

Designs that manipulate independent variables are grouped under the heading *experimental or quasi-experimental* designs. Both experimental and quasi-experimental research designs involve manipulating the independent variable(s) and observing the change in the dependent variable(s). The goal of this genre of design in contrast to others is that researchers try to *control* changes in the variance of the independent variable(s) without allowing the intervention of other unwanted variables. In one of the simpler designs, there is one group of participants that gets the treatment and another group that does not (i.e., the control group). For example, Shapley, Sheehan, Maloney, and Caranikas-Walker (2011) used 21 middle schools as treatment groups where students and teachers received laptop computers, instructional resources, professional development, and technical support while 21 additional middle schools were used as control groups and did not receive this technology immersion. They were interested in exploring if the students and teachers in treatment schools would improve their technology proficiency, the frequency of their technology-based class activities, and small-group interactions as compared with the students and teachers in control group schools.

The difference between experimental and quasi-experimental research has to do with how the sample is selected. If the samples for the treatment and the control groups are randomly selected, then the design is truly experimental. If not, it is quasi-experimental. This is an important difference because any sample that is not randomly sampled could be biased, and thereby could unintentionally allow extraneous variables to affect the results of the study. *Bias*, here, has a specific meaning. If there is a systematic difference in the make up of either the treatment group or the control group that might affect the results of the study, other than the treatment variable, the samples are biased.

Shapely et al.'s (2000) study, mentioned above, would be classified as quasi-experimental because the samples were not randomly chosen. In fact, the treatment middle schools were chosen through a competitive technology grant process. If this is the case, then the question arises as to whether there were any important differences between the treatment and control groups other than receiving or not receiving the treatment.

Purely experimental studies are uncommon in fields of educational research mainly because of the difficulty to randomly select participants from experimentally accessible populations (see Chapter 4). There are two characteristics that identify this design: whether the independent variable was manipulated by the researcher(s) and whether some form of randomization was used in selecting the participants. One example is a study by Bon (2009), which investigated the impact of the applicant's gender and religion on principal's screening decisions for assistant principal applicants. For this project, national random samples of high school principals were asked to evaluate hypothetical applicants whose resumes varied by religion and gender. A list of 400 participant names was generated, using a purely random stratified selection process by an external data retrieval company. The samples were then stratified by gender such that 200 of the participants were male and 200 were female. A total of 274 administrators responded, representing a 64 per cent response rate. By including the details of how participants were chosen they increased the external validity (see Chapter 4) of generalizing the findings of the study to a larger target population.

Random selection of participants is sometimes substituted by another randomization procedure called *random assignment*. Instead of randomly selecting participants from a pool of possible participants, the treatment is randomly assigned to participants who may have been part of a convenient sample. Note, however, that this use of randomization does not necessarily increase the *external validity* of the study. The researcher might assign treatments randomly to participants within intact groups, such as classrooms. Such groups are not usually representative of a larger target population to which generalizations can be made. Conclusions, therefore, may not be directly generalizable to the target population.

Olsen et al.'s (2012) study provide an example of the benefits of using random assignment in an experimental study. They examined the effects of a way to enhance interpretative reading and analytical writing of mainstreamed English learners in secondary schools. Teacher clusters were randomly assigned to the treatment (The Pathway Project) or control group, and students were randomly assigned to classrooms. This study using multilayered random assignment was designed to improve the internal validity (discussed in the next section) of the project, thus allowing the researchers to make stronger conclusions from their results.

Experimental or quasi-experimental studies come in a variety of designs (see Chapters 10 and 11 in McMillan & Schumacher, 2010). The reason there are so many different designs is that there are many extraneous variables, other than the independent variable(s), that might cause the dependent variable to vary. Each design tries to control a specific set of these unwanted variables. We will not go into detail here, but suffice it to say that each design is defined by various combinations and ordering of the treatment and control groups along with random or nonrandom sampling. If you would like more detail, we recommend Gall et al. (1996), McMillan and Schumacher (2010), Mertler and Charles (2011), or websites like: www.socialresearchmethods.net/kb/desexper.php

Internal Validity

When discussing cause and effect in research, no matter where the study fits on the three continua discussed in section "Classifying Research Designs", the internal validity of the study is of critical importance. The extent to which extraneous variables affect the change in the dependent variable is the extent to which the internal validity is influenced. Whereas *external validity* relates to the degree to which findings can be generalized or transferred to populations or situations (see Chapter 4), *internal validity* is concerned with the degree to which the results of the study are due to the independent variable(s) under consideration and not due to anything else. Researchers favoring more qualitative approaches use the term *credibility* to mean the same thing as internal validity (Miles & Huberman, 1994).

Internal and external validity are not mutually exclusive. The degree to which a study lacks internal validity limits the degree to which the findings can be generalized to a target population (i.e., external validity). In other words, for a study that looks at causation, internal validity is a necessary requirement for external validity. Obviously, if the changes in the dependent variable are not due to the independent variable, then you certainly cannot generalize any findings to some target population. Nevertheless, having internal validity is not sufficient for establishing external validity. That is, a study might be designed so that the independent variable is the only thing that could cause change in the dependent variable, but because the sample is not representative of the target population or comparable with any other situation, the results of the study cannot be generalized or transferred to that population or situations. The following may be of some help.

As previously mentioned, there are a number of extraneous factors that can affect the results of a study that will lower the internal and external validity of a study. Gall et al. (1996) gave a very good overview (Chap. 12) of the work done by Campbell and Stanley (1963), Cook and Campbell (1979), Bracht and Glass (1968), and others that try to identify most of the extraneous factors that can play havoc when exploring causal relationships. They listed 12 factors related to internal validity, and 12 factors under external validity. Miles and Huberman (1994, Chapter 10) presented a very similar list of factors from a qualitative research perspective (sections B and C).

We have reworked these lists to try to remove redundancies and make things more manageable. We have also subordinated some of the factors to show how they relate to one another. As a result, we list 14 threats to internal validity along with nine subordinate ones. We illustrate these extraneous factors with the *Research Minefield* presented in Figure 5.3. A well-designed study will weave around these hazards to capture a more accurate picture of how the independent variable(s) influences the dependent variable. The following is a brief explanation for each of the 14 *mines* with examples of studies that have either avoided them or hit them.

History

This refers to the influence of events that take place at different points in time on the dependent variable other than the independent variable. Any study that takes considerable time to be completed can be affected by this if care is not taken. For instance, suppose researchers are running a study on improving young children's math skills using some new teaching methodology over several months. During that time, a new program is put on national TV teaching math for young children. If the researchers found any difference between the treatment and control group, could they be certain that the results were only due to the new methodology? Could the

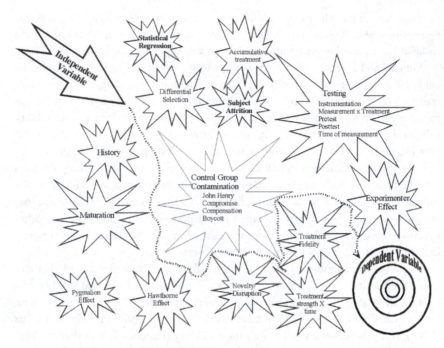

FIGURE 5.3 The Research Minefield

new methodology have interacted with the new TV program in such a way to produce the results? Had the program not appeared when it did, the new methodology might not have produced the same results. Consequently, the researchers could not be sure what caused the changes in language behavior, if any were observed.

Longitudinal studies (i.e., studies that are done over a period) are vulnerable to the History mine. An example is the study done by Giesen, Cavenaugh, and McDonnall et al. (2012), who investigated the effects of academic supports for a national sample of 292 elementary and middle school students who were blind or visually impaired over 6 years. They wanted to investigate the impact of academic supports over time while controlling for differences in grade level, gender, cognitive disability, and family socioeconomic status. The study drew from data beginning in 2000 and running to 2006. The researchers were careful to describe issues with regard to gathering data for such a long period of time when other factors during this time might have affected the results. At times, some historical events can interact with a treatment in different ways than with a control group and produce results that otherwise would not have happened. To give more confidence to the results of longitudinal studies, it is always wise for a researcher to inform the reader if anything of possible importance had occurred historically. Even if nothing happened, this should be reported so that the reader is made aware that this precaution was attended to.

Maturation

This is similar to History but deals with the natural changes that take place over time in participants other than what is under study. Such areas as physical coordination and strength, emotional states, and cognitive structures change as people grow older. Studies that take place over longer periods of time are potentially subject to this interference. For example, according to Piaget, young children who are at the preoperational (Ormrod, 2014) stage, between the ages of 2 and 6, "have some logical thinking but base their thought primarily on hunches and intuition" (p. 29). In the next stage, concrete operational (6–11/12 years), children are able to think logically, but only with visible concrete objects. If Piaget's thinking is valid, we would have to take great care in the use of visual objects when using them to examine concrete materials in learning of children across these stages (McNeil & Uttal, 2009).

The longitudinal study by Giesen et al. (2012) should not have had this problem. Although their participants were different ages, they would have developed physically and cognitively at the same pace. However, if there is something about the treatment that interacts with certain developmental stages, then different results could be found. The authors were also careful to state "the presence of a cognitive disability in addition to visual impairment is critically important to consider" (p. 24) since a combination of disabilities may require specialized academic supports.

Differential Selection

Hitting this mine can occur whenever researchers do not randomly select their samples when forming different groups for comparison purposes. Any preexisting differences between groups caused by choosing dissimilar participants could result in differences between groups not due to the variable being investigated. The classical situation where this might occur is when two intact classrooms are used: one for the treatment group and the other for the control group. Chances are that there are preexisting differences between the classes. Accordingly, these prior differences, and not the treatments, could account for any difference in the dependent variable between groups.

The results of Kesan and Caliskan's (2013) study might have been influenced by *differential selection*. The researchers wanted to explore the effect of learning geometry topics in seventh graders using a specific sketchpad geometry software package. Forty-two 7th grade students were the participants with 21 of these receiving traditional instruction (the control group) and 21 receiving instruction using the experimental software (the treatment group). Although the researchers used sixth grade math scores as an indicator of the presoftware math achievement comparability of the two groups, the participants were not randomly selected to the control or treatment groups. The researchers did not provide any additional information in regard to the potential differences in the two groups other than their pretest geometry ability was comparable. Their findings suggested that the treatment group that used the software had statistically greater achievement when compared with the control group; however, these findings may have been more credible to the research community if random selection had been taking place.

Statistical Regression

This is a fancy name for a phenomenon found in research where participants chosen from either of two opposite ends of an ability continuum, usually based on performance on some test, have a high probability of scoring closer to the middle of the continuum on the second testing without any outside help. This movement of scores toward the middle is referred to as *regression toward the mean* or *statistical regression*. This can manifest itself when a researcher selects participants who initially score very low on an ability test and test them again after administering some form of treatment to raise their ability level. Any increase in performance after the treatment cannot be conclusively attributed to the treatment because it might be due to the statistical phenomenon of regressing upward toward the mean (i.e., the middle of the ability group).

Why does this happen, you might ask? The reason is that test scores are not exact measurements of a person's ability (oops, just gave away a secret). Many people, who initially do badly on a test, may have done badly for a variety of reasons—maybe they were not feeling well or something disturbing happened on the way to the test. If they had taken the test on another day, they might have done better. This is just one possible explanation of this phenomenon.

However, in the case of qualitative research, the extreme cases might be exactly what researchers are focusing on (Miles & Huberman, 1994). If they are trying to obtain a sample that contains information-rich data to answer the research question, then this strategy is the correct one. Statistical regression is not a factor.

Subject Attrition

When there is a loss of participants during a research study, this can occur (also known as *experimental mortality*). The results will be affected and misleading because attrition does not commonly occur randomly. People who drop out of a study often differ from those who remain in ways that distort research findings. For example, researchers might lose some beginning-level learners from their sample because they lose interest and drop out. This might leave the study not only with proportionally more participants of higher ability levels, but with participants who have higher motivation.

A study that might have been affected by attrition was done by Wallinger (2002), who investigated the effects of block scheduling on learning a foreign language. *Block scheduling* is a nontraditional format that varies the classroom schedules during the instructional week. Wallinger was able to obtain 66 classes from various high schools that had a French program for ninth grade. She began the study with classes that could be grouped into three different scheduling strategies. The numbers of classes in each group were 23, 23, and 20. However, she reported that six classes did not complete the study. The problem was that all six were from the same scheduling strategy, which later produced some important differences. The question immediately arises whether this particular scheduling had something to do with the classes dropping out. If so, these data are important to the findings.

Sometimes researchers drop participants from groups to produce equal numbers in each group, often referred to as a *cell*. The reason they do this is that many statistical procedures are easier to interpret when there are equal cell sizes. However, you want to check whether participants are dropped randomly. If this is done, there is less chance that a bias may occur. Another caveat is that, when dealing with smaller numbers of participants, the loss of even one participant can have a significant impact on the results. The conclusion is that when you read a research article, give attention to any irregularities in the sample. There should be clear documentation to show that the results of the study were not contaminated by any participant attrition.

Control Group Contamination

The danger of this is when there is more than one group in a causal study. Many studies use control groups in their designs. Typically, a control group is one that does not receive the novel treatment which is the focus of the study. For instance, a new method for teaching vocabulary might be compared with a traditional method.[2]

However, this effect could better be referred to as *competing group contamination*. The reason is that some studies compare differences between groups possibly · without a control group. These studies have several competing treatment groups. In such studies the following discussion is still applicable.

Celikten, Ipekcioglu, Ertepinar, and Geban's (2012) study, is used in the following discussion as a platform for illustrating the four ways a competing group can affect the results of a study. The researchers compared the effectiveness of conceptual change oriented instruction through cooperative learning and traditional science instruction on fourth grade students' understanding of earth and sky concepts and their attitudes toward these concepts. Fifty-six 4th grade students from the same elementary school took part. One class of 28 students received cooperative learning instruction (the treatment group) while the other class of 28 students received traditional instruction (the control group). The researchers stated that the two instructional methods (not the students) were randomly assigned to each group. They also stated that based upon pretest results, there was no significant difference between these two groups on the students' understanding of sky and earth achievement.

Competing group contamination can take four different directions. They are:

Competing Group Rivalry (John Henry Effect)

When the behaviors of the competing groups differ because they are trying to outdo one another, you cannot be sure the results are due to the difference in treatments, that is, the independent variable(s). This condition might occur if the competing group were explicitly known as *the control group*. Not only might extra effort come from the participants in the group, but the person supervising the control group, such as a teacher, might apply extra effort to compete. The thing to look for is whether the researchers have specified what measures were taken to protect from this effect. Careful researchers will take precautions to keep the groups' identities a secret and report them in their study (see http://en.wikipedia.org/wiki/John_Henry_(folklore)).

In Celikten et al.'s (2012) study, students in the two groups were equivalent in terms of socioeconomic status including the educational level of their parents and their family income indicated by "middle-range" status. The researchers did not state that they took any specific precautions to insulate the two groups from knowing who was in the control or the treatment group. Though there was no mention of the possible *John Henry* problem, had the control group heard about what was going on in the other class, they may have been challenged to compete. This would have been a possible explanation had there been no difference between the experimental group and the control group. However, the experimental group outperformed the control group, so this was not a problem.

Experimental Treatment Diffusion (Compromise)

When the competing groups gain knowledge of the factors making up the differing treatment conditions and employ these factors in there own situations, the results might be corrupted. The extraneous variable here is *not* competition, as in section "Competing Group Rivalry (John Henry Effect)", but rather the mixing up of the treatment factors in the competing groups due to knowledge about what is taking place in the other group(s). This often happens when the competing groups are in close proximity and have time to get to know what the other(s) is doing. Care should be taken to reduce the possibility of participants from the different groups discussing what the other(s) is doing.

Looking at Celikten et al.'s (2012) study, we can conclude that this did not happen since the same teacher taught both classes and could control the type of instruction, although there might have been common awareness of what was happening in the experimental treatment. Similar to the John Henry effect, this problem might have been of concern if there had been no difference between the treatment and control groups, or if the control group outperformed the treatment group.

Compensatory Equalization of Treatments

When attempts are made to give the competing group extra material or special treatment to make up for not receiving the experimental treatment; you no longer have a true control group. In fact, you would have a new treatment group.

The temptation to provide the control group with extra help arises when there is a possibility that the treatment group will have an advantage over the control group in some real-life situation. To illustrate, if researchers were comparing some new method of teaching math (treatment group) with the traditional way (control group) math was being taught during a real math course, they might be tempted to give the control group some extra material or help so that they would not be at an unfair disadvantage at the end of the course. However, in doing so, the differences between treatment and control could be distorted, making the results uninterpretable. Again because the experimental group outperformed the control group in Celikten et al.'s (2012) study, this most likely did not occur.

To prevent *compensatory equalization of treatments* from happening, researchers should use someone to supervise the control group who is unaware of the advantage the treatment group might have during the study. In addition, they should allow time after the experiment to help the control group catch up with those in the treatment group so that the control group is not unduly penalized. A well-written study will report how this problem was addressed.

Demoralization (Boycott) of the Control Group

This potential contaminator occurs when participants in the control group resent the special treatment given to the treatment group and lowers their performance. This is the opposite of the John Henry effect. In Celikten et al.'s (2012) study, if participants in the control group, for example, learn that those in the treatment group are allowed to learn in cooperative groups with their friends rather than independently, their envy might cause them to refuse to cooperate with their instructor. To prevent this, some strategy needs to be used to convince the control group that they are not being deprived.

Here Celikten et al. (2012) study might have had a problem. Since both of the control and treatment groups were in the same school, the control group might have become demoralized if they had news that they were not getting to use cooperative learning. In turn, they might have given less effort to learn than normal. This offers an alternative explanation for the inferior performance of the control group in comparison with the treatment group. Because Celikten and his colleagues did not state whether they tried to prevent this, we are left with this alternative explanation regarding their findings.

Testing

This mine refers to ways in which measuring the dependent variable(s) can distort the results of a study. Under this heading, we list five sources to which the consumer of research needs to pay attention.

Instrumentation

The type of instrument used to measure performance on the dependent variable(s) can have an effect. This can occur if two different types of instruments are used and the performances of the two are compared with each other. In Celikten et al.'s study (2012), if one test of the knowledge of earth and sky concepts were used (e.g., a multiple-choice test) as a pretest and another test of earth and sky concepts (e.g., an essay test) were used as a posttest, you would not know whether any change in test scores was due to increase in ability or difference in the difficulty level between the two tests. Unless the two tests are parallel in all possible ways, the results between the two tests cannot be compared. In Celikten et al.'s study, the same testing instrument Earth and Sky Concepts Test (ESCT) was use for both the pre- and post-test measure of knowledge.

Measurement–Treatment Interaction

Similar to the previous, but in this case the results are only found when using a particular type of measure. To illustrate, we might only be able to find certain effects of a novel method for teaching earth and sky concepts to fourth graders with multiple-choice exams, but not with tests of written compositions. Any attempt to generalize results from only one type of measurement to all types would be groundless.

Almost every study using only one type of instrument to measure the dependent variables could be accused of having this problem. Celikten et al. (2012), for example, used the same test format for pretesting participants' prior knowledge of earth and sky concepts as well as for the posttest after the treatment. The format followed the test design of ESCT, in which participants responded to 15 multiple-choice questions. The discerning reader should ask whether the same results would have been found if test formats had been used. This is not to suggest, however, that the findings of this study are insignificant. They are important, but they are only part of the puzzle. To bolster their conclusions, this study should be replicated using other science assessment formats to see if the findings are replicated.

Pretest Effect

This is caused when a test given before the administration of the treatment interacts with the treatment by heightening participants' awareness of importance of certain material. If this happens, the performance on the test given after the treatment (i.e., the *posttest*) would be higher than if no pretest were given. The question here is whether the pretest alerts the participants to components in the treatment to which they would not normally pay much attention. The only way we would know if this occurred would be if we had another treatment group that did not take the pretest and compared their performance on the posttest with that of the pretest or treatment group. If there was no difference, then we could conclude that there was no pretest effect.

Celikten et al.'s (2012) results might have been influenced by this. They used the exact same test for assessing the prior knowledge of earth and sky concepts in their pretest as they did for their posttest after the treatment. The project was conducted over an 8-week span but the researchers did not allude to any potential problems with a pretest effect. However, had they used an additional group who did not take the pretest prior to the treatment, they could have tested whether there was any pretest effect. That is, if no difference between the two treatment groups (i.e., pretest with treatment vs. treatment without pretest) on the posttest was found, they would have clear evidence that the pretest did not interact with the treatment.

Posttest Effect

Unwittingly, researchers might design their posttest so that it helps participants *make associations* between different concepts at the time of taking the test rather than during the time of treatment. Had another test been used, these associations might not have been made, and the conclusion would be that the treatment had no effect.

Most likely you have experienced this effect when taking an exam sometime in the past, like most of us. It is known as the *click of comprehension* effect. As participants take the posttest, suddenly something in the test brings things together in a way that the participants had not thought of previously, but this effect was something that the treatment was suppose to have done prior to the posttest, not during it.

Time of Measurement Effect

This relates to timing. Many studies apply whatever measurement they are using immediately after the completion of the treatment. To conclude that such results can be interpreted to mean that the treatment also has long-term effects would be misleading. Maybe the results are due to information stored in short-term memory. For us to make any strong conclusions, we would have to have an additional measurement with an appropriate time interval.

To control for the above effect, some studies administer the test without warning a week or more later. Although Glenberg, Brown, and Levin (2007) did not control for this effect, they were interested in enhancing reading comprehension of students in small reading groups by using a manipulation strategy. Participant groups of 6- to 8-year-old children were formed from convenience samples and then 15 three-student groups were randomly assigned either to one of two treatment conditions or a control group. The two conditions consisted of either rereading a sentence aloud or acting out the action sequence (manipulation) in the text.

The results showed that the treatment groups (specifically the manipulation treatment) had greater reading comprehension than the control group immediately after the treatment. If the researchers had delayed their posttest 1week later, they might have found that these differences disappeared. Such findings would provide evidence that the treatment did indeed have a significant effect.

Researcher Effect

This can also be a source for data distortion, which in turn weakens the internal validity of the results. If the results are determined by who does the experiment or who does the interview, the results are questionable. This problem often occurs when researchers are the ones who are either administering the treatment or collecting data that depends on their judgments. A study that exemplifies the care needed to avoid this effect is Holmes' (2012) study, which we looked at previously. The study used a mixed-method approach gathering both quantitative and naturalistic observational data. Holmes used data gatherers and reported that they "made no attempt to interact with the children" (p. 334) they were observing. Had the data gatherers had direct contact or interviewed children, they might have done things in such a way that the results would have been influenced in the direction they predicted.

Under the same heading we include the *data gatherer effect*. In the Holmes' (2012) study, observers "made contact only when the children approached the observers. During the first few visits, some children were curious and ask the observers what they were doing. Observers told the children they were interested in what children do at recess" (p. 334). Most likely the participants became desensitized to the observers' presence during the lengthy time of the project (1 year). Without this lengthy longitudinal data gathering period, the results of the study would be suspect.

Consequently, you need to pay attention to who applies the treatment/control and/or who/what does the data gathering. If the author(s) of the study is the one applying the treatment, while another administers the control, the results are questionable. If the researcher is directly doing the data gathering, there should be at least one other person checking to make sure the data is objectively gathered. More is given about this in the next chapter.

Pygmalion Effect

This is a type of researcher effect. This is caused by a change in the researchers' perception of the behavior of the participants caused by their expectations of the participants' performance. For instance, if the data collectors think that the participants they are observing are high-ability students, they might be more lenient (or demanding) in their observations than if they thought the participants were low-ability students. Any time participants have been divided into ability groups such as high/middle/low proficiency and the data collector is aware of this, there is a danger of this effect. The danger is even greater if the type of data collected requires any form of qualitative judgment on the part of the data collectors, such as when using a rating scale. Researchers need to take precautions that the data collectors are unaware of the ability level of the participants they are observing and clearly state what precautions they have taken in their report.

Hawthorne Effect

When participants behave differently because they know they are in a research study distortions can occur. In a normal classroom environment the same results might not be found. This problem is usually dealt with by masking from the participants the fact that they are involved in a study. To illustrate how this effect might have influence on the results of a study, we use a study by Tze and Chou (2010). They looked at the effects of how background music effects concentration and reading comprehension. They used 133 college students who were randomly assigned to either a control (no background music) or one of two treatment groups (slow classical music or Hip Hop) while completing a reading comprehension task. In this study, it is difficult to determine whether the students were affected by the background music, or whether the students were flattered just to be asked to participate in a research project. However, the results showed that certain music distracted from reading comprehension, so participants' knowledge of being given special treatment did not really influence them.

Treatment Intervention

The results of a study can be affected in at least two undesirable ways: *novelty* and *disruption*. Some treatments are so new that their novelty affects the results on the dependent variable. For example, if a study is looking at the effects of using computers to teach a foreign language in comparison with normal classroom teaching, the students in the computer group may be more motivated to do well because of the novelty of using computers. This novelty may wear off after sustained exposure to computers and their motivation drops. In this study, the improvement would not have been due to the effectiveness of computers but the motivation level of the students caused by something new in the classroom. To avoid this effect, a study needs to have a *cooling-off period*, where the novelty wears off before any measurements are made.

Not all things new are an advantage, however. Disruption in performance can be due to participants being unfamiliar with the new intervention being tried. Using the computer example that we previously discussed, many participants who have not acquired good keyboarding skills may perform more poorly than those using traditional paper and pencil. These results would mask any advantage the computer might have over traditional methods.

The study by Kesan and Caliskan (2013) may have been influenced by some of these issues. They found significant differences when the control and treatment group were compared after using a new geometry software program. However, the researchers recognized this problem in their *Discussion* section in that the differences could be due to unfamiliarity of using the program. They also noted that teachers who worked with the treatment groups actually needed additional training with the software to achieve optimal results. Anytime researchers are willing to present the potential limitations or factors that may have affected the results of their study; they should be applauded for their effort.

Accumulative Treatment Effect

It is also known as *multiple-treatment interference or order effect*. This is the result of the accumulative effect of the particular order in which treatments are presented. Some research designs administer several treatments to the same participants. When this happens, care needs to be taken that the particular order in which the treatments are given does not influence the results. The most common way to control for this effect is using what is called a *counterbalanced* design. This is a simple procedure whereby the order of the treatments is varied across participants so as to attenuate the effects of order.

A study that exemplifies this procedure was completed by Dolan, Hall, Chun, and Strangman (2005), who looked at the influence of computer-based and read–aloud test performance with high school students with learning disabilities. In a counterbalanced design, students were administered one form of assessment via a traditional paper and pencil exam (PPT) and the other via a computer-based system with optional text-to-speech (CBT-TTS). To control for order effects and differences between test forms order of administration (PPT vs. CBT-TTS first) and test form (A vs. B) were counterbalanced across four randomly composed groups. By counterbalancing tasks, Dolan et al. controlled for the effects of order when the data were combined.

Treatment Fidelity

This has to do with whether the treatment was administered in the correct manner as defined by researchers (Gall et al., 1996). Studies that use people other than researchers as the treatment administrators are in danger of the treatment not being administered correctly. If the treatment is not properly given, the results cannot really answer the research question. However, if researchers do the implementation themselves, the researcher effect could play a role. To ensure treatment fidelity and avoid researcher effect, researchers need to train treatment administrators other than themselves to the point where the treatment is administered at the appropriate level.

Tze and Chou (2010) realized this danger in their study so they trained three volunteer teachers who were asked to assist with the experiment and the collection of their data. Adequately training the observers begins to ensure that the treatment was administered in the correct manner and that the effects are due to the treatment rather than researcher error or data collection inconsistency.

Treatment Strength–Time Interaction

Time needed for a treatment to have any noticeable effect. Some treatments require more time than others. This potential problem especially relates to studies that deal with teaching methodology commonly found in applied linguistics. Time is needed for most innovative methods to take effect, which means that these studies need more than 1 or 2 weeks before testing whether an innovation works.

When the results find no effect for a new method being tried out, the reader needs to ask whether there was enough time in the research design to allow the treatment to work. This may have been a factor in a study by Maden (2011) where he explored the effect of a cooperative learning technique on achievement in written expression skills of university students. The quantitative data was captured using a treatment-control-group pretest-posttest design to measure the before and after treatment effects of exposure to Jigsaw, a form of cooperative learning instruction. Students in one class received instruction using the Jigsaw technique and another received traditional teaching method instruction. Learning styles of the groups were determined by the Kolb Learning Style Inventory (LSI) and data in regard to their academic success was collected through the Success Test for Written Expression (STWE). The experimental cooperative learning technique was used for 6 weeks. The researcher determined from his results that no significant variation occurred in favor of the treatment group in terms of changes in learning styles or academic success when compared with the control groups. Since the project only ran for 6 weeks, one has to consider if the short time-frame of the project had an impact on the nonsignificant findings as well as the direct participation of the researcher as instructor for the two groups in the study.

As you can see from the above list of the many things that can cause differences in the dependent variable other than the independent variables, it is a wonder anyone tries to answer the question, *Why*. However, rather than turning you into a cynic, rejecting any research as a waste of time, we hope that you have come to appreciate the challenge researchers face when trying to tease out the answers to the *Why* question. Yes, you should have reservations, but in a healthy sort of way. You should take the results and interpretations of any one single study with a degree of caution, knowing that there most likely is a weakness or two. However, this should encourage you to find more studies that address the same question to find if the results agree. If you find a number of studies producing similar findings, you will have more confidence regarding any answers. In addition, when you find a study that is designed in such a way that it avoids all of the mines mentioned above, you will find yourself admiring the study as though it were a famous painting in the Louvre. Maybe that is taking it too far, but you will appreciate them more when you come across them.

In conclusion, there are many variations in the types of designs you will encounter in your readings. In many cases, you will even find combinations of the above designs included in one study. There is nothing to restrict researchers from using whatever they believe will best answer the research questions.

There has been a lot of material covered here, and you will probably not remember it all the first time through. We certainly did not. However, as you continue to read research, you will want to review this chapter now and again to refresh your memory regarding the rationale for using certain techniques. As you do this, you will sharpen your skills at becoming a very effective discerning consumer.

However, before moving on to the next chapter, take the time to do the following exercise. We have developed an instrument to help you catalogue the information you will be looking for below called the *Internal Validity Evaluation Inventory*.

Table 5.1 Internal Validity Evaluation Inventory

Risk	Risk Factor			Precautions Taken
	Low	Medium	High	
History				
Maturation				
Differential selection				
Statistical regression				
Subject attrition				
Competing group contamination				
1. Competing group rivalry: John Henry effect				
2. Experimental treatment diffusion (compromise)				
3. Compensatory equalization of treatments				
4. Demoralization (boycott) of the control group				
Testing				
1. Instrumentation				
2. Measurement–treatment interaction				
3. Pre-test				
4. Post-test				
5. Time of measurement effects				
Researcher effect				
Pygmalion effect				
Hawthorne effect				
Novelty and disruption effect				
Accumulative treatment effect: (multiple-treatment interference)				
Treatment fidelity				
Treatment strength–time interaction				

EXERCISE 5.5

Find a recent study from a research journal that answers a Why question using an experimental/quasi-experimental design.

1   State the research question(s).
2   Identify the independent variable(s) and the dependent variable(s).
3   State any hypotheses and/or predictions made, if any.
4   Study the *Introduction* and *Methodology* sections. In your own words explain what procedures were used to determine the causal relationship.
5   Using the Internal Validity Evaluation Inventory (Table 5.1) at the end of the chapter, rate the risk level of any one of the possible threats to internal validity. Summarize any precautions the researcher(s) took to prevent any of these effects.

Key Terms and Concepts

accumulative treatment effect
action research
applied research
basic research
case study
causal–comparative design
compensatory equalization of treatments
confirmatory research
control group contamination
conversational analysis
correlational study
demoralization
differential selection
ethnography
experimental design
experimental treatment diffusion
exploratory research
external validity
grounded theory
Hawthorne effect
history
instrumentation
intact groups
internal validity

John Henry effect
longitudinal study
maturation
measurement–treatment interaction
posttest effect
pretest effect
Pygmalion effect
qualitative research
quantitative research
quasi-experimental design
random assignment
researcher effect
shot-gun method
statistical regression
subject attrition
thick description
think-aloud technique
time of measurement effect
treatment fidelity
treatment intervention
treatment strength–time interaction
triangulation

Additional Recommended Reading

Huberman, A. M., & Miles, M. B. (2002). *The qualitative researcher's companion.* Thousand Oaks, CA: Sage.
Johnson, B., & Christensen, L. B. (2003). *Educational research: Quantitative, qualitative, and mixed approaches, research edition* (2nd ed.). Upper Saddle River, NJ: Pearson Education.

Notes

1 There is no precise correct point to place these studies. We are only estimating their placement.
2 Just a note of warning here. What constitutes a *traditional* method varies with each study. You should examine whether the traditional method is clearly defined so that you know exactly what is meant by *traditional*. By doing so, you will be able to understand to what the novel method is being compared (cf. *treatment fidelity* later in this chapter).

References

Blakesley, S. (2011). Defining educational leadership in Canada's Yukon Territory: "Hmmm, that's a good question…". *Canadian Journal of Education, 34*(1), 4–36.

Blumberg, F. C., & Randall, J. D. (2013). What do children and adolescents say they do during video game play? *Journal of Applied Developmental Psychology, 34*(2), 82–88.

Bon, S. C. (2009). Exploring the impact of applicants' gender and religion on principals' screening decisions for assistant principal applicants. *International Journal of Education Policy & Leadership, 4*(1), 1–21.

Boon, H. J. (2008). Risk or resilience? What makes a difference? *Australian Educational Researcher, 35*(1), 81–102.

Bracht, G. H., & Glass, G.V. (1968). The external validity of experiments. *American Educational Research Journal, 5*, 437–474. doi:10.3102/00028312005004437

Burns, A. (2010). *Doing action research in English language teaching: A guide for practitioners.* New York: Routledge.

Burns, B. A. (2010). Pre-service teachers' exposure to using the history of mathematics to enhance their teaching of high school mathematics. *Issues in the Undergraduate Mathematics Preparation of School Teachers, 4*, 1–9.

Campbell, D. T., & Stanley, J. C. (1963). *Experimental and quasi-experimental designs for research.* Chicago, IL: Rand McNally. doi:10.1016/0306-4573(84)90053-0

Celikten, O., Ipekcioglu, S., Ertepinar, H., & Geban, O. (2012). The effect of the conceptual change oriented instruction through cooperative learning on 4th grade students' understanding of earth and sky concepts. *Science Education International, 23*(1), 84–96.

Coladarci, T., Cobb, C. D., Minium, E. W., & Clarke, R. C. (2004). *Fundamentals of statistical reasoning in education.* Hoboken, NJ: John Wiley & Sons Publishers.

Cook, T. D., & Campbell, D. T. (1979). *Quasi-experimental: Design and analysis issues for field settings.* Chicago, IL: Rand McNally.

Creswell, J. W. (2002). *Research design: Qualitative, quantitative, and mixed methods approaches.* Thousand Oaks, CA: Sage.

Creswell, J. W. (2008). *Educational research: Planning, conducting, and evaluating quantitative and qualitative research* (3rd ed.). Upper Saddle River, NJ: Pearson Publishing.

Denzin, N. K., & Lincoln, Y. S. (Eds.). (2000). *Handbook of qualitative research* (2nd ed.). Thousand Oaks, CA: Sage.

Dolan, R. P., Hall, M. B., Chun, E., & Strangman, N. (2005). Applying principles of universal design to test delivery: The effect of computer-based read-aloud on test performance of high school students with learning disabilities. *The Journal of Technology, Learning, and Assessment, 3*(7), 1–33.

Dowden, A. R. (2010). A personal journey in promoting social justice as a school counselor: An action research approach. *Journal of School Counseling, 8*(24), 1–23.

Gall, M. D., Borg, W. R., & Gall, J. P. (1996). *Educational research: An introduction* (6th ed.). White Plains, NY: Longman.

Gall, M. D., Gall, J. P., & Borg, W. R. (2010). *Applying educational research* (6th ed.). Upper Saddle River, NJ: Pearson Publishing.

Glenberg, A. M., Brown, M., & Levin, J. R. (2007). Enhancing comprehension in small reading groups using a manipulation strategy. *Contemporary Educational Psychology, 32*(3), 389–399.

Giesen, J. M., Cavenaugh, B. S., & McDonnall, M. C. (2012). Academic supports, cognitive disability and mathematics achievement for visually impaired youth: A multilevel modeling approach. *International Journal of Special Education, 27*(1), 17–26.

Hickey, M. G. (2013). Our children follow our rules: Family and child rearing in U. S. Muslim migration. *Journal of Interdisciplinary Studies in Education, 1*(2), 4–26.

Holmes, R. M. (2012). The outdoor recess activities of children at an urban school: Longitudinal patterns and intraperiod patterns. *American Journal of Play, 4*(3), 327–351.

Jadallah, M., Anderson, R. C., Nguyen-Jahiel, K., Miller, B. W., Kim, I-H., Kuo, L-J., … Xiaoying, W. (2011). Influence of a teacher's scaffolding moves during child-led small-group discussions. *American Educational Research Journal, 48*(1), 194–230.

Kesan, C., & Caliskan, S. (2013). The effect of learning geometry topics of 7th grade in primary education with dynamic geometer's sketchpad geometry software to success and retention. *The Turkish Online Journal of Educational Technology, 12*(1), 131–138.

LeCompte, M. D., Millroy, W. L., & Preissle, J. (Eds.). (1992). *The handbook of qualitative research in education.* San Diego, CA: Academic Press.

Leedy, P. D., & Ormrod, J. E. (2013). *Practical research: Planning and design* (10th ed.). Upper Saddle River, NJ: Pearson Publishing.

Leonard, T. (2000). *A course in categorical data analysis.* Boca Raton, FL: Chapman & Hall/CRC Press.

Maden, S. (2011). Effect of Jigsaw I technique on achievement in written expression skill. *Educational Studies: Theory & Practice, 11*(2), 911–917.

Margiotta, M. (2011). Parental support in the development of young musicians: A teacher's perspective from a small-scale study of piano students and their parents. *Australian Journal of Music Education, 1,* 16–30.

McCrudden, M. T., & Sparks, P. C. (2014). Exploring the effect of task instructions on topic beliefs and topic belief justifications: A mixed methods study. *Contemporary Educational Psychology, 39*(1), 1–11.

McMillan, J. H., & Schumacher, S. (2010). *Research in education: Evidence-based inquiry.* Upper Saddle River, NJ: Pearson.

McNeil, N. M., & Uttal, D. H. (2009). Rethinking the use of concrete materials in learning: Perspectives from development and education. *Child Development Perspectives, 3,* 137–139.

Mertler, C. A., & Charles, C. M. (2011). *Introduction to educational research* (7th ed.). Upper Saddle River, NJ: Pearson Publishing.

Miles, M. B., & Huberman, A. M. (1994). *Qualitative data analysis: An expanded sourcebook.* Thousand Oaks, CA: Sage. doi:10.1177/109821409902000122

Nieto, S. (2013). Language, literacy, and culture: Aha! moments in personal and sociopolitical understanding. *Journal of Language & Literacy Education, 9*(1), 8–20.

Olsen, C. B., Kim, J. S., Scarcella, R., Kramer, J., Pearson, M., van Dyk, D. A., ... Land, R. E. (2012). Enhancing the interpretive reading and analytical writing of mainstreamed English learners in secondary school: Results from a randomized field trial using a cognitive strategies approach. *American Educational Research Journal, 49*(2), 323–355.

Ormrod, J. E. (2014). *Educational psychology: Developing learners.* Upper Saddle River, NJ: Pearson.

Paltridge, B. (2006). *Discource analysis: An introduction.* New York: Continuum.

Peine, M. E., & Coleman, L. J. (2010). The phenomenon of waiting in class. *Journal for the Education of the Gifted, 34*(2), 220–244.

Shapley, K., Sheehan, D., Maloney, C., & Caranikas-Walker, F. (2011). Effects of technology immersion on middle-school students' learning opportunities and achievement. *The Journal of Educational Research, 104*(5), 299–315.

Silverman, S. K. (2010). What is diversity? An inquiry into preservice teacher beliefs. *American Educational Research Journal, 47,* 2, 292–329.

Singh, L. (2013). Guided assessment or open discourse: A comparative analysis of students' interaction on Facebook Groups. *Turkish Online Journal of Distance Education, 14*(1), 35–43.

Skiba, R. J., Poloni-Staudinger, L., Simmons, A. B., Feggins-Azziz, R., & Chung, C-G. (2005). Unproven links: Can poverty explain ethnic disproportionality in special education? *The Journal of Special Education, 39*(3), 130–144.

Tashakkori, A., & Teddlie, C. (1998). *Mixed methodology.* Thousand Oaks, CA: Sage.

Tashakkori, A., & Teddlie, C. (2003). *Handbook on mixed methods in social and behavior science.* Thousand Oaks, CA: Sage.

Turney, K., & Kao, G. (2009). Barriers to school involvement: Are immigrant parents disadvantaged? *The Journal of Educational Research, 102*(4), 257–271.

Tze, P., & Chou, M. (2010). Attention drainage effect: How background music effects concentration in Taiwanese college students. *Journal of the Scholarship of Teaching and Learning, 10*(1), 36–46.

Wallinger, L. M. (2002). The effects of block scheduling on foreign language learning. *Foreign Language Annals, 33*, 2–50. doi:10.1111/j.1944-9720.2000.tb00888.x

Xu, J., & Wu, H. (2013). Self-regulation of homework behavior: Homework management at the secondary school level. *The Journal of Educational Research, 106*(1), 1–13.

6

UNDERSTANDING DATA GATHERING

Chapter Overview

Once researchers determine the research design, they need to decide exactly how they will gather their data. A brief look at research articles in education will quickly reveal that there are many procedures used for collecting data. Some people argue that certain procedures are superior to others. However, we argue, along with others (e.g., Tashakkori & Teddlie, 1998, Chapter 2), that the value of a data-gathering procedure depends on how well it provides answers to the research questions. As a consumer, you should become familiar with as many of these procedures as possible so that you will not be limited in your search for answers to your questions.

This chapter attempts to condense a body of information that could fill an entire course. Therefore, it is important for you to pause and complete each of the exercises as you work through the chapter. Similar to the Sample subsection in a research article (see Chapter 4), the information typically provided about the strategy used for data collection in a research study does not occupy much space. However, the underlying issues in proper data collection can make or break the value of a study. As with Chapter 5, this chapter is one that you will want to review periodically as you read articles that use different procedures.

The chapter is divided into two sections. The first provides a survey of the different methods by which verbal data are collected and a discussion of the strengths and weaknesses of each. This is followed by a summary of how such data can be evaluated as dependable and credible. Section "Collecting and Evaluating Numerical Data" examines methods that typically gather numerical data followed by a discussion on how these data are judged as reliable and valid. These form the criteria that you, the consumer, need for evaluating whether the data-gathering procedures have been appropriately used.

Collecting and Evaluating Verbal Data

This section summarizes a number of data-collection sources that are commonly used in education research resulting in verbal data. In Table 6.1, we group these under *observational* procedures along with the advantages and disadvantages of each procedure. In the following discussion, each of these procedures is expanded and illustrations from published research are given.

Observational Procedures

The procedures under this heading involve capturing data through visual observation. The use of human observers as data collectors is as old as research itself. It has long been known that the main advantage of human observation, over some form of impersonal instrument, is that the former allows for flexibility when exploring what new, and sometimes unexpected, phenomena might be uncovered.

On the other hand, some believe that observational procedures suffer from three disadvantages. The first is that they generally take more time than instrumental procedures. Consequently, they are usually more costly. Second, they are more limited in the numbers of participants/objects that are used for data gathering. Third, they allow for varying degrees of *subjectivity*. That is, the influence of factors such as attitude, temporary emotional and physical states, and so forth, can distort the perception of the observer. However, others believe that these three weaknesses are, in fact, strengths of this category of procedures. The fact that it takes more time, they argue, means that there is better chance to obtain quality information despite of the cost. Using fewer subjects is not a problem if the purpose is to

Table 6.1 Verbal Data-Collection Procedures

Method	Potential Strengths	Potential Weaknesses
Observational	Discover new phenomena, flexible	Time consuming, observer effects
Self	Firsthand information, inner thoughts	Possible bias
Introspection	Immediate access, accesses inner states	Intrusive, difficult to validate
Retrospection	Not intrusive	Memory loss
Outside Observer		
Full-participant	Elicits natural behavior, not intrusive	Possible bias, deceptive, memory loss
Partial-participant	Not deceptive	Possible bias
Nonparticipant	Objective	Disruptive
Interviewer	Ability to probe, monitors comprehension, 100% feedback	Needs training, standardization, handling data

observe information-rich samples. Last, *subjectivity* is viewed as positive because researchers become personally involved with the data collection. In addition, if multiple observers are used and compared with one another for degree of agreement, subjectivity is controlled. In conclusion, we believe that most everyone would agree that observational procedures are powerful means for gathering data.

Observational procedures have many different formats. First, the one doing the observing can vary considerably. Observers can be researchers, people employed to observe, or participants observing themselves. Second, observers might be very involved with the purpose of the study or totally oblivious to why they are being asked to observe. Third, observers might be recording information that requires no interpretation of the observations or be required to give their own evaluative judgments as to what their observations mean. Fourth, the observation process may or may not be backed up with recording devices. Researchers often use recording devices (audio or video) to aid in further analysis.

In the following discussion, we will show how these different formats are used by surveying the most common observational techniques along with their strengths and limitations. This section is based on the degree to which the observer is personally involved with who or what is being observed, beginning with the most involved observer, the self. It ends with the interviewer.

Self as Observer

Using participants as observers of their own behavior has become more common over the past years under the heading of *protocol analysis* (see Chapter 5). This procedure requires participants to observe their own internal cognitive (or emotional) states and/or processing strategies either during an ongoing task, referred to as *introspection*, or after they have completed the task, known as *retrospection*.

Researchers usually record participants' thoughts on audiotape during a *think-aloud* task, as mentioned in Chapter 5. To illustrate, Perry along with several colleagues did a study where they asked participants to identify what strategies they were using to decode new vocabulary in a reading passage. They recorded participants' introspections during the reading process by audiotape recorder and analyzed the transcribed data later (Perry, Boraie, Kassabgy, & Kassabgy, 2001).

The strength of *introspection* is that it gets researchers as close as possible to the inner workings of the participants' mind. The problem, however, lies in validating whether the participants are providing accurate information. If the study is not done carefully, participants may simply tell the researchers what they think the researchers want to hear. An even greater problem is that the very act of reporting what a participant is thinking can be disruptive. These intrusions can interfere with natural cognitive processes, thus distorting the data and making them less authentic.

A study using the *introspection* technique was done by Nash-Ditzel (2010). She explored the impact of metacognitive reading strategies on the ability of five college students in developmental courses to self-regulate while reading over a

10-week period. As part of the data-collection process, the researchers used two separate think-aloud protocols drawing from Pressley and Afflerbach's (1995) previous verbal protocol research while the students read specific passages. This procedure involved a trained interviewer using a think-aloud interview guide to ask-questions of the students as they read specific passages. For this project, students were asked to self-report freely rather than at specific intervals chosen by the interviewer. Data were initially separated by case and by data source and were coded according to specific themes by the researcher.

As with any study using this approach, there are questions about the final data prior to analysis. First, did the students provide accurate descriptions of the reading strategies they actually used? Second, did the presence of an interviewer asking questions in the midst of reading or writing disturb what the students reported? Third, did the students draw upon previous strategies that they had learned earlier? Last, was any information lost or misinterpreted by comparing the verbal think-aloud feedback to other pieces of data that were collected (interviews, observations, document analysis of reading notes)?

The questions just raised about the Nash-Ditzel (2010) study should not be interpreted as criticisms. Rather, they should give us an appreciation for the complexity of trying to obtain data fresh out of the minds of participants. This is as close as we can get to authentic data. As Nash-Ditzel (2010) clearly states, a study like this takes a great deal of careful planning, commitment, and sustained time. As we keep approaching our research questions from different angles (i.e., triangulation), we begin to form a picture of what is actually happening.

To eliminate the possible intrusive effect of the introversion technique, some researchers use retrospection. In this case, the participant is required to wait until after the task before reflecting on what they had done cognitively. However, as you might have realized, a different problem can potentially affect the data (i.e., loss of memory). If the task is complicated or takes a lot of time, the participant can forget some of the mental processes that occurred. The tendency found in the psychology of memory is that participants remember the first and last parts of the information and forget what is in between.

The study by Cai and Lee (2012) illustrates one of two forms of retrospection: *immediate* versus *delayed*. Before discussing this study, however, we want to mention an important point here in regard to the process of research. Sometimes, researchers will use a qualitative/exploratory/applied approach to follow up a previous quantitative/exploratory/applied study. Typically, the reverse is the normal pattern: qualitative results followed by a quantitative study. The reason is that qualitative methods of data collection often look for information-rich data to build theoretical hypotheses. On the basis of these hypotheses, larger quantitative studies are performed to test the hypotheses and generalize the findings to larger populations.

In the study by Cai and Lee (2012), they examined strategies and knowledge sources that second language learners of English use to process unfamiliar words in listening comprehension and whether the use of strategies or knowledge sources relates to successful text or word comprehension. To do this, 20 Chinese students from a university in Beijing, China were asked to listen to nine texts that were based on popular science topics. Participants were told from the outset that the goal of the listening task was to recall the content of the text. Each participant was interviewed after reading the text and answered questions and recalled the content of the texts. Having participants recall the content ensured that participants focused their attention on comprehending the text, rather than problem words. Each interview session was audio-recorded for later analysis and participants had the liberty to use either English or Chinese to answer questions and recall text contexts. In each interview, participants first received an introduction from the trained interviewer outlining the task and participated in a warmup exercise similar to the actual experiment to familiarize them with the procedure. After listening to the text, the participants were asked to answer questions and were individually asked to reflect (retrospect) on the strategies they used (i.e., immediate retrospection).

Several concerns come to mind for this specific study. First, an interviewer was present during all of the introspection output to guide the restrospective responses. Cai and Lee (2012) also used "two proficient native speakers of American English to translate and edit the language on the audio recordings when necessary" (p. 128). Given the possibility of a researcher effect, the question must be asked regarding whether the participants' verbal output was potentially distorted by the prompting and guiding by the interviewers or by the text translations. It looks like a case of "you're damned if you do and you're damned if you don't." The researchers indicate these limitations of the study along with the small participant sample size and using original written prewritten texts as listening materials. The researchers suggest, "We should be careful not to overstate the generalizability of our claims to spontaneous interactional listening texts" (p. 142). Given these limitations, that is, the interview prompts or guiding questions and the translations of the text data, did the researchers obtained reliable and valid data? Good consumers of research will always consider the methods and the data-collection process to illuminate any potential distortion of the findings.

Outside Observers

The more traditional form of the observational procedure is found in research that uses people other than the participants to make observations. We refer to this type as *outside observers* (see Table 6.1). Whereas the self-observer is the best source to try to access the inner workings of the mind, the outside observer is better used for observing the outward behavior of the participants under study.

However, outside observers vary in how close (i.e., personally involved) they get to the people or events that they are observing and how aware the people being observed are that they are being observed. The closer observers get and/ or more aware the observed person is, the more observers participate in who or what is being observed. Technically, the continuum ranges from full to non-participant observer (see Table 6.1).

The *full-participant observer* is one who is or becomes a full member of the group to which the participants/events being observed belong. This is a procedure commonly used to observe a group/event with someone who is either a member or pretending to be a member as an *informant* (i.e., a person who supplies the information). The group is usually unaware that they are being observed.

The obvious advantage of using a full participant is that the other members of the group will behave naturally, thus providing a clear picture of the objective of the observation. The disadvantages are that (a) the observers may be so much a part of the group that they cannot remain objective in their observations, (b) the researchers are using deception to obtain the data, and (c) the observers may forget information if they have to wait until after the encounter with the group before recording the data. In the case of disadvantage (a), limited and/or biased data may be reported by the observer. For (b), the observers might become ostracized from the group when it is learned that they were informing on it. Problem (c) simply results in incomplete data.

We can imagine a study where researchers enlist the help of one student in a group to find out what attitudes the group has toward cooperative learning. The student is the informant (i.e., a full-participant observer). Of course, the researchers could simply give an attitude survey to the group to determine this type of information. To ensure that the members of the group do not paint a rosy picture on the survey to please the researchers, one of the students is asked to gather information predetermined by the researchers and unknown to the other members. By law in the United States, the other members of the group need to be informed that they were observed and their permission obtained before the data are used—especially if anonymity was not guaranteed. Depending on the sensitivity of the information, this could be threatening to full-participant observers who then may not want to be totally honest in their reporting.

An example of the use of full-participant observers is found in Upitis, Smithrim, Garbati, and Ogden (2008) where they explored how their participation in a weekly art-making practice influenced the personal and professional lives of the members of the team, based on semistandardized interviews with six participants and one observer of the art-making group. Since each of the authors was a participant in the art-making practice and they belonged to the same group, one might say, they believed they avoided the problem of deception. Semistructured interviews were conducted with five of the seven participants by a graduate student who was an occasional member of the group. The interviews were based on views of themselves as artists, their experiences with various media, their views on how their relationships with members of the group evolved over time, and the extent to which these art-making sessions influenced their professional work and personal lives. The interviews were audio-taped and transcribed for purposes of thematic analysis. The researchers stated that by "taking part in the art-making sessions, it contributed to our ability to analyse the data in a collaborative manner" (p. 8). By doing this and being a full participant, the researchers "bring together different kinds of knowledge, experience, and beliefs to forge new meanings through the process of joint inquiry in which they were engaged" (p. 9). By being full-participant observers, Upitis et al. could easily collect and provide data with minimum disturbance. In addition, they tried to control for their observations being influenced by having a non full-participant graduate student conduct the interviews.

At the other end of the degrees of participation continuum is the nonparticipant observer who does not personally interact with the participants in any manner. The best use of this method is when the observer makes observations of participants' outward behavior. For example, an observer may measure the amount of time a teacher talks versus the amount of time students talk in a classroom. In this case, the observer has no need to interact with either the teacher or the students to obtain these data.

The principal advantage of this strategy is that it is more *objective*[1] than the other participant methods. On the downside, the presence of an unknown observer, or any recording devices, may have a disruptive effect on the participants, causing them to deviate from their normal behavior. To avoid this, observers need to desensitize the participants to their presence before collecting the data to be used for the study. To do this, a common method is for the observer to attend the sessions long enough for the participants to disregard the observer's presence.

If you will remember from Chapter 5, a study that used this nonparticipant method was done by Holmes (2012), whose aim was to analyze children's outdoor recess activities at an urban school. The researcher wanted to explore gender and grade-level differences in play activities but also wanted to a take a naturalistic approach to gather both quantitative and qualitative data by being as unobtrusive as possible. Holmes and her assistants made no attempt to have direct interaction with the students with the hope of eliminating any influence they might have. After several weeks of initial observing during the year-long study, the hope was that the children were desensitized to the presence of the researchers.

Somewhere between the full-participant and the nonparticipant observer lies varying degrees of partial-participant observation (see Table 6.1). The advantages are several over the nonparticipant observer. First, access to less obvious data, such as attitudes or intentions, is more available. Second, the closer the participant feels the observer is to him- or herself, the less the chance of falsifying the data. However, the closer the participant is to the observer the greater the possibility of bias on the part of the observer.

Partial-participant observers also have advantages over full-participant observers. First, there is less danger that these observers will become so involved with the participants that they lose objectivity. Second, the participants usually know that they are being observed, so there is no deception. However, partial-participant observers may be denied access to more private information that only full-participant observers would be able to access.

To illustrate the use of a partial-participant observer, Cardona, Jain, and Canfield-Davis (2012) used this strategy in a qualitative study to investigate how families from diverse cultural backgrounds understood family involvement in the context of early childcare and educational settings. The participants in the study included nine members from six families who had children enrolled in three early childhood care and education programs. Although the primary method of data collection involved in-depth interviews with the parents of the children, a secondary data source was obtained through nonparticipant observations at each of the three site programs.

Cardona et al. (2012) conducted multiple interviews with family members during the project using a guided questioning format and also an open-ended, semistructured interview to allow participants to share additional comments of personal value. All of the interviews were tape recorded and then transcribed verbatim for later analysis. To gain additional data, the first author, "attended events organized by each of the programs with the permission of the staff" (p. 6). This participation allowed the researcher to have visibility with personnel and families as well as to capture nonparticipant observations by way of field notes in a naturalistic setting as she explored family involvement. Cardona was a partial-participant observer in that she met and observed family members and site staff in places like classrooms and teacher workrooms where she held informal and formal interviews. She most likely did this to establish personal rapport with her participants to ensure more authentic responses.

One common thing to the Upitis et al. (2008), Holmes (2012), and Cardona et al. (2012) studies, is that the researchers did not limit themselves to only one procedure for gathering data. Rather, they all used a multiprocedural approach, as referred to previously, as *triangulation*. Researchers, who want to protect their research from the weakness of only one approach yet profit from the strengths of that approach, will build into their study several different data-collecting procedures. Researchers may use full, partial, or nonparticipant observers to gather data, but they should triangulate their findings with those of other procedures to increase credibility of their findings.

The consumer of research might ask which of the above procedures is most appropriate. As previously stated, the answer much depends on the research question and the nature of the data needed to best provide the answer. If the research question requires information that cannot be obtained by observing outward behavior, then a method needs to be used where the observer can get closer to the participants. Where easily observed outward behavior is sufficient, there is no need for closeness. Each approach has its strengths and weaknesses.

Regardless of what type of observer is used, observers need training to provide useful data. Of course, if researchers are doing the observing themselves there is no need of training because they know what they are looking for. In addition, to ensure that there is no bias, researchers should keep their observers *blind* to the purpose of the study, especially if any hypothesis is being tested. (This sounds like an oxymoron:

keeping your observer blind.) If they fail to keep them blind, the observers might unconsciously see only what the researchers want to be seen. A well-written study will be very clear about whether training was given to the observers and whether the observers were aware of the ultimate purpose of the study.

The last set of studies we have looked at used researchers as observers. However, a study done by Allsop (2011) used observers other than herself when looking at the use of visible forms of collaboration when children were learning with the support of Wikis-online editable websites. For this project, children ages 9–10 years old were allowed regular access to the wikispace at school and from home, once in a week for six initial weeks. The children were given information on how to edit pages, create links, and how to revise previous work. The students were not guided as to how to collaborate as the researcher wanted to observe the forms of collaboration that may occur naturally while editing the wiki. The independent observers who collected and analyzed data were trained to conduct unstructured observations of student interactions and collaborative efforts via a video recording and were able to track the history of specific pages and entries to the wikispace. The one concern is whether the videotaping influenced the participants' behavior. When it came to interpreting the data and constructing meaning, each independent observer analyzed their own data followed by a group discussion and analysis of the same data. Following good research protocol, the researcher also gathered additional data in the form of an online questionnaire that explored the participants' attitude about the project. Properly training the independent observers and taking precautions to make sure of their limited influence added greatly to the validity of their findings.

Interviewer

As seen in some of the studies discussed earlier, interviews were used to obtain data as well (see Table 6.1). This method is a combination of observation under highly structured conditions and some form of data recording. The difference between the observer and the interviewer is that the interviewer personally interacts with the participant through a series of questions to obtain data, whereas with the observer data is collected as it occurs without probing with questions. The difference between an interview and a questionnaire (which will be discussed in Instrument section) is that an interpersonal connection is formed between the interviewer and the interviewee. This connection allows for direct monitoring for comprehension of the questions and modification in the case of misunderstanding.

The quality of the data coming from an interviewer is determined by the care taken to ensure that the same procedures are used for each interviewee. Strict adherence to directions as to what questions are to be asked and in what order they are to be asked need to be observed. Otherwise the answers cannot be compared.

However, an interview can range from highly structured, to semi-structured, or to open-structured. The *highly structured* interview follows a predetermined set of questions with no allowance for variation. The *semi-structured* interview has a set of predetermined questions, but the interviewer is free to follow up a question with additional questions that probe further. The *open-structured* interview has a general interview plan, but is not tied to predetermined questions. This allows the interviewer to explore whatever path seems appropriate at the time.

All of these techniques are commonly used in research. For example, Nash-Ditzel (2010) as part of her data-collection process, used a highly structured interview guide when asking students how they self-regulate their reading tasks. Cardona et al. (2012) used structured and *loosely structured* interviews (i.e., semi-structured) to be free to generate more questions as the research progressed. Upitis et al. (2008) employed an open-structured technique, to allow the interviewer flexibility to ask anything that they thought appropriate to ask.

When evaluating research studies that use one of the interview techniques, ask yourself these questions. Did the researcher pretest the interview questions with the interviewers? Were the interviewers trained and tested before they gave the interviews? Were the interviews audio- or videotaped to prevent the loss of information? Would the data be the same if another interviewer did the interview? If you answer yes to all of these questions, then the study followed sound interviewing procedures.

Evaluating the Dependability of Verbal Data Procedures

Verbal data cannot be taken simply at face value, as neither can numerical data. Researchers should provide evidence that the data they have used in their study are dependable enough to analyze. Researchers have at least five types of evidence to support the dependability of their data (see Table 6.2). They are as follows:

Representativeness

This is not referring specifically to whether the sample is representative of the population (i.e., external validity) as discussed in Chapter 4, although related. This is more to do with whether the veracity of the information is being influenced by the choice of respondents or events (i.e., internal validity or credibility). Related to the *elite bias* mentioned above, information coming from one particular segment of a larger group of people can be misleading. Similar to the convenience sampling problem mentioned in Chapter 4, the most accessible and willing participants are not usually the best group to provide the most appropriate data.

In addition, researchers need to give evidence that the events on which generalizations are based are the most appropriate. They might not be present at all times for data collection. If not, consumers must ask about the proportion of time the researcher was present? If only a fraction of the events were observed, were they typical of most events? The ultimate question for consumers is whether researchers have provided evidence that data have come from observing an adequate

Table 6.2 Methods for Determining Dependability of Verbal Data Procedures

Evidence
1. Representativeness
Respondents
Events
2. Prolonged engagement and persistent observation
3. Clarifying researcher bias
4. Check for *researcher effects*
Researcher on persons/events
Persons/events on researcher
5. Weighting the evidence
Informants access and proximity
Circumstances:
behavior observed first-hand
adequate exposure
informal settings
trusted field-workers
Continuous vigilance in checking for various biases

number of events to ensure that subsequent inferences and conclusions were not based on the luck of the draw.

Prolonged Engagement and Persistent Observation

Researchers need enough time for interacting with the respondents and/or the event to gather accurate data. This allows time to gain personal access to the information being targeted. However, if too much time is spent on the research site, one of the *researcher effects* discussed below might set in.

Clarifying Researcher Bias

Every researcher has his or her own set of biases. Because the analysis of data in a qualitative study begins and continues during the collection of data, knowing a researcher's particular bias can help the consumer discern why the data is being gathered and interpreted a certain way. Therefore, researchers should disclose any biases that might have an impact on the approach used and any interpretations made on the data. This helps consumers determine how the researchers arrived at their conclusions.

Researcher Effects

These were discussed in Chapter 5 under threats to internal validity. In that chapter, the influence was mainly looking at the unidirectional effect of the researcher on the behavior of the persons from which data were being collected. However, Miles and Huberman (1994) point out that there is a reciprocal relationship between research-ers and the persons/events being observed. In one direction, researchers' presence or actions influence the behavior being observed (Chapter 5). In qualitative work, for example, respondents might change their behavior in the presence of the data gath-erer to meet perceived expectations, and/or hide sensitive information. Miles and Huberman warn that researchers "must assume that people will try to be misleading and must shift into a more investigative mode" (p. 265). To avoid this, they suggested such strategies as: researchers spending as much time as possible on site to become unnoticed, using unobtrusive methods, having an informant monitor the impact the researcher is making, and using informal settings for some data gathering.

In the other direction of the reciprocal relationship, the persons/events being observed can impact researchers. This can happen when researchers spend too much time with the people being researched, and the researchers *go native* by no longer being able to keep their own thinking separate from that of the respondents. This leads to a quandary because, to avoid the first problem of researcher-on-respondent impact mentioned above, the possibility of the respondents impacting the researchers increases. To avoid the respondent-on-researcher effect, Miles and Huberman (1994) proposed tactics such as: use a variety of respondents, include people outside of the group being observed, control site visits, use an informant to monitor events when not present, use triangulation, use peers to critique the work, and so on.

When evaluating the data collected in qualitative research, consumers should look for ways researchers try to control for, or be aware of, the effect they might have had on the people or the situation and vice versa. This does not simply mean the effect on the *product*, in the form of the data, but also on the analysis *process*. If such care is taken and reported, researchers deserve kudos, and the credibility of findings has been enhanced.

Weighting the Evidence

Miles and Huberman (1994) pointed out that some data are stronger (or more valid) than others. They laid down three principles for determining the strength of data. We have summarized them here in the form of questions that the con-sumer can use to evaluate the strength of the data:

a   What information does the researcher provide about the access and proxim-ity of the informants to the targeted data? The closer to the data the stronger.

b   To what extent do the data consist of actual behavior, observed first-hand, after adequate exposure, in informal settings, by trusted field-workers? The more the stronger.

c   What effort did the data gatherer(s) make toward checking for various biases (as outlined above) during the data-gathering process? The greater the stronger.

We use Cardona et al.'s (2012) study to illustrate how a researcher provides evidence for the dependability of verbal data. Remember the researchers examined nine members of six families who had children enrolled in three different early childhood care and education programs. The first author followed these family members over several months to collect data using several techniques from several sources. Information used for the evaluation is listed in the following Box 6.1.

BOX 6.1 SUMMARY OF CARDONA ET AL. (2012) STUDY

Variable of concern: Home–school relationships.

Participants

One Latin
Three Asian
Two European
Three Euro-American
Annual Income US$10,000–40,000
Teachers and administrators: No information given

Data Sources

Demographic survey of participants
Formal interviews with parent participants (1.5 h): Number not specified
Informal interviews with parent participants. Number not specified
Informal interviews with parents and administrators: Number not specified
Transcriptions of formal interviews
Field notes from researcher observations

Institutions

Three early childcare and educational settings
Sites were accredited by the National Association for the Education of Young Children
Ethnically mixed families (32% Asian, 16% European, 16% Latin, 36% Euro-American)
Participants ranged from high school dropouts to those with gradate degrees
Annual income between US$10,000–40,000

Cardona et al. (2012) used five types of evidence from the list given in Table 6.2. Regarding how *representative* their data were, they provided detailed information about the nine parent participants: three Asians, two Europeans, three Euro-Americans, and one Latin who were selected by the administration and staff of the childhood care centers (see Box 6.1). The issue here is whether these nine participants were representative of other parents who rely on early childhood and education facilities.

In addition, Cardona et al. gave a clear description of the economic backgrounds of the participants and a reasonable description of the three institutions (see Box 6.1) that would help any consumer to compare other institutional environments for possible transference of their findings. The sites were chosen based upon "a high degree of commitment to home-school relationships, and student enrollments of different nationality and immigration status" (p. 3).

However, it would have been helpful if Cardona et al. (2012) had provided a more detailed description of the process that administrators and teachers used to choose the participants. Because the teachers and administrators helped to select the participants, a report of their personal characteristics would help the consumer understand how transferrable the participant data are.

The next evidence type listed in Table 6.2 to support the dependability of data is *prolonged engagement and persistent observation* (#2). Cardona et al. (2012) reported that they had ample opportunity to engage the participants over an extended length of time. They collected data over several months as partial-participant observers.

Regarding type 3, *clarifying the researcher's bias*, the first author of Cardona et al. (2012) supplied details about her own philosophical and research biases in the study. She stated that her research disposition was derived from "case study and real-life context theory" (p. 3). She added that her premise is that children's development and learning depends upon the intercontextual nature of relationships between families and schools identities (p. 1). To her credit, she declared that "through this process, she was able to get to know some of the participants in a more intimate way. She was invited to their homes, they shared food with her, their fears and accomplishments since living in this country, and this was probably the turning point in the relationship to permeate the boundary of researcher and co-participant" (p. 10).

For type 4, *check for researcher effects*, Cardona et al. (2012) discussed a technique called *peer debriefing* where they discussed their initial findings with a *disinterested peer* and actually had the colleague scan some of the raw data to assess whether the findings were plausible based on the data (p. 10). The possibility for either *researcher on persons/events*, or *persons/events on researcher* effects could have occurred. One possibility was that the first author became so close to some of the participants that her perceptions were influenced by this personal contact in their homes. These are not to be understood as negative comments. One of the positive points that qualitative researchers make is that they *become* part of the study. They too are participants in the study.

Under evidence type 5, *weighting the evidence*, Cardona et al. (2012) provided evidence that gives weight to the quality of her data. Regarding *informants' access and proximity* to data, they used nine participants from three early childhood care centers used multiple administrators and teachers to identify likely participants. They gathered data from multiple sources using a triangulation technique from participants, administrators and teachers, and personal observations, and used *participant checks* and entailed informal discussions to check the researchers' perceptions of what was said by the participants. Certainly, these participants had good access and proximity to data. The *circumstances* under which Cardona et al. gathered the data also added to the weight. The data were all gathered first-hand over many occasions in both formal and informal settings.

Before moving on to nonpersonal data-gathering methods, we suggest you do the following exercise to help instantiate what we have covered in the first part of section "Collecting and Evaluating Verbal Data." The following provides an outline to guide in what to look for.

EXERCISE 6.1

Find a recent qualitative study that used one of the observational techniques mentioned in the above discussion that resulted in verbal data.

1   Summarize the research question(s).
2   Describe the type of data that is being gathered.
3   Briefly summarize the procedure used in the study.
4   Describe what was done to avoid the potential weaknesses discussed in Table 6.1.
5   Summarize what the research stated to show the dependability of the data from Table 6.2.

Collecting and Evaluating Numerical Data

The second form data come in is numbers—lots and lots of numbers. These numbers can be frequencies, test scores, numbers representing rank order, and so on. Numbers come from two main sources: human judgment and/or some form of impersonal instrument. First, we describe the procedures used to gather these numbers, and then we explain how these procedures are evaluated for reliability and validity (see Table 6.3).

Table 6.3 Numerical Data-Collection Procedures

Procedures	Potential Strengths	Potential Weaknesses
Judges/raters	Expert opinion	Subjectivity, Fatigue, Halo effect, Ambiguous rubrics
Instrumental Questionnaires/Surveys	Large coverage, time efficient	Inflexible
Closed-form	Objective, broad coverage, easy to interpret	Restrictive, low returns
Open-ended	Information revealing	Subjective
Tests		
Discrete Item	Objective scoring, broad coverage, easy to score	Guessing, difficult to construct
Constructed-response	Allows for individuality, limits guessing	Limited coverage, subjective scoring, training of scorers

Procedures for Gathering Numerical Data

The Judge/Rater

A major method for collecting numerical data in education is the use of judges/ raters. (From now on, we will refer to both as judges.) Judges observe the outward behavior of the participant(s) and make evaluative judgments regarding the behavior. They do this by using some form of rating scale that ranges from low to high, poor to excellent, and so forth, and may be expressed numerically.

Judges can vary considerably in their ratings for reasons other than quality of performance, as was seen from the 2002 Winter Olympics figure skating scandal where one judge was pressured for political reasons. However, in the field of educational research, judges are used to rate such things like mathematical, writing, or reading skills of participants, much less high-stakes than a gold metal. So, there should be no reason to allow such things as vote swapping for nationalistic reasons to influence one's rating.

However, the challenge with using judges continues to be *subjectivity*, which is defined here as the influence of judges' particular preferences and beliefs that differ from the criteria that they are supposed to use when judging. For example, one of us examined what criteria judges used when rating the writing ability of people trying to enter a university based on a one-half hour essay test. He found that some judges used grammar as their main criteria while others used the quality of *organization*. There were a few others who were heavily influenced by *writing mechanics*. Obviously, a rating of 4 by one judge did not necessarily mean the same thing as a 4 from another judge. The assumption should hold that judges use the same criteria when rating. If this is not the case, the data is uninterpretable.

To control for subjectivity, three precautions need to be taken: a well-defined *rubric*, *training*, and *multiple judges*. First, the rubric of the rating scale needs to be clearly defined. A well-written rubric clearly defines what each level of the scale means. The quality of these definitions helps judges apply the rubric in a consistent and meaningful way.

In PK-12 education environments today in the United States, most states have created extensive rubrics to define the scoring process on state-mandated achievement exams. For example, the state of Indiana has created writing rubrics to assist in the scoring of the English/Language Arts writing component at each grade level for the annual Indiana Statewide Testing for Educational Progress Plus (ISTEP+) exam. You can access their website (www.doe.in.gov/assessment/english-arts-rubrics) to see their rubrics for the writing portion of the exam. Their most recent version uses a six-level scale for scoring. For each of these levels, a short paragraph or brief statements are provided that defines what a writer should be able to do in terms of their writing skills (e.g., grammar, vocabulary, etc.).

Related to having a good rubric, another method for controlling subjectivity in a judge's decision is training in the use of the rubric. The judge has to keep in mind each level of the rubric with its definition while rating participants. This is a formidable task and needs training to produce consistent results. The validity of the ratings will only be as good as the mastery of the rubric by judges. A well-planned study will report how the judges were trained on the rubric.

Third, at least two judges need to be used when making judgments. By having multiple judges, researchers are able to check whether the judges are using the same criteria. In addition, the judges can be checked for the *severity* of their judgments. If one judge is consistently rating participants higher than other judges, then leniency could be the problem. If the judge rates the participants consistently lower than the others, then the problem might be severity. If only one judge rates performance, researchers could not interpret the data.

The degree to which judges agree is measured by either percentage of agreement or statistical correlation of ratings. When percentage of agreement is the high 80% onwards, or correlations are .80 or higher, the judges are regarded as in agreement. This is referred to as *inter-rater reliability*, which is discussed later in the chapter.

A study that considered the three precautions outlined above when using judges was done by Martins, Albuquerque, Salvador, and Silva (2013). They addressed the question of whether invented spelling activities with preschool-age children help to analyze the oral segments of words to discover the relations between those segments and the corresponding letters. The preschool participants were assigned to either a treatment (participating in a 5-week spelling program) or control group and evaluated with a pre- and posttest rubric where they were asked to write and read a set of words. They did not provide copies of the rubrics in their paper for the reader to peruse but did provide examples of the interaction between the researcher and the participants. They reported that two of the five educational psychologists received special training during the research on how to carry out the research program. Finally, they used different combinations of two raters for each writing sample and averaged the two ratings for the data. They reported that the interscorer agreement in word-by-word classification using the Kappa statistic was .98 on the pretest and .96 on the posttest. As you can see, the researchers followed good procedures in gathering their data.

Besides subjectivity, there are two other obstacles that the research needs to attend to when using judges: *fatigue,* and *halo effect.* Regarding the first, judges become tired if they have to evaluate too many participants at any given time. Judgments made in the early part of rating a large number of participants may be very different from those made later due to judges simply becoming tired. The study by Martins et al. (2013) may not have had this problem. We estimate that the three judges divided 180 participants' invented spelling samples so that each of the five judges had 36 samples to assess. It would be interesting to know how the researchers tried to control for the possible effects of researcher fatigue.

The other obstacle, *halo effect*, is caused by the carryover effect of judging the work of one participant onto the work of a following participant. When judging the quality of writing, for instance, exposure to a well-written (or poorly written) passage may have a positive (or negative) influence on the judgment of the following passage. This is usually controlled for by varying the order of the people or things being rated between judges. The researchers should mention any precautions taken to help the reader to rule out such effects.

Instrumental Procedures

The other method for collecting numerical data is using some form of impersonal instrument that requires participants to supply data to the researcher. Table 6.3 lists two general instrument types that encompass a wide range of devices used to collect data: *questionnaires/surveys*, and *tests*.

The advantage of using instrumental procedures over observational ones is that researchers can gain access to many more participants in more timely and economical ways. However, the main disadvantage is that once they are put into print, they cease to be flexible during the data-collection process. Any new thoughts researchers might have will have to wait until the next study.

Questionnaires/Surveys (Q/S)

These types of instruments consist of various types that can capture a lot of information in a short amount of time. They consist of lists of questions and/or statements presented on paper or through some other media such as computers. Q/Ss are considered instrumental equivalents to interviews. They have two main advantages over interviews. First, they are useful for collecting data from larger numbers of people in fairly short amounts of time. Second, they are more economical than interviews because they do not take as much time or require trained interviewers to administer. As mentioned previously, the main disadvantage is that Q/Ss are not flexible as are interviews in that the questions/statements cannot be modified once they have been given to respondents, nor can they probe respondents for further information.

The items in a Q/S can be closed-form or open-form. *Closed-form* items provide a set of alternative answers to each item from which the respondent must select at least one. For example, a question might require a participant to choose either *yes* or *no*. Or, a statement might be given requiring participants to indicate their level of agreement from a 2 or more point scale. The 5-point scale is often referred to as a Likert-type scale, named after R.A. Likert who used it for measuring attitude (Likert, 1932). The main advantage using the closed-form is that the data elicited are easy to record and analyze with statistical procedures.

On the other hand, *open-form* items allow participants to give their own answers without restrictions. This type works best when there could be a wide variety of answers that participants might give to a question, such as "How old are you?" Another common use is when researchers explore what possible answers might be given, as when asking participants what they think is good about the program they have just completed. These data usually have to undergo verbal analysis.

Typically, most Q/Ss contain both open- and closed-form items. Demographic information about the respondent (e.g., gender, nationality, etc.) and the program (e.g., course level, etc.) use both formats. Even when the rest of the items are closed-form, the last item is almost always an open-form to capture any other comment by the respondent.

A well-prepared Q/S should be *pilot-tested* before administered in a main study. That is, it is tried out on a group of people similar to the target group who will eventually get it. The resulting feedback can provide useful information to make sure that all the items are clearly understood and that the entire instrument is user-friendly.

One of the challenges in using Q/Ss is getting them back from potential respondents. *Response rate* is important because losing respondents is a form of attrition of the sample that can result in a biased sample. Typically, the response rate is much less than the number of people who received the instrument. Trying to chase after people to return it is almost impossible because, to ensure anonymity, these instruments usually do not require respondents to identify themselves.

The rule of thumb is that researchers should get a response rate of at least 70% before the data is considered representative of a target population.[2] However, if the number of Q/Ss sent out is small, the return rate needs to be higher to maintain representativeness. A well-written study should report the number of questionnaires sent out and the return rate to aid the reader in applying this criterion.

An example of the proper use of Q/S is found in Gökalp's (2013) study that investigated web users' preferences and perceptions on the use of the web to see if specific demographics are responsible for differences on web user's perceptions on the use of the web in physics education. The *Perceptions of the Internet and Education Scale* was developed and used by the author for this study. The participants consisted of 340 web users who were drawn from the population using a purposeful sampling method. The author reviewed other studies related to perceptions of the Internet and web-based/assisted instruction and then developed the first version of the instrument which consisted of 30 items that were reviewed for validity by two experts with Ph.D.s in computer science and instructional technology. With this initial version of the scale, 510 web users completed the pilot instrument for providing initial feedback for the development of the final survey. Twenty of the initial items were modified and revised based upon this feedback. In addition, the items were translated into several languages by two language experts (English and Turkish) since the anticipated respondents originated in multiple large cities (Istanbul, Ankara, Izmir, Bursa, etc.). Besides the visitors from search engines, there were also around 27,000 registered uses of the website. The author stated that the generalizability of the results is limited to the populations with similar demographics (e.g., gender, age, residents of large cities, students versus professionals). Gökalp provided extensive demographic information about the participants and also discussed the development and analysis of the instrument items in great detail. The only potential flaw to the project is that Gökalp failed to provide a copy of the final questionnaire at the end of the article for us to see.

Tests

The other main type of instrumentation commonly used in research is under this general heading, also referred to as *assessments*. Although we are sure that no one needs to be told what a test is, due to years of experience taking them, we simply state that a test is an instrument that is designed to assess what participants remember, or do physically, and/or mentally. Because a single test can do all three, depending on the test items that make up the test, we use the term *test items*, rather than simply *tests* or *assessments*.

Test items come in all formats and modalities. They can be administered via paper, computer, or face to face with an examiner. They can assess abilities through observing outward behavior, as when performing some physical feat, or assess cognitive outcomes through responses on paper or a computer screen, not to mention many more applications.

Cognitive test items differ by making different cognitive demands on participants. Some items require participants to *recall* information. Such items as fill-in-the-blank and completion serve this purpose. Other items require participants to recall and integrate information, such as composing an essay. Such items are also referred to as *open-ended* or *constructed response*. Other test items require participants to *recognize* from a set of alternatives the most appropriate answer. Items such as multiple-choice, matching, and alternative-choice are commonly used for this purpose.

Some people have preferences regarding item type. Yet, as with everything else we have discussed so far, the type of test item used in research should be determined by the question being asked. If a research question inquires whether participants can identify the meaning of a sentence or written passage, then recognition-type items are quite appropriate. However, if researchers seek to know whether the target information has been stored in such a way that participants can access the information easily, then a recall-type item would be better. If researchers are trying to assess whether participants can integrate information, then an essay format would be more appropriate.

Accordingly, there are some practical considerations that researchers usually address when choosing item types. Two that are very much related are *time* and *cost*. Some item types take longer to administer than others and usually require trained judges to analyze the responses. For example, the open-ended essay prompt that requires a one- to two-page response from each participant can take 1 or more minutes to score depending on the scoring technique. Not just anyone can evaluate these responses. As with training judges, raters of written compositions also need training. All of this takes time; and whatever takes time usually means greater costs. However, recognition-type items can be given to larger numbers of participants and scored by untrained personnel or even by optical-mark scanning machines in a minimal amount of time.

When evaluating the proper choice of item type, we need to ask ourselves whether the responses from the item type of choice are directly related to answering the research question. To illustrate, if writing ability is being investigated, then multiple-choice items would probably not be appropriate. In contrast, if reading comprehension is the focus of the question, then multiple-choice items could be used effectively. If one's ability to perform a laboratory procedure is being assessed, then some form of performance assessment would be the best approach. Later in this chapter, it will become apparent why choice of item type is important.

There are other terms you might encounter when reading the Instrument section of a study. One common term is *standardized test*. The word *standardized* means that the test has been designed to be given under strict guidelines for administration and scoring. That is, the same instructions are to be given to the respondents at every administration of the instrument. The amount of time that is allowed to finish the test is also held constant for everyone, and the scoring procedure is the same for everyone. Standardization is important for producing data that can be compared. Research has shown that a change in such things as the instructions given by the test administrator can cause changes in the responses to the tests.

Two examples of college aptitude tests used in the United States for college admissions are the Scholastic Aptitude Test (SAT) (http://sat.collegeboard.org)

and the American College Testing (ACT) (http://www.actstudent.org). Wherever these exams are administered, each is given with the same instructions, allowing for the same amount of time for completion, and strictly scored according to specific guidelines. Any changes in these procedures can render the data useless.

Commercially produced (CP) standardized tests, such as the two mentioned above, are usually developed for large-scale assessment and not specifically designed for individual research studies. However, some CP tests are occasionally used by researchers because they are assumed to have been carefully constructed to ensure reliability and validity—issues that are discussed in greater detail later in this chapter.

A study by Nichols, Kim, and Nichols (2013) studied the effect of community volunteerism on early literacy development. Using a before- and after-effect (pre- and posttest) design, the researchers wanted to determine if volunteers from the community could substantially increase the early reading skills of kindergarteners who were at-risk from falling behind (failing to meet a benchmark indicator). The researchers used a nationally based early childhood reading assessment (Dynamic Indicators of Basic Early Literacy [DIBELS]) to determine whether students improved their reading skills after being tutored for 32 weeks compared with students who did not receive additional tutoring. The DIBELS assessment includes seven subcomponents and data was collected at the beginning, middle, and end of the year. In total, Nichols et al. were attempting to measure reading gains owing to extra tutoring. Assuming that the items in these seven subcomponents adequately represent the grammar, reading, and vocabulary proficiency domains, we can accept them as appropriate measures. Despite the positive results, Nichols et al. recognized several potential limitations of the study that included potential inadequate training of the tutoring volunteers.

Although it is convenient to use off-the-shelf CP standardized instruments, they might not be the best instruments to use in a particular research study. The reason is that these tests are designed for specific purposes that often do not match the need of a study. If researchers use the quantitative part of the SAT exam to measure the effect of a new teaching method on improving math ability over one semester; for example, the results would probably not show any noticeable improvement. However, this lack of improvement might not be due to the ineffectiveness of the new method but instead to insensitivity of the SAT to slight changes over a semester. That is, the limited learning outcomes that are targeted in a relatively short period of treatment are lost in the measurement of the broader scope of the SAT. Nevertheless, the SAT would be appropriate for identifying various groupings for quantitative ability of the participants to be used for research purposes.

In contrast to using CP standardized tests, many researchers design their own instruments for gathering data. The advantage is that they can streamline the instruments specifically to the needs of the study. However, this does not mean that the instruments should not be standardized. When a test is given to more than one group of participants, researchers should follow strict standardization guidelines, such as giving the same time to finish the test to all groups, or else any differences between the groups may not be due to the treatment.

Kobayashi (2002), for example, developed her own tests for reading comprehension when examining whether text organization and response format affect performance on tests of reading comprehension. She expressly stated that the study needed texts in the tests that were "specially prepared to maximize control over the variables identified in the pilot study" (p. 199). Obviously, she needed to design her own tests rather than use some off-the-shelf CP test. Eight parallel tests were developed for this study. Items in two components of each test were given in Japanese (L1) to eliminate any variation due to English reading proficiency. She also reported how care was taken to standardize the tests by preparing written instructions for both the test administrators and the students.

In addition to the term *standardization*, you will come into contact with two other terms in some Instrument sections of various studies: *norm-referenced* and *criterion-referenced* tests. Both terms relate to how test scores are interpreted. *Norm-referenced* means that scores on the test are given meaning when compared with some norming group. A *norming group* is a body of people that is supposed to represent the population of all those who might take the test. On the basis of the statistics generated on the norming group, a person's score is interpreted in relation to the degree to which it is above or below the average of the norming group.

When using a norm-referenced test in a research study, it is important that the sample to which the test is given come from a similar pool of participants as the norming group. Otherwise, the measurements cannot be interpreted by referring to the norming group. An example of a study that relates to this issue was done by Brown, Brown, and Brown (2008) who examined the validity of the PRAXIS II exam—a national, norm-referenced exam in the United States used to determine teacher licensing. The researchers, however, did not provide any information to assure that the 200 preservice teachers were similar to a potential norming group of the PRAXIS II. Their purpose was to explore whether test scores that teacher candidates demonstrate prior to and during their teacher preparation programs serve as predictors of the PRAXIS II scores at the conclusion of their program. Previous research is cited in their conclusions to suggest that state-mandated testing results are not necessarily the best predictors of classroom effectiveness or teacher retention. However, due to the extensive use of the PRAXIS II (39 states currently require this exam for their teacher candidates), the researchers assumed that the Educational Testing Service (ETS) used a representative national sample when norming the test.

Some people confuse the two terms *norm-referenced* with *standardized*, but they are not synonymous. The first term, *standardized*, relates to the conditions under which the test is given, while *norm-referenced* has to do with how the scores are interpreted. This confusion is most likely due to the fact that most standardized tests are also norm-referenced, such as the SAT.

On the other hand, a *criterion-referenced* test does not use a norming group to establish guidelines for interpreting test results. Instead, one or more criteria are used to decide how well the examinee has done. These criteria are predetermined before administering the test and are used to establish cut-points. A *cut-point* (also known as, cut-score, cut-off) is a score on the test score scale used to classify people into different categories such as high, middle, or low ability. For instance, all respondents scoring over 80% correct might be considered high ability, those between 50% and 80% average ability, and those below 50% below average.

In concluding this section, procedures that are commonly used in gathering numerical data were reviewed. However, there are a number of criteria the consumer needs to understand to determine whether the data are of sufficient quality. These criteria are covered in the next section. However, to help establish a foundation for understanding the next section, we suggest that you take the opportunity to complete the following exercise.

EXERCISE 6.2

Find a recent study that used one of the instrumental techniques listed in Table 6.3.

1 Describe the purpose of the study.
2 State the research question.
3 State any hypotheses, predictions, or even expectations if present.
4 Briefly summarize the data-gathering procedure in no more than a paragraph.
5 Describe what was done to avoid any of the weaknesses listed in Table 6.3.
6 Evaluate whether you think the procedures used provided the necessary data to answer the research question and/or to test any hypotheses.

Evaluating the Qualities of Numerical Data-Gathering Procedures

When many people think of research, they imagine numbers and statistics. However, the numbers that are gathered are based on various data-gathering techniques as outlined previously. The quality of these procedures is determined by the caliber of the data-gathering strategy. To sharpen our ability to discern between weak and strong research, we must give attention to this aspect of research when evaluating the worth of a study. The purpose of this section is to provide an overview of these qualities and give examples of how they have been applied in research. Our goal is for you to be able to use these criteria to evaluate the quality of a research study in a discerning manner.

The two most important qualities of any data results that have traditionally been considered essential are *reliability* and *validity*. The strong consensus in the research community is that the level of confidence we put into the findings of any given research is directly proportional to the degree to which data-gathering procedures produce reliable and valid data. We begin by discussing reliability, followed by validity. It will become apparent why this order is important.

Reliability

Reliability has to do with the *consistency* of the data results. If we measure or observe something, we want the method used to give the same results no matter whom or what takes the measurement or observations. Researchers that use two or more observers would want those observers to see the same things and give the same or very similar judgments on what they observe or rate. Likewise, researchers utilizing instruments would expect them to give consistent results, regardless of time of administration or the particular set of test items making up those instruments.

The most common indicator used for reporting the reliability of an observational or instrumental procedure is the *correlation coefficient*. A *coefficient* is simply a number that represents the amount of some attribute. A *correlation coefficient* is a number that quantifies the degree to which two sets of numbers relate to one another. Correlation coefficients that are used to indicate reliability are referred to as *reliability coefficients*.

We do not go into the mathematics of this particular statistic, but we want to give enough information to help in understanding the following discussion. Reliability coefficients range between .00 and +1.00. A coefficient of .00 means there is no reliability in the observation or measurement. That is, if we were to make multiple observations/measurements of a particular variable, a coefficient of .00 would mean that the observations/measurements were totally inconsistent. Conversely, a coefficient of 1.00 indicates that there is perfect consistency. This means that the observation/measurement procedure gives the same results on a consistent basis and is not dependent on the researcher or other variables that might impact the results.

Seldom, if ever, do reliability coefficients occur at the extreme ends of the continuum (i.e., .00 or 1.00). So, you might ask, "What is an adequate reliability coefficient?" The rule of thumb is the higher the better (Wow, that was a no-brainer!!!); but *better* depends on the nature of the measurement procedure being used. Researchers using observation techniques involving judges are very happy with reliability coefficients anywhere from .80 on up. Yet achievement and aptitude tests should have reliabilities in the .90s. Other instruments such as interest inventories and attitude scales tend to be lower than achievement tests or aptitude tests. Generally speaking, reliabilities falling below .60 are considered low, no matter what type of procedure is being used (Nitko, 2001).

There are a number of different types of reliability coefficients used in research. The reason is that different measurement procedures require different

Table 6.4 Reliability Coefficients Used in Research

Type of Coefficient	Purpose, Consistency Over	Measurement Procedure	Statistic Used
Inter-rater	Different judges/raters	Observation of performance	Correlation, percentage
Intra-rater	Different times for same judge/rater	Same as above	Same as above
Test–retest	Different times of testing	Standardized tests and inventories	Correlation
Alternate-form	Different sets of test items and different times of testing	Multiple forms of the same instrument	Correlation
Split-half (odd/ even), Kuder–Richardson 20 & 21, Cronbach alpha	Internal consistency of items within a test	All forms of discrete-item instruments	Correlation, Spearman– Brown, Alpha, KR20, KR21

kinds of consistency. Table 6.4 lists the different types of reliability coefficients, purpose of each, corresponding procedure used, and the statistic used.

The first one listed in Table 6.4, *inter-rater* reliability, is required anytime different judges are used to rate participants' behavior. Typically, this type of reliability is determined by either computing a correlation coefficient or calculating a percentage of agreement. The study that we previously discussed by Martins et al. (2013) used two independent raters for their word-by-word classification procedures. They reported inter-rater reliabilities for the pre- and post-test assessment at .98 and .96, respectively. These figures reveal high agreement between the raters, which we are sure, pleased the researchers.

Also related to the use of judges/raters is *intra-rater* reliability. The type of consistency this addresses relates to judges giving the same results if they were given the opportunity to rate participants on more than one occasion. We would expect high agreement within the same person doing the rating over time if the attribute being observed is stable and the judge understood the task. However, if judges are not clear about what they are supposed to rate, there will be different results, and correlations or percentages of agreement will be low. Although this is an important issue, we have not seen many recent studies report this type of reliability due to difficulty of implementation.

One example we did find was Goh's (2002) study used both inter- and intra-rater reliability. Her study looked at listening comprehension techniques and how they interacted with one another. She had two participants read passages with pauses. During each pause they were to reflect on how they attempted to understand the segment they heard. These retrospections were taped and transcribed. The transcriptions were analyzed by Goh, herself, identifying, interpreting, and coding the data. Commendably, she checked the reliability of her observations by enlisting a colleague to follow the same procedures on a portion of the data and computing an inter-rater reliability coefficient (.76). In addition, she computed an intra-rater reliability coefficient (.88) to make sure that there was consistency even within her own observations. As expected, she agreed with herself (intra-rater) more than she agreed with her colleague (inter-rater).

The remainder of the other types of reliabilities in Table 6.4 are used with paper-and-pencil or computer-administered instruments, whether question-naires or tests. *Test–retest* reliability is used to measure the stability of the same instrument over time. The instrument is given at least twice and the scores are correlated. However, this procedure can only work if the trait (i.e., construct) being measured remains stable over the time between the two measurements. For example, if researchers are assessing participants' key-boarding abilities, administering the assessment 2 weeks later should produce very similar results if the assessment is reliable. However, if there is a month or two between testing sessions, any training on key-boarding may create differences between the two sets of scores that would depress the reliability coefficient. Nevertheless, if the time between the two administrations is too little, memory of the test from the first session could help the participants give the same performance, which would inflate the reliability coefficient.

A study that reported test–retest reliability was done by Kaya and Hamamci (2011). The researchers used a 40-item dysfunctional attitude scale questionnaire to collect data on parents to determine their irrational beliefs about parenting. To measure test–retest reliability, the researchers gave 884 parents of primary school children the questionnaire at two times during a 15-day interval. The test–retest reliability for the Expectations and Perfectionism subscales of the instrument were .84 and .80, respectively. This is considered fairly high reliability.

Another type of reliability estimate typically used when a test has several differ-ent forms is the *alternate-form* procedure. Most standardized tests have multiple forms to test the same trait. The forms are different in that the items are not the same, but they are similar in form and content. To ensure that each form is testing the same trait, pairs of different forms are given to the same individuals with several days or more between administrations. The results are then correlated. If the differ-ent forms are testing the same trait, the correlations should be fairly high. Not only does this procedure test stability of results over time, it also tests whether the items in the different forms represent the same general trait being tested.

For example, Lundervold and Dunlap (2006) were interested in examining alter-nate forms of the Behavioral Relaxation Scale (BRS) to determine whether the traditional "long form" of the scale was comparable with several shorter forms of the instrument. Ten participants were participants in the project with BRS scores based on very short (60s), short (120s), medium (180s), and long forms (300s) of observa-tions by the researchers. The researchers reported that interval-by-internal BRS scores using the very short form (one 60-s interval observation) were strongly associated with the long-form (300-s) BRS score with a correlation of .93. The importance of their findings lies in the increased flexibility of observation methods used with the BRS in applied settings, particularly to determine baseline data and to allow this behavior to be observed in one 3-min observation to reliably determine data trends for the observed behaviors.

A practice that you will no doubt see in your perusal of research is that of borrowing parts of commercially produced standardized tests to construct other tests. Researchers doing this seem to be assuming that, because items come from an instrument that has good reliability estimates, any test consisting of a subset of borrowed items will inherit the same reliability. This cannot be taken for granted. Test items often behave differently when put into other configurations. For this reason, subtests consisting of test items coming from such larger, proven instruments should be reevaluated for reliability before use in a study.

Gökalp (2013), mentioned earlier, developed his own 30-item instrument when he explored perceptions of Internet use among physic education web users. However, 12 items were constructed by him while other items were taken and modified based on the work of Hinson et al. (2003). He was careful to state that a Cronbach's alpha coefficient for the first version of the scale was calculated at .88 with the revision calculated at .94, thus adding confidence in the results of his study.

The last four methods of estimating the reliability of a test are concerned with the *internal* consistency of the items within the instrument itself (see Table 6.4). In other words, do all the items in an instrument measure the same general trait? This is important because the responses for the items are normally added up to make a total score. If the items are measuring different traits, then a total score would not make much sense. To illustrate, if researchers try to measure participant attitudes toward going to school, the question is do all of the items in the survey reflect attitude toward this? If some items relate to learning math and some toward learning art, not to mention the other items related to school in general, combining these results would confound the measure of attitude toward school.

The first of these methods is known as *split-half (odd/even)*. As the name suggests, the items in the test are divided in half. Responses on each half are added up to make a subtotal for each half. This can be done by simply splitting the test in half which is appropriate if the items in the second half are not different in difficulty level, or the test is not too long. The reason length is a factor is that respondents might become tired in the later half of the test which would make their responses different from the first half of the test. To get around these problems, the test can compare the subtotals of the odd items with the even items. That is, the odd items (e.g., items 1, 3, 5, etc.) are summed and compared with the sum of the even items (e.g., items 2, 4, 6, etc.). The odd/even method is preferred because it is not influenced by the qualitative change in items that often occur in different sections of the instrument, such as difficulty of item, or fatigue. Whatever the halving method, the two subtotals are then correlated together to produce the reliability coefficient for measuring internal consistency.

The next three methods of computing a coefficient of internal consistency, Kuder-Richardson 20 & 21 and Cronbach alpha, are mathematically related and sometimes symbolized with the Greek letter α (alpha). The first two, Kuder-Richardson 20 and 21, are really two related formulas symbolized as KR-20 and KR-21, respectively. Both are used with items that are scored dichotomously—also referred to as discrete-point items—that is, correct/incorrect, true/false, yes/no, and so forth. Formula KR-21 is a simpler version of KR-20. In laymen's words, these formulas correlate the responses on each item with each of the other items and then average all the correlations. Kablan (2010) explored the effect of using exercise-based computer games during the process of learning on academic achievement among education majors and reported KR-20 reliability coefficients of .79 and .71 for two of the instruments in his study to evaluate learning levels. For tests that are dichotomously scored (i.e., correct/incorrect), both tests had good reliabilities.

The Cronbach alpha (also know as coefficient alpha) does the same thing as the KR formulas except that it is used when the items are scored with more than two possibilities. One use of this method is on rating scales where participants are asked to indicate on a multipoint scale—also referred to as Likert-type scale—the degree to which they agree or disagree. As with the KR formulas, the resulting reliability coefficient is an overall average of the correlations between all possible pairs of items. Mahoney (2010) calculated Cronbach alpha reliability coefficients of .94, .91, .93, and .96 for each subsection of his Attitude Toward Education (STEM) instrument that was interpreted to mean that each had good internal consistency.

Both the Cronbach alpha and the KR-20/KR-21 are conservative estimations of internal consistency. The term *conservative* is used because they take into consideration all the relationships between items that usually produce lower coefficients than the split-half method—it has nothing to do with politics. For this reason, producers of all standardized tests typically report this type to demonstrate internal consistency. Again, a well-written study will include this information in the data-collecting procedure section. But you will be surprised by studies that fail to report this information.

Factors that affect reliability are numerous. One of the major factors is the degree to which the instrument or procedure is affected by *subjectivity* of the people doing the rating or scoring. The more a procedure is vulnerable to perceptual bias, lack of awareness, fatigue, or anything else that influences the ability to rate or score what is happening, the lower reliability.

Other factors that affect reliability are especially related to discrete-point item[3] tests for collecting data. One of these is *length of instrument* (size does matter), which can affect reliability in two different ways. The first involves not having enough items. Instruments with fewer items will automatically produce smaller reliability coefficients. This is not necessarily due to the items being inconsistent, but rather is a simple mathematical limitation inherent to correlation coefficients. However, there is a correction formula known as the *Spearman–Brown prophecy formula* (Nitko, 2001) used to predict what the reliability estimate would be if the test had more items. When researchers use the split-half reliability coefficient (see Table 6.4), they usually report a Spearman–Brown coefficient because the test has been cut into halves which is creating two short tests. (No, it will not predict your future.)

Dupoux, Hammond, Ingalls, and Wolman (2006) followed the previous procedure in their study that looked at teachers' attitudes toward students with disabilities in Haiti. They used the Opinions Relative to Integration (ORI) of Students with Disabilities instrument for collecting data from 183 elementary and secondary teachers in Haiti. The researchers reported the split-half reliability adjusted by the Spearman–Brown reliability formula to be .92 in early studies in 1979 and 1982. The latest revision of the instrument in 1995 showed a reliability of .87. In a pilot study, when the instrument was translated into the French, the reliability dropped to .67. In the results of the current study, the Spearman–Brown reliability coefficient was reported to be .68 for the 12 items in the final instrument. This study is a good example of several factors that may impact reliability including the length of the instrument, the issue of language translation for the purposes of the study, and in this case specifically, modifications of instrument items to establish concept equivalence for the Haitian linguistic context.

The second way that the length of an instrument can affect reliability is when it is too long. Responses to items that are in the later part of the instrument can be affected by fatigue. This introduces an interfering variable, which will lower reliability coefficients. When developing an English language test battery for placing students at the university where Perry taught, his development team noticed that the reliability of the reading component was lower than expected. This component was the last test in the battery. Upon further investigation they found that a number of items in the last part of the test were not being answered. Their conclusion was that the test-takers were running out of time or energy and were not able to finish the last items. They corrected the problem and the reliability of this component increased to the level felt appropriate. This is also a problem with very long surveys.

The final factor that we will mention is the *item quality* used in an instrument. Ambiguous test items will produce inconsistent results and lower reliability. Participants will guess at poorly written items, and this will not give an accurate measure of the trait under observation. Items that have more than one correct answer or are written to trick the participant will have similar negative effects. In the Dupoux et al. (2006) study, for example, 12 items from their original modified instrument of 25 items had reverse wording and were recoded so that high scores represented more favorable attitudes toward integration of special education students. Of these 12 items, five were eventually dropped because these items lowered the Cronbach alpha coefficient. For some reason, these items were not consistently measuring the same attribute as the rest of the instrument. This left them with 20 real-word items that they considered adequate for further analysis.

There are other factors that influence reliability coefficients, but they relate to correlation coefficients in general. We raise these issues in the next chapter when discussing correlation coefficients in greater detail.

However, to emphasize how important knowing what the reliability of an instrument is, we introduce you to the *Standard Error of Measurement* (SEM; Hughes, 2003; Nitko, 2001). (Do not let this term make you nervous; it is not as bad as it looks. We will attempt to explain this in a user-friendly way.) The reliability coefficient is also used to estimate how much error there is in the measurement results—*error* is any variation in the instrument results due to factors other than what is being measured. By performing some simple math on the reliability coefficient, an estimate of the amount of error is calculated, referred to as the SEM. If there is perfect reliability (i.e., 1.00), there is no error in the measurement; that is, there is perfect consistency. This means that any difference in scores on the instrument can be interpreted as true differences between participants. However, if there is no reliability (i.e., .00), then no difference between participant scores can be interpreted as true difference on the trait being measured. To illustrate, if we used a procedure to measure math achievement that had no reliability, although we might get a set of scores differing across individuals, we could not conclude that one person who scored higher than another had a higher proficiency. All differences would be contributed to error from a variety of unknown sources.

What about the real world where reliabilities are somewhere between .00 and 1.00? A rule of thumb that we give to our students is that a measurement procedure that has a reliability coefficient even as high as .75 has a sizeable amount of error. With this reliability coefficient, half of the average variation in measurement between individuals (see discussion on Standard Deviation in Chapter 7—on second thought, wait) can be attributed to error. For instance, if one person scores 55 on an instrument measuring achievement in social science and another person scored 60 with a SEM of 5.0, we cannot conclude with much confidence that the two students really differ. We will come back to this in the next chapter when we discuss descriptive sadistics (i.e., statistics). We add here that very few studies, if any, report SEMs, although you might see one if you are reading a study on testing. However, by using the simple reference point of a reliability equaling .75, which means that half of the variation between people is due to error, you will be able to judge how stable the results of a study are. Knowing this will help in deciding how much weight you put on a study to answer your questions.

Validity

As with reliability, the quality of validity is more complex than initially appears. On the surface, people use it to refer to the ability of an instrument or observational procedure to accurately capture data needed to answer a research question. Unfortunately, many research methodology textbooks continue to distinguish among a number of types of validity, such as *content validity, predictive validity, face validity, construct validity*, and so forth (e.g., McMillan & Schumacher, 2010; Winter, 2000). These different types have led to some confusion. For instance, some people accuse certain data-gathering procedures of being invalid, while others claim that the same procedures are valid. However, when their arguments are examined more closely, one realizes that the two sides of the debate are using different definitions of validity.

Since the early 1990s, the above notions of validity have been subsumed under the heading of *construct validity* (Bachman, 1990; Messick, 1989). Rather than having a set of minivalidities, they are now represented as different *facets* of a more global validity and are summarized in Table 6.5.

In the upper half of Table 6.5 in the left column, validity is shown to be composed of two main facets: trait accuracy and utility. *Trait accuracy*, formerly referred to as *construct validity*, addresses the question as to how accurately the procedure measures the trait under investigation. However, accuracy depends on the definition of the construct being measured or observed. *Self-regulation*, for example, is a trait that is often measured in educational research. Nevertheless, how this trait is measured should be determined by how it is defined. If self-regulation is defined as the students' ability to monitor and complete tasks in a timely manner, then an approach needs to be used that measures the trait as defined. On the other hand, if other researchers define self-regulation as the ability to monitor and

Table 6.5 Multiple Facets of Construct Validity

		Criterion Related		Content Coverage	Face Appearance
F a c e t s	**Trait accuracy**	Capacity to succeed	Current characteristics	Cognitive/ behavioral/ affective change	Consumer satisfaction
	Utility	Predictive	Diagnostic, placement	Achievement of objectives	Public relations
Procedures		Correlate with criterion	Correlate with other instruments, expert opinion	Correspond with learning targets	Surface impression
Types of instruments		Aptitude tests	Personality inventories, proficiency tests, attitude scales...	Tests, quizzes, performance assessments	All above
Examples		SAT, APT	GED, R-MARS	Instruments to test treatment effects	All above

control emotions, then they would have to use procedures to directly assess this definition of self-regulation. In other words, the degree to which a procedure is valid for *trait accuracy* is determined by the degree to which the procedure corresponds to the definition of the trait.

When reading a research article, look for the definitions of the traits being studied then match them to the measurements used to check for the accuracy facet of validity. These definitions should appear in either the Introduction or the Methodology section of the article. To illustrate, in their attempt to develop a self-rating scale, Rizzo, Steinhausen, and Drechsler (2010) defined *self-regulation* as "primarily a volitional cognitive and behavioral process through which an individual maintains levels of emotional, motivational, and cognitive arousal that are conducive to positive adjustment and adaptation, as reflected in positive social relationships, productivity, achievement, and a positive sense of self" (p. 124). To capture all of the constructs in their definition, they created their instrument based on a review of experimental studies on executive function and self-regulation in children from existing rating scales. This practice of defining traits by using already existing instruments is common among researchers. In effect, the instrument provides the operational definition of the trait.

Regarding the second main facet of validity, *utility* is concerned with whether measurement or observational procedures are used for the right purpose. If a procedure is not used for what it was originally intended, there might be a question as to whether it is a valid procedure for obtaining the data needed in a particular study. If it is used for something other than what it was originally designed to do, then researchers must provide additional evidence that the procedure is valid for the purpose of his and her study. For example, if you wanted to use the results from the SAT to measure the affects of a treatment over a 2-week training period, this would be invalid. The reason is that the SAT was designed to measure academic aptitude that develops over long periods of time. It was not designed to measure the specific outcomes that the treatment was targeting.

Note in Table 6.5 that trait accuracy and utility are subdivided into three dimensions: *criterion related*, *content coverage*, and *face appearance*. These used to be referred to as separate validities: criterion-related validity, content validity, and face validity (e.g., Winter, 2000). However, within the current global concept of construct validity, these dimensions further refine the utility nature of validity.

Criterion related simply means that the procedure is validated by being compared with some external criteria. It is divided into two general types of trait accuracy: *capacity to succeed* and *current characteristics*. Capacity to succeed relates to a person having the necessary where-with-all or *aptitude* to succeed in some other endeavor. Typically, this involves carefully defining the aptitude being measured and then constructing or finding an instrument or observational procedure that would accurately obtain the needed data. The *utility* of identifying people's *capacity to succeed* is usually for prediction purposes. For instance, if researchers want to predict people's ability to succeed at the university, they would administer an instrument that would assess whether the examinees had the necessary aptitude to succeed (see Table 6.5) prior to going to the university. Predictive utility is determined by correlating these results with measurements on the criterion that is being predicted, in this case the grade point average (GPA) of the same students after their first semester. A high correlation would provide evidence for predictive utility. Suffice it to say that you can find more about this from any book on assessment (e.g., Nitko, 2001).

A number of measures have been used over the years to predict the success of new teachers. One of the most well-known standardized instruments that has been around for many years is the Teacher Perceiver Interview (TPI) online interview protocol (Gallup Organization, 2004). They developed this protocol for the purpose of assisting schools and administrators to predict objectively, whether applicants to their school districts would eventually become quality teachers. Although many concerns still exist with using this protocol as a singular predictor of teacher effectiveness, the research by Gallup suggested a strong predictive relationship between TeacherInsight scores and principals' ratings of teachers, students' ratings of teachers, and student achievement. The researchers continue to maintain that the instrument is a reliable predictive instrument for both certified and noncertified teachers.

The second general type of criterion-related trait accuracy that is validated against an external criterion is *current characteristics* (see Table 6.5). Such things as math proficiency, personality traits, and attitude are considered characteristics that individuals possess over time. Procedures that measure these are used for (i.e., utility) diagnosing people for placement into different categories such as different proficiency levels.

One method commonly used for providing evidence for being able to validly identify *current characteristics* is by whether the diagnoses given by the procedure matches an expert opinion. Rizzo et al. (2010), for example, took care to use experts (teachers and child psychologists) to judge the construction of the instrument items to measure self-perceptions of self-regulation. By doing so, they begin to supply evidence that their instrument was measuring what they intended to measure.

Another common method for showing the above facet of validity is to correlate the results of the procedure with performance on another instrument that has been accepted by the research community as a good criterion. Often performance on instruments designed for a particular study is correlated with students' performance on recognized standardized tests or instruments to estimate validity. Kaya and Hamamci (2011) developed their parent irrational belief scale and to provide validation support of the instrument, used three additional instruments (the Dysfunctional Attitude Scale, the Beck Depression Inventory, and the Irrational Belief Scale-Short Form) to compare the results. The researchers reported how correlational values among the three existing scales and the new instrument were positive indicating the new instrument agreed with the existing measures. By doing so, they were able to provide evidence that irrational beliefs were accurately being measured.

The second dimension in Table 6.5 is *content coverage*. The general traits being assessed here are *cognitive, behavioral,* or *affective change*. In *experimental* research, the main question looks at cause-and-effect relationships in the form of treatment effects. Often the objective of the treatment is to increase learning or change the participants' behavior or attitude. This same objective needs to be used when planning the measurement procedure because its main utility is to assess whether the treatment objective has been achieved. Thus, the validity of the measurement procedure is determined by how well its content aligns with the treatment objectives. In this case, validity is not assessed by computing a correlation coefficient, as with other validity procedures, but by matching various components of the measurement procedure with the treatment objectives.

For example, Kayiran and Karabay (2012) examined the effects of learning basic reading and writing skills through a phonics-based sentence method or a decoding method. The researchers' reasoning was based on the thinking that reading and writing instruction leads to significant changes in students' intellectual, affective, and social skills. Their central goal was to explore if one of these approaches may be more effective in encouraging reading comprehension achievement. The reading comprehension achievement test included seven texts in different genres (informative, narrative, descriptive, and poem) and 25 questions based on similar reading comprehension tests, Turkish course books, and the IOWA silent reading test. For this reading comprehension instrument to have been valid for measuring the effects of the two learning methods, the researchers needed to show that the learning methods or treatments were designed to increase participants' reading comprehension. Without this information, there is little way of knowing whether the measuring instrument was sensitive to any changes due to the treatment. The principle here is that when a study has a treatment that is designed to affect cognitive/behavioral/attitude change, researchers should show how the measurement procedure is sensitive to change in these areas to establish that the procedure has appropriate utility (i.e., one facet of validity).

The third dimension in Table 6.5 that qualifies trait accuracy and utility is *face appearance*, which some refer to as *face validity*. Related to accuracy, the key issue is whether a measurement procedure appears to measure what it is suppose to measure. The closer it appears to be gathering the correct data, the more valid it looks. In regards to utility, face appearance is important for public relations with participant as well as with the outside community. Participants who do not feel that the procedure is measuring what they think it should measure might not be motivated to do their best. This, in turn, will affect the results of the study. People outside a study might not see the relevance of a particular measurement technique and, therefore, not consider the results from such measurement useful for answering the researchers' question (i.e., the consumer). Although this dimension of validity is of lesser theoretical importance from a research perspective, it is the one that many practitioners in education give most attention to. This has led some people to make incorrect conclusions about the validity of data that result from some measurement procedures.

To illustrate how easy it is to allow the facet of *face appearance* to overshadow other aspects of validity, Perry relates this somewhat bizarre, but true, story. One of his former professors once said something like this.

> If I were to tell you that I found a correlation of +0.95 (a very high correlation) between shoe size and success in learning a foreign language, and that I have found this high correlation in a number of studies with different groups of participants, would you use shoe size as a test to predict future success for entrants to your foreign language program?

Most likely, you would agree with this professor with an emphatic "no way." However, Perry asked, "Why not?" His answer was "The test is not valid." If you agree with him, what aspect of validity would you have in mind? Most likely, you would be considering face appearance as he was. Perry, in contrast, argued that the test is valid on the basis of its predictive utility. Anything, no matter what it looks like, that correlates with something else as high as .95 is a powerful predictor. We certainly agree that shoe size does not appear at face value to relate to the ability to learn a language. For prediction purposes, however, face appearance is not necessary, although desired. Understanding *why* something can predict something else does not have to be clear either, although we would certainly try to find out the reason. We argue that if the data are correct, we should use shoe size as an entrance test because it was shown to have high predictive utility. Certainly, it would be the cheapest and quickest test to administer, although not very popular with people whose foot size predicted failure.

Before concluding this section of the chapter, we need to point out a very important principle. The relationship between validity and reliability is *unidirectional*. There are two aspects to this: (a) reliability does not depend on validity, but (b) validity depends on reliability. Regarding the former, an instrument or observational procedure can be reliable (i.e., consistent) when measuring something, but not necessarily measuring the right thing. To illustrate, if we measure a person's height with a measuring tape, the results will be consistent (i.e., reliable) every time. No matter how many times we measure that person's height, we will get the same results. Yet if we claim that our measurement is an accurate assessment of a person's weight, our procedure is not very valid. Notice that we said *not very* and refrained from using *invalid*. The reason is that height is related to weight: Tall people are usually heavier than short people. Although related, height would not be a valid direct measurement of weight.

However, the opposite is not true. We cannot have a valid instrument that is not reliable, see (b) above. Accuracy implies consistency but not vice versa. Obviously, if we cannot depend on a procedure to give us consistent (i.e., reliable) results, accuracy will also fluctuate. In fact, *the validity of an instrument will never exceed its reliability*. If a measurement procedure has low reliability, its validity will be low as well—regardless of how valid the developer wishes it might be. On the other hand, a high reliability coefficient does not automatically mean that the instrument is also highly valid. Therefore, reliability is necessary, but not sufficient for defining validity. Once the instrument is determined reliable, researchers must then show with separate information that it is valid.

As you can see from the previous discussion validity is not a static concept. Because it is tied very much to the facet of utility, it changes with every research design (cf. Chapelle, Enright, & Jamieson, 2008).

In summary, when you read or hear the term *validity* being used, refer to Table 6.5 and try to determine what aspect of validity is being considered. Then ask yourself if the term is being used correctly. Remember that if a measurement has low reliability, regardless of its face appearance, it also has low validity. However, too few studies report how the validity of the procedures used was determined. Yet the results of a study depend heavily on whether the measurement procedures are valid. The weaker the validity, the less we can depend on the results.

In conclusion, the last section of this chapter has introduced the two principal qualities of numerical data-gathering procedures: reliability and validity. Regardless of what procedure researchers use, they need to report to the reader evidence that the procedure used provides reliable and valid data. If not, there is no way the reader will know whether the conclusions made based on the data have any credibility. With this basic information in hand, you should now be able to read the section about data-gathering with understanding. In addition, you should have enough confidence to evaluate whether the procedure a researcher used provided reliable and valid information.

You are now ready to grapple with how data are analyzed. This is the subject of the next chapter. However, before you leave this chapter, try the following exercise so that you can gain firsthand experience in evaluating the data-gathering procedures used in a study of your choice.

EXERCISE 6.3

Task: Find a research study of interest in a recent journal related to some aspect of education. Do the following:

1 List the research question(s).
2 Look at the data-collection procedure used: (i.e., tests, surveys, raters, observers, etc.). Does the procedure seem appropriate for answering the research question(s)?
3 What information was given relating to reliability?

   a Type?
   b Amount?
   c How reliable was the procedure being used?

4 What facet of validity was examined?

5 How well did the procedure correspond to identifying the trait being measured in your opinion?

6 Did statements about validity correspond to evidence of reliability?

Key Terms and Concepts

Collecting and Evaluating Verbal Data

automatic response patterns
closed-form questionnaire items
open-form questionnaire items
constructed response items
criterion-referenced tests
discrete-point items
full-participant observer
halo-effect
highly structured interviews
informant
instrumental procedures
introspection
judge/rater
nonparticipant observer
norm-referenced test
objective
observational procedure
open-structured interviews
partial-participant observer
participant observers
retrospection
rubric
semistructured interviews
standardized test
subjectivity
think-aloud procedure
triangulation

Collecting and Evaluating Numerical Data

alternate-form reliability
coefficient
construct validity
content coverage
criterion related
Cronbach alpha
face appearance
internal consistency
inter-rater reliability
intra-rater reliability
item quality
Kuder-Richardson 20 and 21
predictive utility
reliability
reliability coefficient
Spearman–Brown prophecy formula
split-half (odd/even) reliability
standard error of measurement (SEM)
test–retest reliability
trait accuracy
utility
validity

Additional Recommended Reading

Freeman, J. D. (1983). *Margaret Mead and Samoa: The making and unmaking of an anthropological myth.* Cambridge, MA: Harvard University Press.

Mackintosh, N. J. (1995). *Cyril Burt: Fraud or framed?* New York: Oxford University Press.

Scholfield, P. (1995). *Quantifying language: A researcher's and teacher's guide to gathering language data and reducing it to figures.* Philadelphia, PA: Multilingual Matters.

Teddlie, C., & Yu, F. (2007). Mixed methods sampling: A typology with examples. *Journal of Mixed Methods Research, 1,* 77–100.

Tekinarslan, C., Pinar, E. S., & Sucuoglu, B. (2012). Teachers' and mothers' assessment of social skills of students with mental retardation. *Educational Sciences: Theory & Practice, 12*(4), 2783–2788.

Notes

1 *Objective* is at the other end of the continuum from *subjective*, in that the observer's observations are not influenced by bias due to attitude, temporary emotional states, etc. In actual fact, there is no 100% purely objective or subjective observation.
2 Go to http://nces.ed.gov/statprog/statisticalstandards, and look for Survey Response Rate Parameters.
3 This item tests only one thing and is scored correct or incorrect.

References

Allsop, Y. (2011). Does collaboration occur when children are learning with the support of a wiki? *The Turkish Online Journal of Educational Technology, 10*(4), 130–137.

Bachman, L. F. (1990). *Fundamental considerations in language testing.* New York: Oxford University Press.

Brown, J. R., Brown, L.J., & Brown, C. (2008). "Signs, Signs, Everywhere There's Signs… and the Sign Says": You got to have a PRAXIS II membership card to get inside. *Teacher Education Quarterly, 35*, 29–42.

Cai, W., & Lee, B. P. H. (2012). Processing unfamiliar words: Strategies, knowledge sources, and the relationship to text and word comprehension. *The Canadian Journal of Applied Linguistics, 15*(1), 122–145.

Cardona, B., Jain, S., & Canfield-Davis, K. (2012). Home-school relationships: A qualitative study with diverse families. *The Qualitative Report, 17*(70), 1–20.

Chapelle, C. A., Enright, M. K., & Jamieson, J. M. (2008). Test score interpretation and us, In C. A. Chapelle, M. K. Enright, & J. M. Jamieson (Eds.), *Building a validity argument for the Test of English as a Foreign Language* (pp. 1–25). New York: Routledge.

Dupoux, E., Hammond, H., Ingalls, L., & Wolman, C. (2006). Teachers' attitudes toward students with disabilities in Haiti. *International Journal of Special Education, 21*(3), 1–14.

Gallup Organization. (2004). *TeacherInsight interview: Predictive validity study 2003–2004 School Year.* Princeton, NJ: Author.

Goh, C. C. M. (2002). Exploring listening comprehension tactics and their interaction patterns. *System, 30*, 185–206.

Gökalp, M. S. (2013). Perceptions of the Internet and education: A study with physics education website users. *International Journal of Environmental & Science Education, 8*(2), 289–302.

Hinson, J., Distefano, C., & Daniel, C. (2003). The internet self-perception scale: Measuring elementary students' levels of self-efficacy regarding internet use. *Journal of Educational Computing Research, 29*(2), 209–228.

Holmes, R. M. (2012). The outdoor recess activities of children at an urban school: Longitudinal patterns and intraperiod patterns. *American Journal of Play, 4*(3), 327–351.

Hughes, A. (2003). *Testing for language teachers* (2nd ed.). Cambridge, UK: Cambridge University Press.

Kablan, Z. (2010). The effect of using exercised-based computer games during the process of learning on academic achievement among education majors. *Educational Sciences: Theory & Practice, 10*(1), 352–364.

Kaya, I., & Hamamci, Z. (2011). Development of the parent irrational beliefs scale. *Educational Sciences: Theory & Practice, 11*(3), 1160–1165.

Kayiran, B. K., & Karabay, A. (2012). A study of reading comprehension skills of primary school 5th grade students-learning basic reading and writing skills through phonics-based sentence method or decoding method. *Educational Sciences: Theory & Practice, 12*(4), 2854–2860.

Kobayashi, M. (2002). Method effects on reading comprehension test performance: Text organization and response format. *Language Testing, 19*, 193–220.

Likert, R. (1932). A technique for the measurement of attitudes. *Archives in Psychology, 140,* 1–55.

Lundervold, D. A., & Dunlap, A. L. (2006). Alternate forms of reliability of the Behavioral Relaxation Scale: Preliminary results. *International Journal of Behavioral Consultation and Therapy 2*(2), 240–245.

Mahoney, M. P. (2010). Students' attitudes toward STEM: Development of an instrument for high school STEM-based programs. *The Journal of Technology Studies,* 24–34.

Martins, M. A., Albuquerque, A., Salvador, L., & Silva, C. (2013). The impact of invented spelling on early spelling and reading. *The Journal of Writing Research, 5*(2), 215–237.

McMillan, J. H., & Schumacher, S. (2010). *Research in Education* (7th ed.). Upper Saddle River, NJ: Pearson Publishing.

Messick, S. (1989). Validity. In R. L. Linn (Ed.), *Educational measurement* (3rd ed., pp. 13–103). New York: Macmillan.

Miles, M. B., & Huberman, A. M. (1994). *Qualitative data analysis: An expanded sourcebook.* Thousand Oaks, CA: Sage.

Nash-Ditzel, S. (2010). Metacognitive reading strategies can improve self-regulation. *Journal of College Reading and Learning, 40*(2), 45–63.

Nichols, J. D., Kim, I-H., & Nichols, G. W. (2013). *The effect of community volunteerism on early literacy development.* Paper presented at the annual meeting of the American Educational Research Association, San Francisco, CA.

Nitko, A. J. (2001). *Educational assessment of students* (3rd ed.). Upper Saddle River, NJ: Prentice-Hall.

Perry, F. L., Boraie, D.; Kassabgy, N.; & Kassabgy, O. (2001). *How EFL learners deal with unknown words.* Paper presented at the American Association for Applied Linguistics Annual Conference, St. Louis, MO.

Pressley, M., & Afflerbach, P. (1995). *Verbal protocols of reading: The nature of constructively responsive reading.* Hillsdale, NJ: Erlbaum.

Rizzo, O., Steinhausen, H-C., Drechsler, R. (2010). Self perceptions of self-regulatory skills in children aged eight to 10 years: Development and Evaluation of a new self-rating scale. *Australian Journal of Educational & Developmental Psychology, 10,* 123–143.

Tashakkori, A., & Teddlie, C. (1998). *Mixed methodology.* Thousand Oaks, CA: Sage.

Upitis, R., Smithrim, K., Garbati, J., & Ogden, H. (2008). The impact of art-making in the university workplace. *International Journal of Education and the Arts, 9*(8), 1–25.

Winter, G. (2000). A comparative discussion of the notion of "validity" in qualitative and quantitative research. *The Qualitative Report, 4*(3/4). Retrieved from http://www.nova.edu/ssss/QR/QR4-3/winter.html

7

UNDERSTANDING RESEARCH RESULTS

Chapter Overview

Once researchers collect their data, they must determine whether the results answer their research questions. If they are "What" questions, the answers will be in the form of information that (a) describes what variables are important, (b) identifies the context in which certain phenomena occur, and/or (c) uncovers important relationships between phenomena. If the questions are "Why" types, then the results will attempt to explain the cause behind certain phenomena. In either case, the analysis of the data will be presented verbally, numerically, or a combination of the two.

In this chapter, various types of data and data analysis procedures that appear in Results sections of research are discussed. Following a short introduction to data analysis, there are two main sections: the first relates to how verbal data are presented and analyzed, and the second introduces how numerical data are presented and analyzed. Although somewhat technical, this latter section does not require a math background. It furnishes you with the concepts needed to understand the statistical procedures found in many Results sections.

By the end of this chapter, our goal is you are able to read Results sections of research articles with enough confidence to critically evaluate whether appropriate procedures have been used and correct interpretations have been made.

Introduction to Data Analysis

Numerical Versus Verbal Data

Some people think that numerical data are more scientific—and therefore more important—than verbal data because of the statistical analyses that can be performed on numerical data. However, this is a false conclusion. We must not forget that numbers are only as good as the constructs they represent. In other words, when we use statistics, we have basically transferred verbally defined constructs into numbers so that we can analyze the data more easily. We must not forget that these statistical results must again be transferred back into terminology that represents these verbal constructs to make any sense.[1] Consider, for thought, the following statement by Miles and Huberman (1994) as an argument for the importance of verbal data:

> We argue that although words may be more unwieldy than numbers, they render more meaning than numbers alone and should be hung on to throughout data analysis. Converting words into numbers and then tossing away the words get a researcher into all kinds of mischief. You thus are assuming that the chief property of the words is that there are more of some than of others. Focusing solely on numbers shifts attention from substance to arithmetic, throwing out the whole notion of "qualities" or "essential characteristics." (p. 56)

Nevertheless, be careful not to swing to the other side of the pendulum, thinking that verbal data are superior to numerical data. Both types of data have their place and are equally important. Miles and Huberman provide a very powerful discussion in their statement on how the two types of data complement each other. This concurs with our position presented in Chapter 5 of this book.

Common Procedure

In almost all studies, all of the data that have been gathered are not presented in the research report. Whether verbal or numerical, the data presented have gone through some form of selection and reduction. The reason is that both verbal and numerical data typically are voluminous in their rawest forms. What you see reported in research journals are results of the raw data having been boiled down into manageable units for display to the public. Verbal data commonly appear as selections of excerpts, narrative vignettes, quotations from interviews, and so forth. Whereas, numerical data are often condensed into tables of frequencies, averages, and so forth. There are some interesting differences, however, which we describe in the following two sections.

Analysis of Verbal Data

Most of the credit in recent years for developing criteria for presenting and analyzing verbal data must go to researchers who have emphasized the use of qualitative research strategies. However, because of the variety of qualitative approaches used, there are differing opinions about the analytical steps that should be followed when analyzing verbal data. For instance, Creswell (1998) identified only three out of 13 general analysis strategies common to three different authors of qualitative research methods (Bogdan & Biklen, 1992; Huberman & Miles, 1994; Wolcott, 1994). This makes it difficult to set standards for evaluating the Results section of a qualitative research article.

In addition, unlike work with numerical data, presentation of verbal data and their analyses appear very much intertwined together in Results sections of research reports. That is, separating the data from the analysis is difficult. Numerical data, in contrast, are presented in some type of summarized form (e.g., tables of descriptive statistics) and followed with the analysis in the form of inferential statistics (see the following Analysis of Numerical Data section).

Consequently, the analysis of verbal data is not quite as straightforward as analyzing numerical data. The reason is that analysis of verbal data is initiated at the beginning of the data–collection process and continues throughout the study. This process involves the researcher interacting with the data symbiotically. Literally, the researcher becomes the "main 'measurement device'" (Miles & Huberman, 1994, p. 7). Creswell (1998, pp. 142, 143) likened data analysis to a "contour" in the form of a "data analysis spiral," where the researcher engages the data, reflects, makes notes, reengages the data, organizes, codes, reduces the data, looks for relationships and themes, makes checks on the credibility of the emerging system, and eventually draws conclusions.

However, when we read published qualitative research, we seldom are given a clear description of how this *data analysis spiral* transpired. In Miles and Huberman's (1994) words, "We rarely see data displays—only the conclusions. In most cases we do not see a procedural account of the analysis, explaining just how the researcher got from 500 pages of field notes to the main conclusions drawn" (p. 262).

If the researcher is working alone during the data analysis spiral, serious questions arise concerning the credibility of any conclusions made. First, there is the problem mentioned in Chapter 6 regarding possible bias when gathering data through observation and other noninstrumental procedures. However, because analysis begins during the data–collection stage in qualitative research, *analytical biases* become a possible threat to the validity of conclusions. Miles and Huberman (1994) identified three archetypical ones: *the holistic fallacy, elite bias*, and *going native*. The first has to do with seeing patterns and themes that are not really there. The second is concerned with giving too much weight to informants who are more articulate and better informed, making the data unrepresentative. The third, *going native*, occurs when researchers get so close to the respondents that they are "co-opted into [their] perceptions and explanations" (p. 264).

So how are we, the consumers of qualitative research, supposed to determine whether the information in the Results section is credible? Miles and Huberman (1994) list 13 tactics for enhancing credibility. Four of these tactics relate to quality of data, which we included in Table 6.2. We place triangulation (#1 in Table 7.1) under patterns and themes based on Creswell's (1998) use of the term, although Miles and Huberman included it with data quality. We listed

Table 7.1 Methods for Evaluating Credibility of Patterns and Explanations Drawn from Verbal Data

Evidence for...	Tactic
Patterns/Themes	1. Triangulation
	2. Outliers & Extreme cases
	3. Surprises
	4. Negative evidence
	5. Peer review
Explanations/Conclusions	6. Spurious relationships
	7. If–then tests
	8. Rival explanations
	9. Replicating findings
	10. Informant feedback
	11. Rich/thick description
	12. External audits

three[2] (2–4) to evaluate patterns/themes, and five (6–10) for appraising their explanations and conclusions.

Creswell (1998) provided eight verification procedures that he and a colleague extrapolated from a number of differing types of qualitative studies. Three of these overlapped with Miles and Huberman's (1994) list—triangulation, negative evidence, and member checks (i.e., informant feedback)—leaving five. Three relate to evaluating data quality, so we put them in Table 6.2 and discussed them there. The third, *peer review* (#5 in Table 7.1), is useful for checking whether the perceived patterns are credible, although also useful for evaluating explanations. The last two, rich/thick descriptions (#11) and external audits (# 12), are powerful tactics for evaluating explanations. Each of these tactics is further explained below.

Few studies will use all 12 of these tactics to enhance credibility. However, the more a study has in each category, the more evidence is put forward for strengthening the credibility of the results. There should be at least one tactic used in each of the two general categories in Table 7.1.

Evaluating Patterns and Themes

One of the main goals of much qualitative research is to extrapolate patterns and themes from the verbal data. The question for the consumer is whether these patterns are plausible based on the data. The first five tactics listed in Table 7.1 can be used to support these patterns proposed by researchers (cf. Creswell, 1998; Miles & Huberman, 1994). The first, *triangulation*, shows how the same patterns are seen in the data from different sources. The next three involve atypical data that might not fit the patterns or themes being proposed by the researcher. The temptation is to avoid these *hiccups* in the data, referred to in quantitative analysis as *data smoothing*. However, for the qualitative researcher, these exceptions are excellent means to test the perceived patterns or themes being formulated. The last tactic, peer review, involves getting a second opinion, which corresponds to criterion-related validity discussed in Chapter 6.

Triangulation (see Chapters 5 and 6)

This procedure involves using data from multiple sources to converge on themes and patterns. For the purpose of increasing credibility to an argument, the more evidence coming from independent sources, the better. As in law courts, one witness is not enough. The more independent witnesses the stronger the case. The same holds true for qualitative research; the more data coming from a variety of sources, the better the research. This, of course, assumes that data from each source can stand the test of the other data quality criteria discussed in Chapter 6.

Leung and Choi (2010) completed a qualitative study where they studied the self-esteem, peer affiliation, and academic outcome among low-achieving students in Hong Kong. Their specific interest was to explore the transition of low-achieving students from primary schools to secondary schools. This study used *triangulation* where the researchers collected data from multiple sources including observational field notes, conversations with students, teacher interviews, interrater checklists, and student portfolio samples of written work. Once the data was collected, the researchers transformed the data into working documents that could be coded into more quantifiable terms of the major themes that emerged from the data. Using multiple researchers to gather and analyze the data, and multiple sources that generated data, the researchers attempted to increase the credibility and validity of their findings.

Simply stating, using triangulation of different data sources in a study, however, does not necessarily increase credibility of the conclusions. Researchers need to inform us how and why triangulation was used. Questions such as the following need to be answered: How does data from each source contribute to the convergence of a perceived pattern or theme? In what way do the researchers believe this particular combination of data adds to the overall credibility of the conclusions? These are questions researchers are obligated to answer to add weight to the overall credibility.

Outliers and Extreme Cases

Examining such data seems to be counterintuitive to the tactic of checking for representativeness at the top of the list (see Table 6.2). However, these are very effective ways to check whether the patterns and themes perceived by the research are not due to some form of bias. Most qualitative studies limit themselves when it comes to how many people or situations are studied. Because of this, the perceived patterns and themes may be unique to the sample being used. However, once these patterns and themes have been formulated from the original sample, comparing them with samples of people or events that differ considerably is an excellent way to check credibility. Prior and Niesz (2013) explored refugee children's adaptation to American early childhood classrooms and observed and collected data from three early childhood students from Myanmar. The researchers interviewed the families of these children as part of their data collection process. They also discovered that with one of the children, the family felt a "cultural dissonance" in that the child often struggled at different times of the year and would only speak English rather than her native language. Despite the researchers' findings of other similar themes throughout their analysis, this one participant might represent a more extreme case when compared with her peers.

In some studies, the opposite might be true. Researchers deliberately use extreme cases compared with the original sample. The reason is that such samples are information-rich (see Chapter 4). However, once the patterns/themes have been extrapolated, it seems imperative that researchers would want to compare their findings with a sample that is less extreme. If the patterns/themes hold for the more general sample, they are made more credible.

Surprises

Another tactic for promoting the credibility of perceived patterns/themes is examining unexpected findings. Reporting unexpected findings gives some confirmation that researchers are not so focused on what they want to find that they cannot recognize any anomalies. Of course, once the surprise has been noted by the researchers, they need to explain how it confirms or forces adjustment to the proposed pattern or theme. One example is Bond's study (2011) which explored how school principals react to unexpected public confrontation. Some of their results supported a theory of how professionals mentally process information during surprise situations while some comments from principals were a surprise to the researcher that suggested more professional development might be needed to help principals react to these types of situations.

Negative Evidence

Here researchers actively seek evidence that will go against their patterns or themes. One would not think that researchers would want to find evidence contradicting their proposals. It is certainly not something that happens automatically as the data are being analyzed by researchers. They would have to make a planned effort to do this after beginning to formulate any patterns or themes. Just the fact that researchers made this effort would be impressive. However, it is not sufficient to simply report that negative evidence was found. Researchers need to identify the evidence and discuss the implications. This type of information reported by researchers in a published report adds more weight to the prosed patterns/themes. Examine Rott's study (2005) to see how she used two pieces of negative evidence to enhance the credibility of the patterns she extrapolated from her data.

Peer Review

A *peer* is someone on the same level of the researcher "who keeps the researcher honest; asks the hard questions about methods, meanings, and interpretations" (Creswell, 1998, p. 202). The researcher, especially if doing the study alone, needs someone, such as a colleague, to evaluate proposed patterns as well as themes to prevent influences from such analytical biases as *holistic fallacy* mentioned previously. We suggest you look at McKenna and Millen's (2013) study that used both multiple sources of data collection and peer review to establish the credibility of the patterns they saw in their data.

Evaluating Explanations and Conclusions

The last phase of evaluating a qualitative study is examining the explanations/conclusions of the study. Table 7.1 presents seven tactics that researchers can use to bolster credibility: five from Miles and Huberman (1994) and two from Creswell (1998). These are useful for consumers of qualitative research for evaluation, as well. However, the burden of proof is on the researcher, not the consumer. The more tactics used by the researcher the more credibility given to the interpretations of the findings.

Spurious Relationships

Not all things that appear to be related are directly related. For example, lung cancer and the number of ashtrays a person owns are related. However, this relationship is spurious (i.e., misleading). Another variable directly related to each of these—amount of cigarettes smoked—produces an indirect relationship between ashtray and lung cancer. So when researchers propose a direct relationship between constructs, they should provide a convincing argument that there are not other variables producing this relationship.

If–Then Tests

These tests "are the workhorses of qualitative data analysis" (Miles & Huberman, 1994, p. 271). In the fuller version an *if–then test* is a conditional sentence in the form of, *if the hypothesis is true, and then there should be a specific consequence.* Every explanation based on data is a type of hypothesis, usually in the form of relationships among variables, underlying principles, or processes. Researchers test their hypothesized explanations by predicting that some consequence would occur with a novel sample of people or set of events. This strategy is built into the grounded theory method discussed in Chapter 5. Hatcher, Numer, and Paulsel's (2012) study demonstrated how this was used to support their explanations to their data when looking at teachers' and parents' beliefs about the role of pre-schools in preparing students for kindergarten.

Rival Explanations

Eliminating competing explanations is a powerful way to add weight to a theoretical conclusion. The researcher formulates at least one plausible competing explanation and applies the *if–then* test. The explanation that best explains the data is the most plausible. The researcher can then report how the weaker explanations could not compete.

However, the consumer must beware that the competing explanations offered are not *straw men*; that is, explanations that were not plausible in the first place—easy to refute. This might occur if researchers are so bent on their own explanation that they do not address more plausible alternatives, but still want to give the appearance that they have used this technique to gain credibility.

Another caveat for consumers is to not conclude that, just because the competing explanations were not as robust as the one proposed by the researcher, the proposed one is a good one. The one proposed may not be a good one, although better than the others. On a more practical note, researchers must provide evidence that not only their explanation is better than the competition, but it is also good in itself. For example, based on some earlier research and Native American stereotypes, Bordelon, Opatrny, Turner, and Williams (2011) originally had negative impressions of an annual Native American cultural fair. Going into the project, they assumed that the cultural fair was a frivolous and unimportant activity that unfortunately, over the years, had become over commercialized. On the basis of the analysis of the themes that appeared in their data, the researchers changed their views and concluded that the cultural fair had a deeper purpose and meaning to the participants.

Replicating Findings

This strategy is recognized by both qualitative and quantitative researchers as an excellent way to support hypotheses and theories. The more the same findings occur despite different samples and conditions, the more confidence we can have in the conclusions. Hypothesized relationships that can only be supported by one sample of individuals in only one setting have little use in the practical world. Occasionally, researchers will report several replications of the study in the same report. It is a good way to provide evidence for the robustness of their explanations. Garvis (2012) added to the credibility of her conclusions by showing how they were similar to previous theories and published research.

Informant Feedback

This relates to the reactions that the informants have to the conclusions of the study. Such feedback can be used to check the plausibility of conclusions drawn by the researcher. The researcher needs to take care here, however, due to possible *researcher effects*. Respondents may simply agree with the researcher just to please the researcher, or the researcher may give the informant a final report which is too technical. This could result in agreement to hide the embarrassment from not understanding or produce a negative response because of misunderstanding. In either case, the researcher needs to inform the consumer of the report regarding the manner in which the feedback was obtained. The more effort the researcher makes to facilitate the understanding of the informant, the more weight the consumer can give to the feedback. Darvin (2011) showed the 17 informants in her study, video, and transcripts to solicit feedback on drafts of her conclusions to add to the credibility of her interpretations.

Rich/Thick Description

This involves a detailed description of the participants, context, and all that goes on during the data-gathering and analysis stages. The purpose is to provide the reader of the study with enough information to decide whether the explanations and conclusions of the study are warranted. When this is done, you will notice that the researcher will follow each proposed explanation with excerpts from the data. The more excerpts, the more support—one excerpt does not establish a pattern or support an explanation. Be careful, however, not to fall in the opposite trap by mistaking quantity with quality. That is, the excerpts that are used to support an explanation need to be truly supportive. This strategy is so important that almost every study cited in this section provided many excerpts from their data pools to warrant their conclusions—take Bond (2011) for example.

External Audits

A seldom used, but powerful method (Creswell, 1998) to increase the credibility of the interpretations of a study is to hire an outsider to evaluate the study. A well-funded research project may employ such a person to add credibility to the findings and conclusions. Many studies have unpaid external reviewers critic them out of academic courtesy. Such people are usually recognized in the acknowledgements at the end of a study. Carrier (2011), for instance, thanked two people for detailed reviews and comments on earlier drafts of her work. It is safe to assume that these people provided feedback on her interpretations of the data that was collected.

Cardona, Jain, and Canfield-Davis (2012) illustrate (see Chapter 6) how explanations coming from verbal data might be evaluated using the 12 tactics presented in Table 7.1. Remember in Chapter 6, we looked at Cardona et al.'s qualitative case study that explored how families from diverse cultural backgrounds under-stood family involvement in the context of early childhood care and educational settings. A summary of the Tactics we found in their study is presented in Table 7.2 followed by an expanded explanation.

Cardona et al. (2012) made extensive use of triangulation to identify patterns in the data to draw her conclusions. The researchers used data from three primary sources (parents, teachers, and administrators) and several secondary sources (observations at three preschool sites) to provide evidence to understand the "lived experiences of other people, and how they interpret meaning to that expe-rience" (p. 5). The preschool sites' data representation, for example, was supported with data from sources like field notes of site observations, and parent, teacher and administrator interviews, some of these occurring in the home of the parents.

Cardona et al. (2012) reported one *outlier and extreme cases* (#2) where the parents of one student would only communicate in English rather than their native language, thus raising some questions about the parent responses. The researchers did not report any use of a *surprise* tactic (#3) in any of the data. Cardona et al. also provided some *negative or contradictory* evidence (#4) where some parents felt that their opinions and wishes were valued by the teachers and administrators while others felt that all decisions were being controlled by the administration. All of these tactics eventually contributed to the credibility of her construct of positive home–school relationships she was aiming to demonstrate.

Cardona et al.'s (2012) argument for the *believability* of their interpretations are relatively strong in that they reported a *peer review* (#5) by early childhood profes-sionals, family therapists, and counselor education faculty (p. 5) during their

Table 7.2 Evaluation Tactics for Verbal Data Applied to Cardona et al.'s Study (2012)

Checking for…	Tactics	Check
Patterns/Themes		
	1. Triangulation	☺
	2. Outliers & Extreme cases	☺
	3. Surprises	
	4. Negative evidence	☺
	5. Peer review	☺
Explanations/Conclusions		
	6. Spurious relationships	
	7. If–then tests	
	8. Rival explanations	☺
	9. Replicating findings	
	10. Informant feedback	☺
	11. Rich/thick description	☺
	12. External audits	

☺ means that the tactic was effectively used.

construct formation and in the early stages of their data collection. Using someone, like colleagues, to check their interpretations of the data, they could potentially avoid the possibility of a number of biases, one being *holistic fallacy* previously mentioned. Early on in the project, the researchers felt some parents were disconnected to the questions being asked during the interviews and based on this *informant feedback* (#10), the researchers consulted again with colleagues and changed the questioning protocol.

The final stage for evaluating verbal data analysis is *Explanations and Conclusions* (see Table 7.1). There are seven tactics under this heading that a researcher can choose from for heightening credibility. Cardona et al. (2012) used one of these in their study: *rich/thick description* (#11). Regarding the first, although the first author maintained a research journal and used multiple sources of information including nonparticipant observations and peer debriefing, the data sources and results were discussed within the research team and not with the informants. There is no evidence that they shared their conclusions with the parent, teacher, or administrator participants or that they provided them with a copy of the final report.

Cardona et al. (2012) clearly used rich/thick descriptions in their study. This is required if the researchers hoped to back up their explanations regarding home–school relationship development within diverse families. For each of the conclusions that were made, the researchers back them up with rich and plentiful quotations from different individuals they interviewed. They also summarized some of the nonverbal behavior that was observed during the interviews. In many ways, this is similar to a lawyer arguing a case in a court of law.

Tactic #8, *rival explanations*, is one that few researchers have used but is a powerful addition to bolster the credibility of the researchers' conclusions. For Cardona et al.'s study, for example, one plausible explanation that the researchers recognize is that this was a short-term project with formal interviews taken from only nine informants recommended by the administration at three sites and therefore the findings may not be representative of a larger population. Although the informants were recommended by the administration, it could very well be that the administration may have only chosen participants that they knew would reflect the teaching staff and school site in a positive manner. Cardona et al. fails to address this issue and if they had, it may have contributed greatly to their conclusions.

The example of Cardona et al.'s study shows how the 12 tactics drawn from combining the work of Miles and Huberman (1994) and Creswell (1998) are a reasonable way to evaluate the analysis of verbal data found in the Results section of studies using qualitative approaches. As mentioned previously, not all of the tactics need to be used before the analysis is deemed credible by consumers. However, having some in each of the two categories certainly helps. Cardona et al. (2012) clearly presented credible evidence in both areas, which has definitely added to the main argument of their paper.

EXERCISE 7.1

Find a recent study of interest that used a qualitative research design that resulted in verbal data. Complete the following using these points.

1   Begin by stating what qualitative procedure was used by the researcher(s).
2   Describe the data that were the bases of any patterns or explanations.
3   Summarize any patterns/themes that the research found in the data.
4   Use Table 7.1 to describe the tactics used by the researcher to verify any proposed patterns or themes.
5   Summarize any explanations and conclusions the researcher proposed to explain the patterns/themes observed.
6   Use Table 7.1 to describe any strategies used to add credibility to any proposed explanations and conclusions made by the research.

Analysis of Numerical Data

Many researchers try to answer their research questions by first converting their ideas and constructs into some form of numerical data before analysis. The main reason is that numerical data are generally easier to work with than verbal data. Not only are there a number of statistical procedures available to quickly identify patterns and relationships in large sets of data, these procedures are also able to estimate whether the findings are greater than random chance. The purpose of this section is to introduce you to some of the most common procedures used to analyze numerical data and some of the basic concepts that underpin them.

However, before going any further, we want to address some of the reservations people have toward this topic. One word that seems to strike some trepidation in many of our students and some of our colleagues is *statistics*. Some jokingly refer to it as *sadistics*. We have the strong impression that many avoid reading the Results section of research studies because of the statistical terms that they might encounter. They see things like $p < .001$, df, Σ, r, t, and F and say to themselves "No way, it's all Greek to me!"

Typically, we find much of the reluctance toward statistics more a result of some traumatic experience people have had in their past. The result is that they have become *math-phobics* and are developing into *stat-phobics*.

We believe that there are two things that turn a lot of people off about statistics: math formulas and a lot of technical jargon. Fortunately, understanding statistical formulas is not necessary for the consumer of research. Instead, the important things to know are whether an appropriate statistical procedure was used for answering the research questions, and whether the results of the study were interpreted correctly. After reading this section, we trust that you will be able to make these decisions.

The second hurdle that people must cross when dealing with statistics is the jargon that statisticians use. This is not as easy as it should be because different terms are used for the same thing depending on the discipline in which the statistician is working—as you will see later, alpha (α) does not always mean a Cronbach α. This section will give you a good grasp of the terminology as you see these terms applied in actual research situations.

Overview of Statistics

To understand the basic concept behind statistics, we need to review the concepts of *sample* and *population* discussed in Chapter 4. Recall that the population is the entire number of people to which researchers want to generalize their conclusions. The sample is a subgroup of that total number. Statistics are quantities (or numbers) gathered on a sample. They are estimates of what would be found if the whole population were used. Quantities that are gathered directly from the entire population are referred to as *parameters*. Parameters are the *true* values. They exactly describe the population. Because we are almost always dealing with samples, we use statistics rather than parameters.

However, when statistics (i.e., estimates) are used, we have to make inferences about what exists in the population (see Figure 7.1 to illustrate this process). As with any inference, mistakes can be made. Using statistics helps us understand what chance we are taking of making a mistake when inferring from the sample to the population. (Now, if you understand what you have just read, you are well on your way to grasping a useful understanding of statistics.)

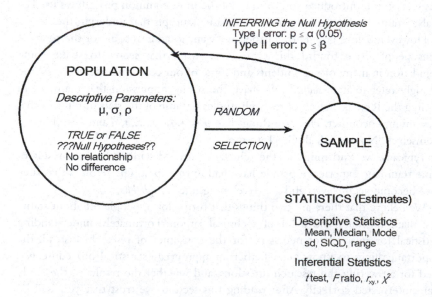

FIGURE 7.1 The Inferential Process from Sample to Population

Statistics can be divided into two main categories: *descriptive* and *inferential*. As the name implies, *descriptive statistics* are those that describe a set of data. They are the fuel used by *inferential statistics* to generate answers to research questions. Inferential statistics not only produce answers in the forms of numbers, they also provide information that determines whether researchers can generalize their findings (i.e., the descriptive statistics) to a target population.

The following subsections of this chapter expand these two general types of statistics. Obviously, they will not exhaust all that there is about these topics. In this regard, we see statistics like an onion; there are many layers. This section will only deal with the outer layers, at most. However, we have added another layer in Appendix B that takes you a little deeper into some of the more technical aspects of each of these statistical types if you want to gain some deeper insights. We also include in this appendix some more less-common procedures that you may want to continue with after mastering the following sections. The outer layers presented below give you enough information to be able to understand and evaluate the majority of the studies that you will read. When you come across something not mentioned in the following, it most likely has been treated in Appendix B.

Understanding Descriptive Statistics

There are three basic concerns that should be addressed when using descriptive statistics to describe numerical data: the shape of the distribution, measures of average, and measures of variation (see Table 7.3).

The first is regarding the shape of the data. The concern is whether the data are symmetrically distributed and approximate a normal curve.[3] The importance of knowing this directly relates to researchers' choice of the statistics used in their study, both descriptive and inferential. This is seldom mentioned in most research articles, but it is important. Suffice it to state here that if a distribution of data is severely skewed (i.e., lopsided), rectangular (i.e., no curve at all), or multimodal (i.e., more than one cluster of data; see Table 7.3), certain statistics should not be used. If you want to go to the next level of the onion on this matter, see Appendix B.

On the basis of shape of the data, the second concern is about the statistic to be used to describe *average*. There are three: mean, median, and mode (see Table 7.3). Briefly defined, the *mean* is computed by adding up all the scores

Table 7.3 Three Important Areas in Descriptive Statistics

Shape of Data	Averageness	Variance
Symmetrical	Mean............	Standard deviation
Skewness	Median.........	Interquartile range
Multimodal	Mode...........	Range

and dividing by the total number of scores. The *median* is the middle point in the distribution of data that divides the number of people in half. The *mode* is the most frequent score.

The reason there are three measures used for average is discussed more fully in Appendix B. However, for research purposes, the mean is the most common estimate of average used by researchers for numerical data. However, on the occasion that the data distribution does not approximate a normal distribution, other indicators of average more accurately represent the data distribution.

The third concern also affected by the shape of the data, is what statistic to use to indicate how much the data varies (i.e., the *variance*). There are also three different measures of variation (see Table 7.3): standard deviation, interquartile range, and range. The first, related to the mean, is the average deviation of scores from the mean. The second, related to the median, estimates where the middle 50% of the scores are located in the data distribution. The third is the distance from the lowest to the highest scores in the distribution. More detailed discussion is in Appendix B regarding how these three are used and related to one another. However, because the standard deviation (*SD*) is the one most commonly used in research, it will get more treatment in the following discussions. Similar to the use of the mean, the *SD* is only appropriate for describing data if the distribution does not vary too much from normalcy.

Understanding Inferential Statistics

We began this section on statistics with the discussion about how researchers attempt to infer their findings to a population based on a sample of participants/objects (see Figure 7.1). This process is where inferential statistics plays a crucial role. The main goal for the remainder of this chapter is to describe the various inferential statistical procedures that are commonly used, explain why they are used, and provide examples from the published research that have used these procedures. However, before going on, we must first discuss the meaning of the *null hypothesis* and *statistical significance*. In our opinion, the need for the consumer to understand these two concepts is more important than remembering the names of the statistical procedures that will be described afterward.

The Null Hypothesis

The notion of statistical significance directly relates to the testing of the null hypothesis. Therefore, we first discuss this famous hypothesis (although you may have never heard of it) that all studies test when using inferential statistics, regardless of whether they say, followed by the meaning of *statistical significance*.

In essence, inferential statistics procedures can be boiled down to answering two types of questions: *are there relationships* between variables or *are there differences* between groups of data? The null hypothesis, as the word *null* suggests, states that there is either *no* relationship or that there is *no* difference between groups. Regardless of whether there is a research hypothesis (also known as an alternative hypothesis), the null hypothesis is lurking in the background to be tested. In exploratory studies, for instance, where there are no stated hypotheses, behind every relationship being studied there lies a null hypothesis that assumes there is no relationship in the population. For every study that explores whether there is a difference between groups of people, there is a null hypothesis that assumes that there is no real difference between the groups.

Few published studies explicitly state their null hypotheses these days. Yet, whether stated or not, they are always lurking behind the scene. A good example of study where a null hypothesis was clearly stated without any stated research hypothesis is one by Young, Edwards, and Leising (2009). These researchers were interested in determining whether a math-enhanced curriculum and instructional approach would diminish students' attainment of technical skills. Young et al. used a control and treatment group design with a posttest assessment at the end of the year to compare the two groups. The researchers specifically stated their null hypothesis as they were predicting that no difference between the two groups on technical competence as measured by the posttest would occur. Using the results of their data analysis, they failed to reject their null hypothesis by finding no statistical difference between the two groups.

Now why would some one want to state their hypothesis in the null form? Why not state the hypothesis in the positive: There will be a significant difference between programs? In practice, many researchers state their hypothesis in the positive. However, it is more accurate to state the hypothesis in the negative because it is this hypothesis that inferential statistics tests, not the positively stated hypotheses. Be that as it may, the answer to our question lies in making valid logical arguments. For those who would like to understand more about the logical argument that is the bases for using the null hypothesis, go to Appendix B.

Statistical Significance

You will encounter the term *statistical significance* much more often than *null hypothesis* when reading the Results section of an article; however, the two terms are very much interrelated. When researchers refer to some result as *statistically significant*, they are referring to the *null hypothesis*, regardless of whether they are aware of it.

Statistical significance has to do with the probability of making a mistake in inferring that the results found in a sample reflect some truth about the target population (see Figure 7.1). This mistake (or error) is directly related to the null hypothesis (Figure 7.2 should help illustrate this discussion). The heading over the columns of the 2 x 2 matrix[4] is labeled, *Reality* (what is true in the population). There are only two possibilities: the null hypothesis is true (Column 1) or it is false (Column 2). That is, there is either no true relationship or difference

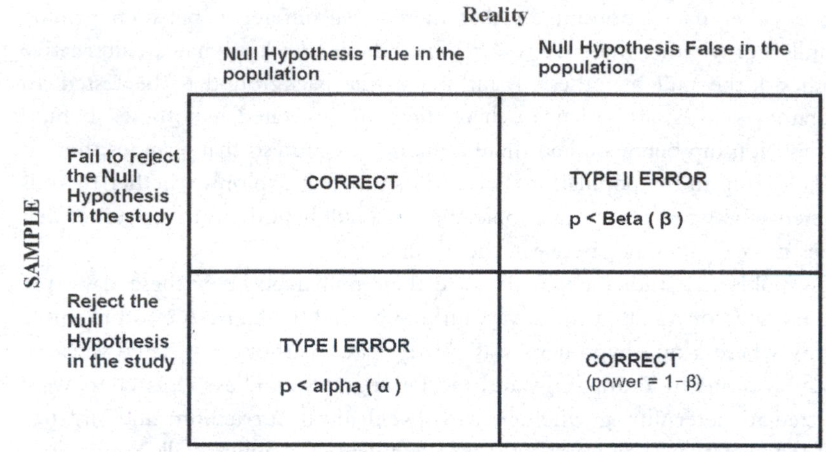

Reality

	Null Hypothesis True in the population	Null Hypothesis False in the population
Fail to reject the Null Hypothesis in the study	CORRECT	TYPE II ERROR $p <$ Beta (β)
Reject the Null Hypothesis in the study	TYPE I ERROR $p <$ alpha (α)	CORRECT (power = $1-\beta$)

SAMPLE

FIGURE 7.2 Testing the Null Hypothesis

between variables in the population (i.e., the null hypothesis is true), or there is a relationship or difference in the population (i.e., the null hypothesis is false). There is no middle ground.

However, in research using samples, it is impossible to know for sure whether the null hypothesis is true unless the research is done on the whole population. This means that the truth about the null hypothesis is inferred from the sample to the population.

The heading for the rows of the matrix in Figure 7.2 is labeled, *Sample*. Again there are only two possibilities: The results either *fail to reject* the null hypothesis or they *reject* the null hypothesis. If the results show that no relation or difference was found, then the findings fail to reject the null hypothesis (i.e., no statistical significance was found). In this case, no error was made (see Figure 7.2, Column 1, Row 1). However, if the null hypothesis is, in fact, false in the population (i.e., there is a true relationship or difference between variables), the results from the sample are misleading and an error has been made. This is known as a *Type II error* (Figure 7.2, Column 2, Row 1). That is, the results of the study failed to reveal that the null hypothesis was false in the population. Moving down to Row 2, the other possible finding from the sample is that the results reject the null hypothesis. Translated, this means that a statistically significant relationship or difference was found in the results. Yet if in the population (i.e., reality) there was no relation or difference (Column 1), then to infer from the sample to the population that the null hypothesis was false would be erroneous. This is referred to as a *Type I error*. However, if the null hypothesis was truly false in the population (Column 2), it would be correct to infer that there was probably a relationship or difference in the population based on the findings from the sample. (At this point, we suggest that you stop and meditate on all of this. Very few grasp the above in one reading.)

We are sure you did not fail to notice in Column 1/Row 2 and Column 2/ Row 1 the p < alpha $(\alpha)^5$ and p < beta (β), respectively. These have to do with the probabilities of making a Type I and a Type II error. The most common one cited in Results sections is the probability of making a Type I error ($p < \alpha$). Statistical significance is based on this estimate.

Statistical significance has been somewhat arbitrarily defined by statisticians (and probably some gamblers) as the probability of making a Type I error either equal to or less than 5% (i.e., $p \leq .05$). Translated, this means that there is a 5% chance or less that a mistake has been made when inferring that the null hypothesis (i.e., no relationship or no difference) is not true in the population (i.e., the null hypothesis is rejected). Sometimes you will see other probabilities such as p < .01 or p < .001. These of course are even smaller than p < .05, which means that the probability of making a Type I error is even less (1% or 0.1%, respectively). Bagheri and Aeen (2011) for example, found statistically significant mean differences between two groups on writing assessment at the end the treatment period at the p < .05 level. This does not mean that their findings were 95% true—a common misunderstanding of what statistical significance means. What it means is that she can have a lot of confidence that she did not make a Type I error.

Two other misconceptions are common regarding statistical significance. One is to think that because something is statistically significant, there is a strong relationship between variables or a big difference between groups. This may not, in fact, be the case. It is not uncommon to see small relationships or small differences statistically significant. The reason is that statistical significance is directly related to the size of the sample. If the sample size is fairly large, then small relationships or small differences may come out to be statistically significant. When the sample size is smaller, the same statistical value found for a relationship or a difference will not be statistically significant.

Here is where the probability of making a Type II error becomes important. When the sample size is relatively small and the results were found not to be statistically significant (i.e., the null hypothesis failed to be rejected), the probability of making a Type II error is higher than when a larger sample is used. Thus, in reality, the null hypothesis may be false (i.e., there is a relationship or difference), but due to a small sample size the results failed to reveal this. Another way to say this is that researchers might have found a statistically significant relationship or difference had they used a larger sample. For more information on the Type II error and a discussion on the related topic of *power*, go to Appendix B.

The other common misunderstanding regarding statistical significance is confusing it with *practical significance*. As mentioned above, a relationship may be weak but still statistically significant; or a difference between groups may be small but still statistically significant. Here is where we can be misled if we are not careful when reading statistics results. If a relationship is weak or a difference between groups is small, regardless of how statistically significant it is, there may be no practical use for the results. For example, who wants to spend money and time making curricular changes if students using a new method only increase by a few test points compared with those using a traditional method, although the result was statistically significant. This point is illustrated in several research studies mentioned later in the chapter. Related to this is the concept of *effect size* which many journals require when reporting statistical significance (e.g., gains in math or reading achievement). See Appendix B for more information on this.

Although the previous discussion seems to be beyond what a consumer might need to understand in a Results section, the issues discussed above are the foundation stones to build an understanding of the statistical procedures about to be outlined. However, before going on to the more interesting stuff, we suggest you do the following exercise to give yourself feedback on how well you have understood this last section. Rushing ahead without grasping what we have just read will hinder understanding the following section.

EXERCISE 7.2

Choose a study that uses numerical data.

1   Was the study looking for relationships or differences between groups?
2   Look for any mention of a null hypothesis.
3   Now examine the Results section and look for values like $p < .05$, $p < .01$.
4   How does the researcher interpret these results?
5   What is the probability of the Type I error being made in this study?
6   Explain what this means in your own words.

Inferential Statistical Procedures

There seems to be no end of all the statistical procedures that are available for analyzing numerical data. To describe them all would take several large volumes. Therefore, we have selected the most common statistical procedures that are presented in educational literature in this section. These procedures look at several more layers of the statistical onion, but there are others that lie deeper. For those who would like to go further than what is presented here, a number of issues and procedures are presented in Appendix B along with a discussion on how they are used.

At the end of this current section, the consumer should be able to understand what some common statistical procedures are used for, what their results mean, and whether they are used appropriately. There are no formulas to understand or calculate: only definitions, applications, and interpretations. Examples from research are given to show how these procedures have been applied.

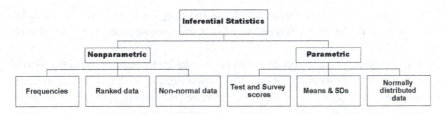

FIGURE 7.3 The Two Main Categories of Inferential Statistics With Corresponding Data Types

Inferential statistics can be divided into two general categories: *nonparametric* and *parametric* statistics (see Figure 7.3). Nonparametric statistics are used for analyzing data in the form of frequencies, ranked data,[6] and data that do not approximate a normal distribution. Parametric statistics are used for any data that do not stray too far from a normal distribution and typically involve the use of means and standard deviations, such as scores on tests and surveys.

As previously mentioned, the objectives of most researchers are to find relationships between variables or differences between groups. Under each of these objectives there are both nonparametric and parametric procedures for analyzing data.

Relationships Between Variables

Figure 7.4 summarizes some of the more frequently used procedures according to the two types of statistical procedures: nonparametric and parametric.

Nonparametric Procedures

Under the *relationships/nonparametric* heading on the left side of Figure 7.4, there are two procedures that are frequently seen in research: *chi-square* and *Spearman*

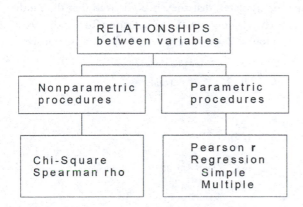

FIGURE 7.4 Statistical Procedures for Analyzing Relationships

rank correlation (rho). There are several others, but they are less commonly used. All of them have to do with assessing whether a relationship exists between at least two variables.

The Pearson *chi-square* (pronounced Ky-square and portrayed with the Greek symbol χ^2) is the procedure of preference when dealing with data in the form of frequencies (or relative frequencies in the form of percentages). In its simplest form, the chi-square procedure compares the observed frequency (or percentages) of different levels of a variable with what would be expected if no relationship existed (i.e., the null hypothesis).

For example, if researchers ask the question "Is there a relationship between gender and success in learning math?" they would compare a random sample of males and females on their success rate. Figure 7.5 illustrates what the data might look like if there were 40 females and 40 males sampled. Note that the null hypothesis would predict that there would be no difference between the number of males and females who pass or fail. If this was true, then the expected frequency should be 20/20 for each sex, which is indicated by the numbers in parentheses. However, in our fictional data the researcher found that 27 females versus 17 males passed as opposed to 13 females versus 23 males failed. Can researchers conclude that there is a relationship? Although the frequencies appear to differ, do they differ from what would be expected if the null hypothesis were true? Rather than rely on an *eyeball* analysis, researchers could do a chi-square analysis. Out of curiosity, we did an analysis on this data and obtained a chi-square value 5.05 which is statistically significant at $p < .03$. The null hypothesis is rejected with a 3% probability of making a Type I error. Researchers can therefore conclude that there is most probably a relationship between gender and success rate at learning math.

To illustrate, Bornsheuer, Polonyi, Andrews, Fore, and Onwuegbuzie (2011) were concerned with exploring the relationship between ninth grade retention and on-time graduation in a southeast Texas high school. For this study, on-time graduation was defined as completion of high school within 4 years after entering as a freshman. The researchers specifically stated that they hypothesized that the ninth grade retention would be negatively related to on-time graduation. To test this, they performed a 2 (ninth grade retention) × 2 (on-time graduation) chi-square analysis

	Passed	Failed	Total
Males	17 (20)	23 (20)	40
Females	27 (20)	13 (20)	40

FIGURE 7.5 Comparison of Males Versus Females Who Passed and Failed in Frequencies

where they compared the percentages of students retained and those who graduated in 4 years. This resulted in a chi-square value of 447.64, statistically significant at $p < .0001$. Simply stated, the researchers determined that students who were retained in the ninth grade were more than six times less likely to graduate on time in 4 years than students who were not retained. In this case the null hypothesis was rejected, giving support to the researchers' hypothesis that there is most probably a relationship.

The second method for examining relationships under nonparametric statistics is computing a *Spearman rank-order* correlation coefficient, also known as the Spearman *rho* correlation coefficient. This procedure analyzes data in the form of ranks, and the correlation coefficient is symbolized by either r or the Greek symbol ρ_{rank} (rho). This coefficient ranges from $\rho_{rank} = -1.0$ to $+1.0$. The first value (-1.0) means that there is a perfect negative relationship: as ranking of one variable goes up, the other goes down in perfect order. The value of $+1.0$ is a perfect positive relationship where rankings of both variables correspond perfectly in the same direction. A coefficient of 0.00 means that there is no relationship. As a coefficient increases between 0.00 and 1.00, in spite of whether $+$ or $-$ is in front of it, the relationship between the two variables increases—the $+$ increases in a positive direction, and the $-$ increases in a negative direction.

A very practical example of using Spearman's rho procedure comes from the work of Bonner (2009). The biology department at a university in Maryland had become concerned that students were entering into the biology major without adequate academic preparation. The researcher analyzed data from the past five cohorts of biology majors, and using Spearman's rho procedure determined that there was a significant correlation between their success in the introductory course in their major and their math SAT score (Spearman's rho $= .58, p < .001$). The researcher was confident enough in her findings to encourage the university to develop a required preparatory course for students whose Math Scholastic Aptitude Test (MSAT) score was below a prescribed cutoff value.

Based on what was stated previously about statistical significance, this correlation was significant even though Bonner used a fairly small sample ($N = 71$). Large samples can produce statistically significant correlation coefficients even though small, whereas small samples require a larger correlation coefficient to be considered significant. Therefore, considering the size of the sample and the resulting correlation always becomes an important consideration for a consumer of research. More will be stated about this under parametric procedures.

There are other nonparametric measures of relationships that you will occasionally see in research such as the Cohen's Kappa, phi-coefficient, Cramer's *V*, Somer's *d*, and so on (see Appendix B for more information). To give proper treatment to all of these procedures it would require a separate book; however, if you are interested in knowing more about these other procedures, search your favorite web browser by entering *nonparametric statistics*, or enter the specific name of the procedure you are interested in.

Before moving to parametric procedures for relationships, look at a study related to your interest that has used some form of nonparametric statistic to examine a relationship. The following exercise gives you steps to follow to guide you in this task. Enjoy!!

EXERCISE 7.3

Find a study that looked for a relationship between two or more variables using either chi-square or the Spearman rho in its statistical analysis.

1 What form are the data in (frequencies, percentages, ranks)?
2 What is the null hypothesis being tested (explicit or implicit)?
3 Are the results statistically significant? At what level? What does this mean regarding making inferences?

Parametric Procedures

One of the most common statistics used to examine relationships (see Figure 7.4) between variables is the *Pearson product-moment correlation* (PPMC) *coefficient*. With a name like this, it is no wonder people do not like to look at statistics. It is more commonly referred to the Pearson r after Karl Pearson. You will also see it reported simply as r or r_{xy}. This coefficient, like the Spearman rho, is computed on two variables for every participant, such as measures of numerical ability and verbal ability. The end product is an r that ranges from -1.00 to +1.00, indicating a perfect negative or perfect positive relationship, respectively. As with all coefficients of correlation a .00 means no relationship. The null hypothesis states that the relationship is .00 in the population.

A study done by Gregory, Cornell, and Fan (2011) examined the relationship between structure and support in the high school climate and suspension rates of ninth-grade students. Among other statistical procedures they also obtained PPMC coefficients to test multiple relationships. The researchers correlated measures of high schools with authoritative structures and other variables like the percentage of students on free and reduced lunch, the percentage of Black and White students and their suspension rates, and students' experiences of several authoritative school attributes. They found statistically significant correlations for a number of comparisons. For instance, one result showed that correlations among the suspension rates show that schools with high rates of Black students were more likely to have high rates of White student suspension, $r = .76$ ($p < .001$) indicating statistical significance. Note that $r < .76$ is positive and more than half way between .00 and 1.00. This should be interpreted as fairly strong positive relationship, suggesting that there is a relationship between White and Black student suspensions based on the school structure and support.

Using the above results, we want to illustrate two misapplications of the correlation coefficient that occasionally appear in the literature (see Chapter 5)—correlation means causation and improper application. To think that correlations can be interpreted to mean causation would be crazy enough to think that Gregory et al. findings support that Black student suspensions cause (i.e., influences, increases, changes, etc.) White student suspensions. This should illustrate the erroneous application of a simple correlational coefficient.

Another thing to keep in mind is that correlations are bidirectional (i.e., symmetrical), which means that both of the following statements are correct: A correlates with B, and B correlates with A. In other words, to show a causal relationship, they would have had to use an experimental design that could perhaps compare both Black and White student suspension rates and the potential causes of these outcomes, in this case, perhaps school climate, using a control and treatment group design. At most, a correlational analysis can see if there is a potential causal relationship, before going to the more arduous task of doing a full blown experiment. If there is no statistically significant correlation, a causal relationship can be ruled out right from the start.

The second important misuse of the correlation coefficient is assuming that, because a correlation coefficient is statistically significant, it has important practical use. Gregory et al. (2011) found another correlation of $r = .18$ between the Black student–White student suspension gap and the percentage of White student suspensions significant at the $p < .05$ level. Even though statistically significant, is a correlation of .18 of any practical use? The answer is made clear when you square the correlation coefficient. This is signified by r^2 and is a measure of the *percentage of common variance* between the two variables. Another way to say this is that r^2 represents the amount of variation the two variables have in common. This value is commonly used to determine the importance of the relationship. We can see clearly in this case that $r = .18$ becomes $r^2 = .03$, or that the two variables only have 3% in common—not much to warrant any practical significance. However, Gregory et al. (2011) found another significant correlation (i.e., $r = .47$) between supportive climate and experience of school rules that shows a little more potential for practical use. The $r^2 = .22$ indicates 22% common variance.

The issue of amount of common variance is important, because some people may try to push their own agenda based on statistically significant correlations which are not strong enough to justify an agenda that cost time and money to implement—Gregory et al. did not do this, by the way. Therefore, when you want to make your own evaluation of the strength of a correlation coefficient, simply square the correlation and interpret the result as the strength of the relationship.

The next common parametric statistical procedure used to explore relationships is *regression analysis*. This is highly related to the Pearson r coefficient and r^2. Regression analysis is used to identify variables (referred to as *independent variables*,

IVs) that either predict or explain another variable (the *dependent variable*, DV). There are two forms of regression analysis: *simple* and *multiple*. In its *simple* form, there is only one IV and one DV. The independent variable is the predictor or the variable that explains, and the DV is the variable being predicted or explained. For example, if we want to find out whether we can predict success in university for foreign students defined by their GPA with their Test of English as a Foreign Language (TOEFL) results, we would use a simple regression procedure. The TOEFL score would be the IV (i.e., the predictor) and student GPA after the first semester or year at university would be the DV.

On the other hand, we might want to know how much students scores on an essay exam (i.e., the DV) can be explained by their grammar ability (i.e., the IV). The first addresses a prediction question, the second an explanation question. It is important to note here that in neither case are we suggesting that the IVs are causing the variation in the DV.

In its *multiple* form, regression analysis is used to determine which combination of independent variables best predicts or explains the variation in one dependent variable. For instance, we might want to know what combination of independent variables such as academic aptitude, motivation, high school GPA, and so forth, best predicts or explains success in university. The multiple regression procedure will be the correct procedure.

The key statistic for regression analysis is R^2. It means the same thing as the Pearson r^2 mentioned previously. In fact, the $R^2 = r^2$ when there is only one predictor variable. The R^2 is the percentage of variance of the DV that is related to one or more predictor variables (IVs) and ranges from 0% to 100%. The first thing that is tested for statistical significance is the R^2. If it is found to be statistically significant, the null hypothesis (i.e., no variance can be predicted or explained by the IVs) is rejected. When this happens, each predictor variable (IV) in the equation is tested individually for statistical significance to see if it contributes to the overall prediction (or explanation) of the DV.

An interesting study using multiple regression by Onwuegbuzie, Bailey, and Daley (2000) illustrated this method. The purpose of their study was to test a number of hypotheses regarding the best combination of variables (IVs) that might predict foreign language achievement (DV) among university students. They included six batteries of instruments that measured various components of cognitive, affective, personality, and demographic factors, totaling 18 independent variables. As for their dependent variable, foreign-language achievement in four different foreign languages, they used adjusted average grades for their university language courses. As a side note, the researchers pointed out an important principle regarding the number of independent variables one should use in multiple regression. If the ratio of participants to independent variables is too small the resulting statistics will be unstable. Their ratio was 10 participants to each independent variable, which is more than necessary. Onwuegbuzie et al. used a multiple regression procedure to examine all possible subsets of variables to determine which combination best predicts language achievement. For each combination, an R^2 was calculated and tested for statistical significance. Onwuegbuzie et al. found that a combination of two cognitive, one affective, one personality, and one demographic variable resulted in an R^2 of .34, $p < .001$. That is, 34% of the variance of language achievement was predicted by this combination of variables. This is a moderate R^2 in magnitude. Realize that only 34% of the variance of foreign-language achievement was accounted for. However, for prediction purposes, this is better than random guessing.

There are more complex methods using correlational procedures for dealing with more specialized questions that we will not cover here. So when you come across terms like *factor analysis, discrimination analysis, latent trait analysis, structural equation modeling*, and so on, remember that these involve correlating variables with other variables for the purpose of identifying which variables share common variance. Not only that, but the last procedure listed is actually used to determine cause-and-effect relationships! You might think we just contradicted ourselves after all that ranting and raving about correlation not meaning causation. Not really. When this procedure is used to determine cause-and-effect relationships, it is guided by specific hypotheses that instruct the researcher where to place each variable in the equation to manipulate all the variances. If we go any further than this, you might close the book and run, so we will move on.

EXERCISE 7.4

Find a study that looks for relationships between variables using either the Pearson *r* or one of the two regression procedures.

1   What are the variables? (In the case of regression, what are the IVs and the DV?)
2   Describe the data used in the analysis.
3   What is the null hypothesis being tested (explicit or implicit)?
4   Are the results statistically significant? At what level? What does this mean regarding making inferences?

Differences Between Groups of Data

The second type of research objective is to find whether groups of individuals differ from one another. As with relationships, there are both nonparametric and parametric procedures used to analyze these differences (see Figure 7.6).

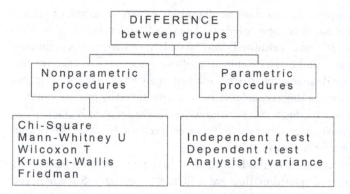

FIGURE 7.6   Statistical Procedures for Analyzing Differences Between Groups

Nonparametric Procedures

Chi-square analysis is also used for finding differences between groups. It is used when data is in the form of frequencies (or relative frequencies in the form of percentages). Koyoma, Plash, and Davis's (2012) study for example was concerned with a cross-cultural comparison of multicultural self-awareness among K-12 in-service school teachers. The researchers wanted to explore the self-awareness among 134 teacher participants using the Cultural Diversity Awareness Inventory (CDAI) and compare the results to a previous study by Yeung (2006) who used Chinese participants. By doing this, it allowed the researchers to compare Eastern and Western perspectives. The data consisted partly of 27 opinion statements using a 5-point Likert scale categorized into five areas: (1) general cultural awareness, (2) culturally diverse family, (3) cross-cultural communications, (4) assessment, and (5) creating a multicultural environment using multicultural methods and materials. A chi-square analysis for each of the five areas was then computed to compare the Eastern and Western participants' responses. Three of the five chi-square values (χ^2) were statistically significant at the $p < .05$, level, providing evidence that there was a difference. Koyoma et al. did not adjust the probability level for committing a Type I error due to the multiple comparisons.

By adjusting for the Type I error, we mean that for each comparison (i.e., χ^2 computed) there is a 5% probability of making a Type I error ($p < .05$). When multiple comparisons are made with the same level of 5% for each comparison, the probability of making a Type I error increases. For 10 comparisons, for instance, the overall probability increases to 40% (put "familywise error rates" into Google search for more information). Koyoma et al. reported the probability level for each of the five chi-squares that were computed. The researchers helped to limit the overall probability of making a Type I error to a much lower level, in some cases $p < .001$, for each comparison by reporting these as separate results.

When the data are other than frequencies and do not approximate a normal distribution, the difference between two independent samples[7] of participants on some dependent variable is typically analyzed using the *Mann–Whitney U test*. This procedure converts the data into ranks within each group for analysis. There are no means or SDs involved. The statistic computed is a U value, which, if statistically significant at the $p < .05$ level, means that the difference between the two groups is statistically significant.

A study done by Kennedy, Russom, and Kevorkian (2012) illustrates the use of Mann–Whitney. They investigated teachers' and administrators' perceptions of bulling in schools and compared these two groups. The researchers recognized that their data were ordinal in nature and were not normally distributed; therefore, they used nonparametric statistical procedures (the Mann–Whitney) to test for differences between the two groups. They found in their results that for the Bullying Perception Survey (BPS-10), the perceptions of teachers and administrators were significantly different regarding their role in bullying prevention ($p < .02$). Teachers felt more strongly that educators played an important role in bullying prevention; however, administrators felt more comfortable communicating with the parents of bullying victims. Teachers were also significantly more likely than administrators to perceive a need for increased bullying prevention training.

When two sets of data are not independent, the *Wilcoxon matched-pairs signed rank test* (also known as the *Wilcoxon T test*) is used to test for differences. This means that the two sets of data are *dependent* or *correlated* with one another in some way. This can occur in two different situations. The first is when the two sets of data are gathered from the same group of participants. The second occurs when two different groups of participants are compared on one variable while matched on some other variable. The first situation can occur, for instance, when data are gathered on a pretest before some treatment is given and compared with data from a similar measurement after the treatment on a posttest. Both measurements are made on the same participants. The second situation could occur when the researcher tries to control for (or eliminate) the effects of an extraneous variable, such as intelligence, on the dependent variable by pairing up participants from the two groups based on that extraneous variable.

An example of the first situation is found in Ray and Coulter's (2010) study that examined preservice teachers' perceptions of the value of using digital minigames in middle school social studies classrooms. The dependent variable was a pre- and posttest measure of the perceptions of the use of digital games developed by the researchers. They tested the participants once before the use of digital gaming in the course, and once near the end to see if there was any positive gain in perceptions of the value of using digital games as a pedagogy of instruction. Therefore, they had two measures on each participant. The researchers stated that they used the Wilcoxon matched-pairs procedure test to examine the change in perception from the pre- and posttest assessment. Given the small sample of participants ($N = 18$) and the use of a Likert scale for the assessment, the data would not fit the assumptions of normalcy required for a parametric procedure. Ray and Coulter reported that there was a statistically significant increase from the pretest to the posttest ($T = 5.5, p < .01$) in positive perceptions of the preservice teachers after they experienced the use of minigames.

An example for the second situation occurs when researchers want to control for (i.e., eliminate) the effects of an extraneous variable while testing for differences between two groups. They would do this by using the Wilcoxon procedure on the dependent variable by *matching* participants in pairs from the two groups based on the extraneous variable. For this reason, the Wilcoxon procedure is sometimes referred to as the *Wilcoxon matched-pairs signed-rank test.*

However, a quick hypothetical example of using the matching procedure would be to measure attitudes of two different groups of participants (Treatment vs. Control) toward learning a second language. However, we might want to make sure that our results are not due to differences in language proficiency between the two groups. Thus, we match participants before we begin the treatment by finding two participants with the same language proficiency, however measured, and put one participant into the treatment group and the other in the control group. We do this for the rest of the participants, producing matched pairs. Now we apply the treatment and compare the two groups on a measure of attitude. When using the Wilcoxon method, we would measure the difference in attitude for each matched-pair of participants and then compute the Wilcoxon statistic based on those differences.

What happens if a researcher wants to compare more than two sets of data that do not fit the normalcy criterion? The *Kruskal–Wallis test* is typically used for this purpose. This method is an extension of the Mann–Whitney test; however, it compares more than two independent groups of participants using the same procedure of ranking data prior to analysis. The study by Yu and Kim (2010) used the Kruskal–Wallis for testing the differences in interactions and behaviors of teachers and students between three groups all at once: elementary school physical education classes, middle school physical education classes, and high school physical education classes. Since 11 schools from five different school districts in Seoul, South Korea were randomly selected to gather data from, we assume that the researchers did not feel the data fit the assumption of normalcy. However, all the Kruskal–Wallis method does when statistical significance is found is to show that somewhere between the groups there is a difference. So when Yu and Kim found a significant Kruskal–Wallis (usually signified with H or put into a χ^2 format), they had to use the Mann–Whitney test to look at the difference between each pair of groups (e.g., elementary vs. middle school, middle school vs. high school, and elementary vs. high school). The reason they used the Kruskal–Wallis first, rather than going straight to making pairwise comparisons with the Mann–Whitney, was to control for the Type I error when making multiple comparisons. For each statistical test there is the probability of making a Type I error. So if one uses the shot-gun approach of making all possible pairwise comparisons, the probability of making a Type I error increases rapidly. Yu and Kim avoided this problem by following the procedure they used.

There is also a nonparametric procedure for testing the difference between three or more sets of dependent data. The *Friedman test* does exactly this. It is very similar to the Wilcoxon T test, in that it tests the differences between different measures on the same set of participants, referred to as *repeated measures* or a *nested design* (see Appendix B).

An example of a study using this procedure was done by Al-Seghayer (2001), who investigated the effects of three annotation modalities for presenting glosses on vocabulary acquisition via the computer. Although he clearly hypothesized that the video mode would be superior to the two others (i.e., text only and text with pictures), he also explicitly stated that the null hypothesis of no difference was what was being statistically tested. All of the participants received all three conditions in the study and three measures of vocabulary acquisition were made, making it a *repeated measures* design (i.e., the variable of modality of presentation was *nested* within the participants). He also clearly stated that he used the Friedman test because his data did not meet the normalcy assumption and that the data were ordinal (i.e., ranked data) in nature. Al-Seghayer found a statistically significant difference (Friedman $\chi^2 = 28.88$, $p < .001$). However, similar to the Kruskal–Wallis test, finding a significant difference only indicated that somewhere there was a difference between data sets. Al-Seghayer followed up this finding with several pairwise comparisons using the Wilcoxon T test, comparing each modality against the other on measures of vocabulary acquisition. He was also careful to adjust the probability level for making a Type I error due to making multiple comparisons to $p < .017$ for each comparison—an issue which we discussed previously.

There is a lot more that could be included about nonparametric statistics. In fact, there are entire books that only address nonparametric statistics. However, we have introduced you to some commonly used procedures that you will come across in the research. If there are others you see and want to know more about what they do, you can find needed information by searching the web. Before moving on to parametric statistics, the following exercise provides you with an opportunity to find a study of your own to apply what you have read.

EXERCISE 7.5

Find a study that looked for differences between groups of data that uses one of the nonparametric procedures discussed above.

1   Describe the data and any reasons why the researcher used the procedure.
2   What are the independent and dependent variables?
3   What is the null hypothesis being tested (explicit or implicit)?
4   What statistical procedure is used?
5   Are the results statistically significant? At what level? What does this mean regarding making inferences?

Parametric Statistics

When the assumptions regarding the data distribution are met (i.e., the distributions of data do not depart too much from normalcy or the variation in each set of data [i.e., SDs] does not differ too much from one another), parametric procedures can be used to analyze differences between groups. The statistical procedures discussed below are almost a mirror image of the ones discussed under the above nonparametric section. One difference is in the type of data that is analyzed, and another is that means and SDs are being compared.

The parametric equivalent to the Mann–Whitney and the Wilcoxon T tests is the t test. It is used to test the difference between two sets of measures on one dependent variable. (Just think of the song *Tea for Two* to help remember this.) Corresponding to the two nonparametric procedures above, the t test comes in two forms: *independent* and *dependent*.

The independent t test analyzes the difference between the averages (i.e., means) on one dependent variable for two independent groups. This is similar to the Mann–Whitney test on the nonparametric side, except that the t test deals with means and variances, not rankings. The two independent groups usually represent two levels of one independent variable, such as male and female for the variable of gender; and the measure used for comparison represents one dependent variable such as the scores on a single reading test.

As a part of the initial analysis, Gurbuz, Catlioglu, Birgin, and Erdem (2010) provide an example of this procedure when they investigated fifth grade students' conceptual development of probability through activity-based instruction. They used a pretest/ posttest, control and treatment group design with type of instruction as their independent variable. The treatment was *activity-based instruction* and the control group received traditional teacher-led instruction. The dependent variable, *conceptual knowledge of probability*, was measured by the Conceptual Development Test (CDT) which included three components, sample space (SS), probability of an event (PE), and probability comparisons (PC). This resulted in three different measures of their one dependent variable. Independent t tests were used to compare the control and treatment groups prior to the treatments. The t test pretest results on all three components of the CDT were found to be not statistically significant different ($p > .05$), suggesting that all groups were at the same level prior to the implementation the treatments. From here, the researchers continued on with their analysis with another procedure to determine the impact the instructional treatments on the posttest scores for both groups.

A side note regarding the difference in the size of the SDs between the two groups at the pretest phase. Besides the criterion of normalcy of the data distribution, another criterion for using parametric statistics is that the variances are similar (i.e., homogeneity of variance). If you square the SD you have a measure of variance; and in the above case, these groups look fairly homogeneous. If their data had violated the assumption of homogeneity of variance then they would have most probably used the nonparametric Mann–Whitney test, which would have been a better way to go.

The *dependent t test* (also known as, *correlated t test* or *paired t test*) assesses the difference between the means of two sets of scores for either the same group of participants or two groups whose participants have been matched in some way (cf. Wilcoxon *T* test). An example of the first scenario would be when one group of participants have been given a pretest, followed by a treatment, and then given a posttest. The difference between the means of the two tests was tested using this procedure.

The second scenario would occur if two groups (e.g., males vs. females) were being tested on reading achievement, but the participants were matched on some other variable such as intelligence. That is, one male is matched with a female based on an intelligence test and then placed in their corresponding group. By doing this, the researcher eliminates any difference between the two groups due to intelligence. The means for the two groups are then analyzed for difference by the dependent *t* test. It is comparable with the Wilcoxon test discussed in the nonparametric section, except that means and variances are used.

Tseng, Chang, Lou, and Chen (2013) explored students' attitudes toward four disciplines of science, technology, engineering, and mathematics (STEM) before and after they were exposed to a project-based learning activity (PjBL). The participants were 30 college freshmen and all of them were exposed to the treatment, in this case, a PjBL. They used one-sample *t* tests (or dependent *t* tests) to compare the participants' responses on a pretest, followed by the PjBL activity, and then a posttest questionnaire to determine whether PjBL had any significant effect on the participants' attitudes about STEM subjects. The researchers completed five dependent *t* tests, one for each of the discipline areas and one for the four disciplines combined. Tseng et al.'s results showed that student attitudes toward all four STEM disciplines combined were greater after the PjBL activity and so were their attitudes toward the individual modules.

Before moving on to a more complex procedure, use the following exercise to help you apply what you have just read.

EXERCISE 7.6

Find a study that looked for differences between two data sets that used some form of the parametric *t* test.

1   What are the independent and dependent variables?
2   What form are the data in?
3   What is the null hypothesis being tested (explicit or implicit)?
4   What statistical procedures are used (dependent or independent *t* tests)?
5   Are the results statistically significant? At what level? What does this mean regarding making inferences?

The statistic that is commonly used in the research literature is *analysis of variance* (ANOVA). As is the Kruskal–Wallis and the Friedman test are to the Mann–Whitney and the Wilcoxon *T* tests, respectively, the ANOVA is to the independent and dependent *t* tests. The *t* test compares two sets of data, whereas ANOVA is used to compare more than two sets.

The simplest form of ANOVA involves the use of one independent variable and one dependent variable. This is referred to as a *one-way ANOVA*. The IV may have three or more levels with one DV. The objective is to find whether the means for the groups on the dependent variable differ from one another. For instance, say researchers want to study whether there is any difference on reading proficiency (DV) based on social economic status (SES). They would take equal random samples from three or more SES groups, obtain measures of reading ability, and perform a one-way ANOVA. In effect, the researcher would be comparing the means of the groups with one another. The statistic reported is the *F ratio* which is determined to be statistically significant by the same criterion for all inferential statistics ($p \le .05$).

If the *F* ratio in the above example is statistically significant, it only indicates that somewhere there is at least one difference between the group means that is statistically significant. It does not identify where the differences are. The researcher must now find out where those differences are by performing pairwise comparisons (also known as, *post hoc comparisons*). Two of the most common that are used in the literature are the Tukey's honestly significant difference (HSD) and Newman–Keuls[8] (sounds like a brand of cigarettes) tests. You can think of these tests like you would a series of *t* tests, only they are more stringent regarding making a Type I error for multiple comparisons. There is another procedure used if the researcher wants to combine several groups to compare with one other or with another combination of groups called the *Scheffé's* test.

By now you should realize why we would not simply do a whole bunch of *t* tests. The reason is that the probability of making a Type I error increases with the number of statistical tests. If we do a lot of *t* tests at the $p < .05$ level, we multiply this probability by the number of tests made, as mentioned previously in several places. The ANOVA approach, along with subsequent pairwise procedures, control for this by keeping the overall probability of a Type I error at the 5% level or less. (There is a repeated measures ANOVA [cf. Friedman test], that is discussed in Appendix B.)

A good illustration of the use of a one-way ANOVA is a study by Bang and Luft (2013) who investigated secondary science teachers' use of technology in the classroom during their first 5 years of teaching. The study used 60 females and 35 males beginning secondary science teachers from five states and followed them for 5 years. Each of the participants was involved in one of four types of mentoring induction programs. The data was collected in two forms, interviews with the participants about their practice and observations of that practice. For the classroom observations, the researchers coded the classroom instruction in

5-min increments following the Collaboratives for Excellence in Teacher Preparation protocol. Four types of technology use were also investigated (e.g., the use of PowerPoint). The researchers performed four types of statistical tests including a one-way ANOVA to test for differences in technology use between induction groups, the extent a teacher taught in-field/out-field, the SES of the schools in which the teacher taught, and gender. To summarize some of their findings, the results indicated that the type of induction group had a significant impact on the dependent variable of software use (F [3,91] = 7.78, p < .001). Post hoc comparisons showed that the intern induction group used software over the 5 years of the study significantly less when compared with the other induction groups. The researchers also found a significant difference between male and female beginning science teachers in their uses of technology. Means' comparisons showed that male science teachers used PowerPoint and software significantly more than female science teachers, $F(1,51.475) = 5.40, p < .05$, and $F(1,94) = 4.57, p < .05$, respectively. In summary, the researchers concluded from their findings that gender and SES were significant factors that either facilitated or inhibited the use of technology specifically PowerPoint and software use.

A slightly more complicated form of ANOVA is the *two-way* ANOVA. This approach is used when a researcher wants to look at the effects of two independent variables on one dependent variable at the same time. Each of the independent variables can have two or more levels. For example, the first independent variable might be nationality with four levels: French, Egyptian, Chinese, and Russian. The second independent variable might have two levels, such as gender (male and female). If this study was found in the literature, the analysis would be referred to as a 4 × 2 ANOVA, meaning that it has two independent variables with the first having four levels and the second having two levels. The DV might be reading ability.

The order of the independent variables is not important, although in the above study nationality would come first and gender second. They can be switched around. In our example, we might have a 2 × 4 ANOVA (gender by nationality) rather than a nationality (4) by gender (2) ANOVA. However, with any type of ANOVA, you can always assume that there is only one dependent variable (also referred to as *univariate*).

When a two-way ANOVA is performed on the data, there are three things that are being tested. The first is the main effect for the first IV. The second is the main effect for the second IV. The third is the *interaction* between the two IVs. *Main effect* can be translated into the question, Are there any differences between the levels of an independent variable taken one at a time, ignoring all else? In effect, it is like doing a one-way ANOVA on each independent variable. In our example above, the main effect for the IV, nationality, would test whether there are any differences on the dependent variable (e.g., test scores for reading ability) between the four nationalities. If there are, and there are more than two levels of the IV, some form of post hoc pairwise comparison would need to be made to find out exactly where the differences lie. For each main effect, there will be a separate F ratio and $p < \alpha$ for statistical significance.

The third thing to be tested is whether there is any *interaction* between the two IVs. The interaction can be more informative than the main effects, although often they are treated as secondary. The interaction informs us whether the dependent variable behaves differently at the different meeting points of the two IVs. Again using our nationality by gender example, it would be more informative to know whether males and females of one nationality perform differently on reading ability tests than males and females do of other nationalities. A statistically significant interaction would suggest that they do. Figure 7.7 contains two graphs (a and b) that illustrate this. Figure 7.7(a) shows what data might look like when there are two main effects but no interaction, and Figure 7.7(b) shows what a significant interaction might look like. In the top graph there is a significant main effect for gender, but no significant interaction

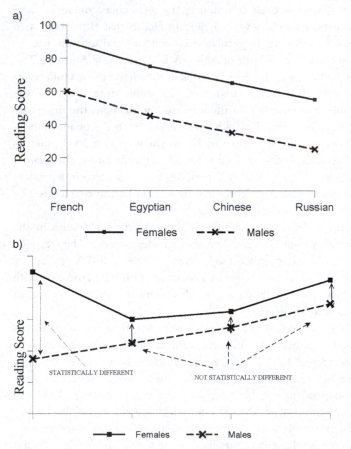

FIGURE 7.7 (a) Illustration of a Main Effect Between Gender and Nationality With no Interaction. (b) A Two-Way Interaction Between Gender and Nationality

between gender and nationality. Note that the females outperform the males for all the four nationality groups by about the same difference. This graph shows that there is probably a statistically significant main effect for nationality as well. The French, in general, performed higher than the Russians and possibly higher than the Chinese.

In contrast, the lower graph illustrates what a significant interaction might look like. Observe that females outperformed males in the French group but not in the other nationalities, although they were still slightly superior. For illustration sake, we have added information in the graph that would not normally appear in such a graph in a published article. A significant interaction would be determined by an F ratio for the interaction effect $p < .05$. But this F ratio does not tell the researcher where the difference lies. To find this out, the researcher would have to compare the difference between female and male means for each nationality using some form of post hoc comparison. As you can see, finding this differential effect would be more informative then simply knowing that nationalities or gender differ on reading ability as a whole.

Gkouvatzi, Mantis, and Kambas (2010) provide a good example of the use of a two-way ANOVA when they pursued a comparative study of motor performance of deaf and hard of hearing students in reaction time, visual-motor control and upper limb speed and dexterity ability. They used an experimental design and performed three separate 2 × 4 ANOVAs with two independent variables Level of Disability (LD) and Age. The variable LD had two levels (deaf and hard-of-hearing) and the variable Age had four age groups: 7–8, 9–10, 11–12, 13–14 years. The dependent variables were three subscales (reaction time, visual-motor control, and upper limb speed and dexterity ability) as defined in the Bruininks–Oseretsky Test of Motor Proficiency (BOT).

On the basis of the previous discussion, we would expect three things to be tested: main effect for LD (deaf vs. hard-of-hearing), a main effect for Age, and a test for the interaction between the LD × Age on each of the subscales. The researchers did not find any main effect for LD for any of the subscales. Age was found to be significantly different for visual-motor control and upper limb speed and dexterity. They found a statistically significant interaction between LD and Age for visual-motor control which illustrates the importance of interactions. Using the Scheffé's multiple comparison post hoc procedure, they found that two of the older groups of the hard of hearing participants scored higher than the lowest age group. This information is more informative than just the main effect for Age.

There are many more permutations of ANOVA that will not be discussed here. However, in Appendix B some other more complex designs that can be found in research are presented. If you come across the terms three-way or four-way ANOVA, ANCOVA, MANOVA, or MANCOVA, look in Appendix B for brief explanations with some examples. However, before moving on to the last chapter, do the following exercise. In our opinion, there is nothing better than to find a study of one's own interest to see how these procedures work.

EXERCISE 7.7

Find a study that looks for differences between different levels of independent variables, using either a one-way or two-way ANOVA.

1   Identify the independent variable(s). How many levels are in each IV? Identify the dependent variable.
2   Describe the nature of the data that is used.
3   What is the null hypothesis being tested (explicit or implicit)?
4   What statistical procedure(s) is used (one-way ANOVA, two-way ANOVA)?
5   Are the results statistically significant? At what level? What does this mean regarding making inferences?

We trust that you have been able to follow through this chapter and feel more confident that you can read through the Results section of a study with some understanding as to what is happening. We promise that as you continue to do so, the information discussed here will become clearer. We have not covered everything there is to cover. To do so would require at least one book by itself, and there are plenty on the market. However, we believe you have enough information in this chapter to handle at least 80% of what you will see in the studies you will come across. Now, on to the last piece of the typical research study—the Discussion and Conclusions section.

Key Terms and Concepts

Analysis Verbal Data
external audits
if-then tests
information feedback
negative evidence
outliers & extreme cases
peer review
replicating findings
rich/thick description
rival explanations
spurious relationships
surprises
triangulation

Analysis of Numerical Data
analysis of variance (ANOVA)
average
Chi-square
dependent t tests
descriptive statistics
F ratio
Friedman test
homogeneity of variance
independent t test
inferential statistics
interquartile range
Kruskal-Wallis test
Mann–Whitney U test
mean
median
mode
multiple regression
nonparametric statistical procedures
normal distribution null hypothesis
one-way ANOVA
pair-wise comparisons

parameters
Pearson product moment correlation
practical significance
range
regression analysis
skewed distribution
Spearman rank correlation (rho)
standard deviation

statistical significance
two-way ANOVA
Wilcoxon matched-pairs signed rank test
Wilcoxon *T* test

Additional Recommended Reading

Gonick, L., & Smith, W. (1993). *Cartoon guide to statistics*. New York: Harper Perennial Edition.
Huff, D., & Geis, I. (1993). *How to lie with statistics*. New York: W.W. Norton.
Jaisingh, L. J. (2000). *Statistics for the utterly confused*. New York: McGraw-Hill.
Rumsey, D. (2003). *Statistics for dummies*. New York: Wiley.
Weitzman, E. A, & Miles, M. B. (1995). *Computer programs for qualitative data analysis: A software sourcebook*. Thousand Oaks, CA: Sage.

Notes

1 See Miles and Huberman (1994, chap. 3) for further discussion.
2 Miles and Huberman originally treated outliers and extreme cases as separate tactics. However, because they stated that the latter was a type of the former, we combined them into one.
3 This is a bell-shaped curve that has many properties used by research. There is a more detailed discussion in Appendix B.
4 Figure 7.2 is an adaptation of a similar matrix in Hopkins and Glass's (1978, p. 280) work.
5 This is not the Cronbach α, referred to in Chapter 6.
6 Ranked data are data that has been converted into ordinal numbers, that is, first, second, third, etc.
7 By *independent samples*, it is meant that the participants in one group are different individuals than those in the other group.
8 See http://davidmlane.com/hyperstat/intro_ANOVA.html for more information.

References

Al-Seghayer, K. (2001). The effect of multimedia annotation modes on L2 vocabulary acquisition: A comparative study. *Language Learning & Technology, 5*(1), 202–232.
Bagheri, M., & Aeen, L. (2011). The impact of practicing autonomy on the writing proficiency of Iranian intermediate EFL learners. *Pan-Pacific Association of Applied Linguistics, 15*(1), 1–13.
Bang, E., & Luft, J. A. (2013). Secondary science teachers' use of technology in the classroom during their first 5 years. *Journal of Digital Learning in Teacher Education, 29*(4), 118–126.
Bogdan, R. C., & Biklen, S. K. (1992). *Qualitative research for education: An introduction to theory and methods*. Boston, MA: Allyn & Bacon.

Bond, J. (2011). Thinking on your feet: Principals' reflection-in-action. *International Journal of Educational Leadership Preparation,* 6(4), ISSN 2155-9635.

Bonner, J. M. (2009). A biology course for the less-than-prepared prospective biology major. *Biosciene, 35*(1), 74–81.

Bordelon, T. D., Opatrny, M., Turner, W. G., & Williams, S. D. (2011). Culture for sale? An exploratory study of the Crow fair. *The Qualitative Report, 16*(1), 10–38.

Bornsheuer, J. N., Polonyi, M. A., Andrews, M., Fore, B., & Onwuegbuzie, A. J. (2011). The relationship between ninth-grade retention and on-time graduation in a southeast Texas high school. *The Journal of At-Risk Issues, 16*(2), 9–16.

Cardona, B., Jain, S., & Canfield-Davis, K. (2012). Home-school relationships: A qualitative study with diverse families. *The Qualitative Report, 17*(70), 1–20.

Carrier, S. J. (2011). Implementing and integrating effective teachers strategies including features of lesson study in an elementary science methods course. *The Teacher Educator, 46,* 145–160.

Creswell, J. W. (1998). *Qualitative inquiry and research design: Choosing among five traditions.* Thousand Oaks, CA: Sage.

Darvin, J. (2011). "I don't feel comfortable reading those books in my classroom": A qualitative study of the impact of cultural and political vignettes in a teacher education course. *The Teacher Educator, 46,* 274–298.

Garvis, S. (2012). "You are my sunshine my only sunshine": Current music activities in kindergarten classrooms in Queensland, Australia. *Australian Journal of Music Education, 1,* 14–21.

Gkouvatzi, A. N., Mantis, K., & Kambas, A. (2010). Comparative study of motor performance of deaf and hard of hearing students in reaction time, visual-motor control and upper limb speed and dexterity abilities. *International Journal of Special Education, 25*(2), 15–25.

Gregory, A., Cornell, D., & Fan, X. (2011). The relationship of school structure and support to suspension rates for black and white high school students. *American Educational Research Journal, 48*(4), 904–934.

Gurbuz, R., Catlioglu, H., Birgin, O., & Erdem, E. (2010). An investigation of fifth grade students' conceptual development of probability through activity based instruction: A quasi-experimental study. *Education Sciences: Theory & Practice, 10*(2), 1053–1068.

Hatcher, B., Numer, J., & Paulsel, J. (2012). Kindergarten readiness and preschools: Teachers' and parents' beliefs within and across programs. *Early Childhood Research and Practice,* 1–17.

Hopkins, K.D., & Glass, G.V. (1978). *Basic statistics for the behavioral sciences.* Englewood Cliffs, NJ: Prentice-Hall.

Huberman, A. M., & Miles, M. B. (1994). Data management and analysis methods. In N. K. Denzin & Y. S. Lincoln (Eds.), *Handbook of qualitative research* (pp. 428–444). Thousand Oaks, CA: Sage.

Kennedy, T. D., Russom, A. G., & Kevorkian, M. M. (2012). Teacher and administrator perceptions of bullying in schools. *International Journal of Education Policy & Leadership,* 7(5), 1–12.

Koyoma, C., Plash, S., Davis, K. (2012). Comparing cross-cultural multicultural self-awareness among K-12 in-service school teachers. *SRATE Journal, 21*(1), 29–36.

Leung, C-H., & Choi, E. (2010). A qualitative study of self-esteem, peer affiliation, and academic outcome among low achieving students in Hong Kong. *New Horizons in Education,* 58(1), 22–42.

McKenna, M. K., & Millen, J. (2013). Look! Listen! Learn! Parent narratives and grounded theory models of parent voice, presence, and engagement in K-12 education. *School Community Journal, 23*(1), 9–18.

Miles, M. B., & Huberman, A. M. (1994). *Qualitative data analysis: An expanded sourcebook.* Thousand Oaks, CA: Sage.

Onwuegbuzie, A. J., Bailey, P., & Daley, C. E. (2000). Cognitive, affective, personality, and demographic predictors of foreign-language achievement. *The Journal of Educational Research, 94*, 3–15.

Prior, M. A., & Niesz, T. (2013). Refugee children's adaptation to American early childhood classrooms: A narrative inquiry. *The Qualitative Report, 18*(39), 1–17.

Ray, B., & Coulter, G. A. (2010). Perceptions of the value of digital mini-games: Implications for middle school classrooms. *Journal of Digital Learning in Teacher Education, 26*(3), 92–100.

Rott, S. (2005). Processing glosses: Qualitative exploration of how form-meaning connections are established and strengthened. *Reading in a Foreign Language, 17*, 45–74.

Tseng, K-H., Chang, C-C., Lou, S-J., & Chen, W-P. (2013). Attitudes toward science, technology, engineering, and mathematics (STEM) in a project-based learning (PjBL) environment. *International Journal of Technology and Design Education, 23*, 87–102.

Wolcott, H. F. (1994). *Transforming qualitative data: Description, analysis, and interpretation.* Thousand Oaks, CA: Sage.

Yeung, A. S. W. (2006). Teachers' conceptions of borderless: A cross-cultural study on multicultural sensitivity of the Chinese Teachers. *Educational Research for Policy and Practice, 5*, 33–53.

Young, R. B., Edwards, M. C., & Leising, J. G. (2009). Does a math-enhanced curriculum and instructional approach diminish students' attainment of technical skills? A yearlong experimental study in agricultural power and technology. *Journal of Agricultural Education, 50*(1), 116–126.

Yu, J-H., & Kim, J. K. (2010). Patterns of interactions and behaviors: Physical education in Korean elementary, middle, and high schools. *International Council for Health, Physical Education, Recreation, Sport and Dance: Journal of Research, 5*(1), 26–32.

8

DISCERNING DISCUSSIONS AND CONCLUSIONS

Completing the Picture

Chapter Overview

The final section of a research article is the Discussion and Conclusion sections where researchers interpret their findings, make practical applications, and try to fit them into a big picture to answer their research questions. No matter what research design was used, no matter what type of data (verbal or numerical) were gathered, no matter how the data were analyzed (looking for patterns or statistics), researchers arrive at the same place: they have to make sense of what they found. They have to interpret their results and provide explanations, draw conclusions, and make applications. Therefore, after the abstract at the beginning of the study, this section is the most read part of the average study.

Many reasons are given as to why the stuff between the Abstract and the Discussion and Conclusion sections is jumped over. We often hear, "Why bother with the rest? Let us just go to the conclusion and find out what we can use for our purposes." However, if this *lazy route* is taken, the consumer will never be able to evaluate whether proper conclusions have been made based on solid research, which in turn will lead to faulty applications. Such slothfulness has resulted in a lot of money and time being wasted based on conclusions that have been drawn from faulty research.

The purpose of this final chapter is to facilitate in developing the consumer's ability to discern whether researchers are making valid interpretations and conclusions based on their data, and whether appropriate applications are being suggested. We first explain what the Discussion and Conclusion sections are supposed to do, and then summarize a number of concerns to which the consumer should give attention. To illustrate these principles, we will close the chapter with two examples from two different types of research designs.

The Needed Ingredients

Researchers vary in the format they use to wrap up their studies. Some will only have a Discussion section, whereas others have both Discussion and Conclusion sections. You might also see additional subheadings, such as Summary and/or Implications. Some attach their Discussion section to their Results section, labeled something like Results and Discussion followed by a final Conclusion. Regardless of the format they use, they usually include the following components in the Discussion and Conclusion sections of their paper.

- *An overview of the study*: The purpose of the study is restated, the questions under investigation are summarized, and any propounded hypotheses reiterated.
- *Overview of the findings*: The researchers should show how the findings address the research question(s) and/or support or fail to support any hypothesis being proposed.
- *Relation of findings*: The researchers should relate the findings of their study to previous research findings and theoretical thinking.
- *Attention to limitations*: The researchers should evaluate their own study and point out any weaknesses and/or limitations regarding the study.
- *Possible applications*: The researchers should suggest in their conclusions how the results can be applied to practical situations.
- *Future possibilities*: The researchers should suggest topics for future research.

Questions Every Consumer Should Ask

When evaluating the Discussion and Conclusion sections of a study, there are a set of questions that the consumer should address:

1   *Do the findings logically answer the research questions or support the research hypothesis?* Here is where the consumer must be wary. Many, if not all, researchers have their biases and would love to find answers to their questions, or support their hypothesis from the results of their studies. Because this final section gives researchers the right to conjecture about what the findings mean, it is easy to unintentionally suggest things that the results do not support.

2   *Does the nature of the study remain consistent from beginning to end?* Our students have noticed that some studies begin as exploratory studies, but end up as confirmatory ones. In such cases, the Introduction section has one or more research questions with no specific hypothesis stated. However, in the Discussion section we suddenly read, "and so our hypothesis is confirmed by the results." Another variation of this is that the researchers generate a hypothesis in the discussion section—which is their right—but then go on to suggest that their results now support the hypothesis. This is circular reasoning (see Figure 2.1). We cannot use

the same data to support a hypothesis from which it has been formulated. A new study must be undertaken to test this hypothesis.

3 *Are the findings generalized to the correct population or situations?* Most studies, in fact, cannot be generalized to a broadly defined population. The reason is that most samples are not randomly selected, nor are they typically large enough to adequately represent a target population. Consequently, results of such studies are suggestive at most and need to be followed up with a number of replications. If the same findings are repeated using different samples from the target population, then we can have more assurance that we are on the right track. This is where a *Meta-analysis* plays an important role. A well-written Discussion section will be careful to warn readers of this problem.

4 *Are the conclusions consistent with the type of research design used?* The main concern here is whether *causation* is being inferred from research designs that are not geared to demonstrate this effect. Having an idea of the type of design being used will help the consumer know whether this error is made when reading the discussion and conclusions. Nonexperimental designs such as descriptive or correlational ones cannot be used to directly show causation. Yet, especially in the latter case, some researchers have slipped into implying that their findings indicate that one variable influences another. When researchers apply their findings, they are often tempted to recommend that people manipulate one variable to cause changes in another. Unless their research design warrants this application, they have made a logical error.

5 *Are the findings and conclusions related to theory or previous research?* To help contribute to the big picture, a well-written Discussion and Conclusion sections should attempt to tie the findings and interpretations to any current theoretical thinking or previous research. This might be done through showing how the findings support what has gone before or by providing evidence to refute some theory or challenge previous research.

6 *Are any limitations of the study made clear?* There are very few, if any, perfect studies in the literature. Regardless of how good a study is, a conscientious researcher will mention what the limitations are to caution the reader from being overly confident about the results.

7 *Is there consistency between the findings and the applications?* As previously mentioned, some researchers confuse statistical significance with practical significance when discussing inferential statistics. We repeat the warning here. Just because a finding is *statistically significant*, this does not mean that it has *practical significance*. We have seen relatively small correlations, such as $r = 0.30$, interpreted as an important finding because it was statistically significant, or the difference of 5 points between a treatment and a control group given importance for the same reason. Yet is either of these findings large enough to get excited about? Maybe, but much depends on the cost in time, human resources, and finance to get that 0.30 correlation or those extra 5 points due

to the treatment. The consumer needs to be on alert when a researcher advocates costly changes based on statistical significance. This is where *effect size* is applied, as mentioned in Chapter 7 and elaborated in Appendix B.

In the following, the Discussion and Conclusion sections of two studies have been evaluated using the above set of questions. The criteria we used for choosing these articles were that they were used previously in former chapters, and they each represented a different type of research: qualitative and quantitative. Both articles were discussed in Chapter 6. The first is an example of a qualitative study using a case study design and verbal data. The second is an example of a comparative or predictive study using numerical data.

Cardona, Jain, and Canfield-Davis (2012) completed a qualitative case study project that explored how families from diverse cultural backgrounds understood family involvement in the context of early childcare and educational settings. Their Results section consisted of observations from multiple different sources (i.e., triangulation), and all of their data were in the form of verbal descriptions other than some informative descriptive indicators. In line with a purely qualitative study, no inferential statistics were used in their study. Their Results and Discussion section provided two themes that emerged from this study: (a) home–school relationships, and (b) families' wishes and wants for their children. The researchers also identified several subthemes within the home–school relationships that included: social respect, personal regard, and perceived competence based on their data observations. Here we will draw attention to the exact words they used to indicate how the researchers were trying to draw meaning from their data. This is exactly what a discussion section is supposed to do. For example, they stated:

> Programs that provide opportunities and spaces for families to connect can support the desires and efforts to maintain social relationships. In the three programs that participated in this study, there was no space other than the entrance or hallways where families could meet without interruptions. Providing the space can enable families to form acquaintances and friendships with other families. This strategy was identified as particularly supportive for families who felt isolated in their community. (p. 15)

Within this text, you can see the researchers are attempting to condense and summarize their hours of collecting data into findings that are meaningful and representative of the data that was collected. This is what researchers do when they are trying to make sense out of their findings regardless of whether the data are verbal or numerical. However, be careful if you see the word *significant* in a study apart from *statistical significance*. If the researchers use this term in their Discussion or Conclusion, they are not talking about statistical significance. Most likely they mean *an important difference*.

Cardona et al. (2012) continued their discussion by providing additional summaries of the themes that were discovered and also provided a Limitations section that discussed some potential drawbacks to their study. For one, they noted that the project was limited to six families who currently have children enrolled in three different early childhood programs. This sample, and the potential differences that existed in the preschool sites, made it difficult for the researchers to generalize their results to other families. They were careful to include in their discussion that a prolonged engagement to collect data was not the aim of the study and, therefore, limits the understanding of family involvement and the factors that enhance connections in the context of early childhood programs. They were careful to include this warning, recognizing the short-term scope of their data collection procedure.

Cardona et al. (2012) also included an Implications section suggesting that their results have important implications particularly for school counselors to help families build social networks and to provide greater understanding of the different perspectives of family involvement. This conclusion seems to be a bit of a stretch beyond the results of their data. However, the data more clearly suggests the positive and negative perceptions of the families rather than the impact that the staff may have on the parents' perceptions.

Cardona et al. (2012) end with a Future Directions section where they suggest additional research using an ecological framework is warranted. Their suggestions for future research that explores how issues of race, social class, and gender impact family involvement practices in urban areas are all excellent ideas that could eventually contribute to the findings of this project.

In addition to the seven questions listed above, keep in mind the criteria listed in section "Evaluating Explanations and Conclusions" of Chapter 7 (see Table 7.1). They should also be considered when evaluating the final Discussion and Conclusion section of a qualitative study. However, because interpretations and conclusions are ongoing during the data collection stages in a qualitative study, these criteria apply both then and in the final discussion.

The second example is by Dupoux, Hammond, Ingalls, and Wolman (2006) who focused on comparing attitudes of urban and rural teachers in Haiti toward inclusion. They formed the following hypotheses: (a) attitudes between urban and rural teachers toward integration in Haiti are similar, (b) attitudes toward integration are positively correlated with number of years of teaching experience, (c) level of education is positively related to attitudes toward integration, and (d) teaching experience is a less powerful predictor of attitudes toward integration of students with disabilities than teachers' cognitions and beliefs. "The predictive variables used in the study included gender, education level, years of teaching experience, number of students in the classroom, type of teacher (regular or special education), number of students with disabilities taught, categories of disability served, range of effective accommodation, and teachers' perceptions of other teachers' attitudes" (p. 6). The researchers used the

Opinions Relative to Integration (ORI) instrument to collect their data and an additional demographic instrument.

Dupoux et al. (2006) began their Discussion section by stating that their results supported their first hypothesis; rural teachers did not differ from urban teachers in their attitudes toward integrating students with disabilities. The researchers used a multiple regression analysis (an advanced statistical procedure) to test which variables were significant predictors of teachers' attitudes toward inclusion. As they progressed through the Discussion section, the researchers were careful to restate their findings and in the narrative, stated that "predictors of attitudes toward integration of students with disabilities were grouped into categories of actual teaching experience and teachers' own cognitions and beliefs. Out of almost 9% of the variance in teachers' attitudes, 5% was explained by variables representing the teachers' cognitions and beliefs" (p. 9). Since their findings suggested that almost 90% of the variance in teachers' attitudes was unexplained in this study, the researchers were wise to include in their discussion why this might have been the case. The researchers examined this in their discussion by arguing that teaching requires complex thinking and the consideration of multiple factors may determine how they respond to the inclusion movement. They also suggest that although valuable information came from the data in this project, there may also be personal unobservable variations that the survey of teachers' attitudes failed to capture. Overall, the researchers' comments matched their outcomes that appear in the Results section, and their discussion did not embellish any of their findings.

Dupoux et al. (2006) conclude their Discussion section by including recommendations for future research and a section on the practical implications of their findings. Under their recommendations for future research, Dupoux et al. maintain that teaching is a multidimensional construct and therefore future research should explore other constructs that may impact teachers' attitudes (i.e., personality, locus of control). This was good for them to note since they clearly were not able to explain much of the variation they found with regard to teachers' attitudes. As the discussion concludes with practical implications of their results, the narrative begins to drift slightly away from the original topic and hypotheses and becomes more of a political discussion that explores the recent plights of the Haitian political system.

If there is any constructive criticism to offer regarding this study, the central drawback to the Dupoux et al.'s (2006) discussion is that it fails to provide evidence of any potential limitations of the project. As we have noted earlier, there is no perfect research project and if you look close enough, every study has potential limitations that should be noted to the research community.

As you can see, the Discussion and Conclusion sections of an article cannot be treated lightly. But to discern its quality, you, the consumer, must be able to evaluate how the preceding sections of a research study logically develop to support the interpretations and conclusions a researcher makes. Without understanding and evaluating each building block leading to the final result, it is impossible to evaluate the end product. Hopefully, the above discussion has provided you with guidelines to help you determine whether the end product (i.e., the conclusions) is warranted. If it is, you are able to make your own conclusions regarding the worth of the study for answering your own questions. Therefore, the best recommendation at this point is to provide you with an exercise that will help you apply what you have just read.

EXERCISE 8.1

Use one of the recent studies you have used in previous exercises.

Evaluate the Discussion and Conclusion sections of the study by answering the following questions. Provide a quick rationale for each answer.

1   Do the findings logically answer the research questions or support the research hypothesis?
2   Does the nature of the study remain consistent from beginning to end?
3   Are the findings generalized to the correct population?
4   Are the conclusions consistent to the type of research design?
5   Are the findings and conclusions related to theory for previous research?
6   Are any limitations made clear regarding the study?
7   Is there consistency between the findings and the applications?

Congratulations!! You have come a long way. Welcome to the Association for Consumers of Educational Research—*whenever we get around to starting such an organization.* Let us close with this analogy. Research is like scuba diving, sky diving, or running a marathon, which we love to do. Many people are afraid to participate in these activities because they think that they will drown, their chute will not open, or their legs will not continue to operate for 26.2 miles. We find that the opposite is true. When we are under the water, in the air, or at the 20-mile marker in a foot race, it is one of the most relaxing experiences we have ever had. We get to see the underwater beauty of sea life, the expanse of the sky, and feel the thrill of accomplishment from a perspective that many will never see. The only danger is not following the principles that we studied when we trained for these experiences. Studying research is similar. There are those who stand on the edge of the ocean, the door of the plane, or at the starting line of research afraid to jump in and experience for themselves the treasures that await them. Their excuses are a fear of drowning or becoming enveloped in a sea of data and statistics. But as with any adventurous activity, if they follow the principles discussed in this book, they will find themselves not only discovering many important pieces of information, but will begin to enjoy swimming in the depths, soaring like a bird, and experiencing great accomplishments. Now it is your turn to make the jump into research and begin finding the treasures of information that awaits you. Appendix A provides a set of guidelines for completing your own review of the research literature that will address any research question you might have. May you approach it with great confidence.

References

Cardona, B., Jain, S., & Canfield-Davis, K. (2012). Home-school relationships: A qualitative study with diverse families. *The Qualitative Report, 17*(70), 1–20.

Dupoux, E., Hammond, H., Ingalls, L., & Wolman, C. (2006). Teachers' attitudes toward students with disabilities in Haiti. *International Journal of Special Education, 21*(3), 1–14.

APPENDIX A
Constructing a Literature Review

If you have grasped the content presented in the chapters of this book, you are ready to complete a review of the research literature that focuses on some topic in which you are interested. Whether you are trying to answer a practical problem about learning, teaching, or schools; preparing a paper on some topic for colleagues; or trying to fulfill the requirements of a course assignment, the ability to do an effective research review is necessary. The purpose of this chapter is to provide guidelines for developing a useful review for answering whatever research question you might have. First, however, we discuss the importance of producing a good literature review.

Why Do a Review of Research?

The main benefit of doing a literature review is to provide the consumer with a mosaic of what is happening concerning a given topic. No research study exhausts all there is to know about a given topic. However, when you can integrate various recent research articles into a meaningful picture, you will be able to discover a number of interesting things.

First, you will realize whether there are any plausible answers to your questions when you see the bigger picture. On first blush, your impression might be that there are no clear answers, and you might be tempted to give up your search. However, as you weave the studies together in an integrated review, you might find answers for practical use.

In addition, you might find conflicting results between studies. This might tempt you to give up with the conclusion that no one can agree on anything. However, this is when being a discerning consumer will pay off. On careful scrutiny of the studies, you will begin to see why there are conflicting results. You might realize that the differences in the samples used in the studies produced the differing results. Or, there might have been a difference in the procedures or the materials used in the treatment. You now have to decide which study best corresponds to the context surrounding your particular research question. The closer the correspondence, the more applicable the findings might be to your situation.

However, if you find that the same results are replicated over a variety of studies, you can have more confidence that you are on the right track. Here is where *external validity* comes into play. If, regardless of the sample, procedures, materials, or type of tests used, the same findings keep appearing, you can be confident that you have a workable answer for your question. Without a well-done literature review, you cannot have this assurance.

Occasionally, you will discover that there is little recent research on a particular question. When this happens, you should take care. Maybe your research question is stated in such a way that your search accessed only a few studies. If this is the case, you will have to adjust the key concepts in your question to produce more rewarding searches. You might have to go back further in time to see whether there was anything done earlier. Then again, your question may be so novel that there is little research available to date.

To illustrate, one of our students who is an elementary teacher, raised a question concerning the usefulness of *looping classrooms* in her school. When teachers teach the same cohort group of students for more than 1 year, for example, first and second grades, and then move back to pick up a new first-grade class for the next 2-year cycle, the teacher is considered a looping teacher and the classrooms, looping classrooms. Our student wanted to know whether there was research to support the use of looping in schools. However, when looking over the past 5 years, she could not find enough research to fill a short one-page review. She first asked whether this topic had been researched out—that is, had research gone as far as possible, whether by sufficiently answering the question or by being limited due to various constraints. Most probably, the latter might be the case. The variables used to test to see whether looping can actually improve student achievement might be beyond current capabilities to manipulate or measure them. If this is the case, we cannot make strong conclusions about its impact on freshmen students. Possibly new approaches will be developed that will move research ahead on this topic in the future.

Second, doing a research review is important if you plan to do a study yourself. Such a review will give you an overview of the different kinds of methodologies, instruments for collecting data, and ways in which to analyze data that have been commonly used in the research for a given area. This knowledge can help you decide whether your proposed study is even feasible given your time, material, and financial constraints. Many fledgling researchers could have saved themselves needless angst if they would have realized that the study they were interested in doing required more time and resources than were available before launching into the task.

Where to Begin

As described in Chapter 2, the first place to begin is searching for studies using *preliminary* sources. These are used to find documents that report research studies or theoretical positions, and we suggest you review Chapter 2 regarding how to make the best use of these valuable tools. Most modern university libraries, as well as some public libraries, have such computerized search capabilities. Now that the Internet is available in most countries, you should be able to obtain a list of research studies pertinent to your questions even from your home computer.

Again, as mentioned in Chapter 2, your search will be as good as the *keywords* (or descriptors) you use. You might have to try different combinations of these words to obtain sufficient results for your review, or you might have to use a *thesaurus* from the preliminary source you are using to identify related keywords to guide your search.

Your goal is to access firsthand research studies (i.e., *primary studies*) that relate to your questions. How many studies you include will depend on the nature of your question(s). If you want to do an exhaustive literature review, you will want to cover as many studies as you can find. However, most people want to put some limitations on their literature review, such as time constraints and/or only journal articles, to confine their search to studies with only certain characteristics.

Figure A.1 illustrates the results of a search we made for research articles using the ERIC database on the Internet. We put *time limits* and *location limits* for studies published in the last 10 years in research journals only. Since social networks are a hot topic today, we first began with the very broad search only using the keywords *Social Networking*. The results were 676 documents. We then narrowed it down to articles dealing with *Social Networking* and *Writing* resulting in 43 references. If we wanted to narrow our search even further we could use *Social Networking* and *Writing* and *Learning* to generate only 27 sources. If our question of interest was something like "Does the use of social networking sites impact student writing and learning?", we might want to stop here and scan through all of these references or go back and broaden our thinking to gather more information. (Note that not all of these references are primary research studies. Some could be position papers or literature reviews.)

Most likely, we would want to narrow our search even more to specifically focus on student achievement. For instance, we are interested in finding research studies about strategies that students use when using social networking sites that may improve their writing skills. So we restated our search terms to be *Social Networking* and *Writing*. As shown in Figure A.1, this captured 43 articles. As you can see, the way we word our keywords for our search did not prevent us from seeing some study that might be using different terminology. We could even get more specific and use a specific social networking site (for example, Facebook) to either expand or narrow our search for more or less articles.

You might ask the question, "How far back in time do you go in your search?" Our recommendation is that you begin by looking at the last 5 years of research. Usually this will result in enough current research to provide viable information

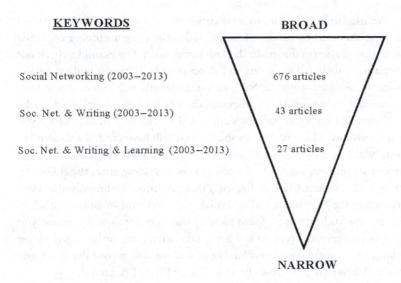

KEYWORDS	BROAD
Social Networking (2003–2013)	676 articles
Soc. Net. & Writing (2003–2013)	43 articles
Soc. Net. & Writing & Learning (2003–2013)	27 articles
	NARROW

FIGURE A.1 Results of Using Different Combinations of Keywords in a Literature Search Using ERIC for Years 2003–2013

addressing your question(s). We then suggest that you begin with the most recent research and work backward in time. This way, you will stay abreast with the most recent issues and findings with which researchers are currently working. In the case of searching for Facebook, since it is a relatively new phenomenon, most of the research is relatively recent. It is a good rule of thumb to use current literature in any search so that you can eliminate getting involved with outdated issues with which people in the discipline are no longer concerned.

Once you have identified the studies you want to consider for inclusion in your review, you face the challenge of getting your hands on the actual articles. Hopefully, you will be near a good library that carries the journals so that you can have ready access to the studies. If the library does not subscribe to the journal, they may have a library loan agreement with other libraries that do have the journals. Some journals such as the *Journal of Educational Research* have electronic versions to which your library might have access. In such cases, you can download full articles for reviewing. If all else fails, you can order journal articles through databases such as ERIC, and they will mail them to you either through your library or to your address. If you do this, we strongly suggest that you order the microfiche version to keep the cost down and help save trees. You will need a microfiche reader for this, but these should be available at your library.

Abstracting Primary Literature

In preparation to constructing your review of the research literature, you will need to formulate a systematic procedure for cataloging and storing your information for each study. We used to have to put our information on 5″ × 8″ (i.e., 12 cm × 20 cm) cards that were awkward to handle. However, today there are a number of online information storage systems that make this task much easier. For example, check out Web research tools such as Diigo.com and Zotero.org to help you build databases and organize research information. Such online programs will revolutionize your research gathering endeavors. These programs allow you to highlight, attach sticky notes, store, sort, and aggregate various studies at the click of a mouse. Once you enter the information, which we discuss shortly, you will have created a database of studies from which you can draw information for you literature review.

When you set up your database of studies for your review, enter the following information in the format (APA, MLA, etc.) that you most commonly use. First, record accurately the last names and all initials for every author of each study. If you have only one author, it is useful to identify their gender as well, because you might want to use personal pronouns when summarizing his or her study rather than speaking in the formal *the researcher*. Next, you want to record the exact title of the article. When doing this, use the style (e.g., APA, MLA, etc.) that you plan to use for your literature review. (*Note:* Web 2 systems like Zotero do this automatically.) This will save you time when you prepare the table of references because you will not have to retype them. At most, you will only have to cut and paste with your word processor software. Following this you will need to record the year published the exact title of the journal (in italics), the volume number (in italics), the issue number, and the page numbers from beginning of the article to the very last page.

If you have read a published literature review, you might have noticed that the author basically looks for 10 things when summarizing the main body of the study. They are as follows:

1 The focus of the study: What area and/or issue is/are being studied?
2 The research question(s) being asked.
3 The hypothesis(es) being tested (if any).
4 The size of the sample and important characteristics such as age and gender; how the sample was chosen or assigned to the study, whether randomly or by some other procedure.
5 The variables in the study such as

    a   descriptive
    b   independent
    c   dependent
    d   moderating.

6 The procedures followed, including any materials, test instruments, or observational techniques.
7 The overall findings of the study.
8 The conclusion(s) that the researcher draws from the findings.

9   Any other observations they have made that pertain to their interests.

10 Any concerns they have with the study that they want to point out in their review.

Writing a Review of Research

The outline we recommend for writing a good review of research is one that we have adapted based on Chapter 6 of Cooper's book, *Synthesizing Research* (1998). This pattern seems to be the one followed by many reviewers of research published in journals. Interestingly, this outline has the same headings that are used in reporting most primary research studies: introduction, method, results, and discussion.

I   Introduction

    A   The research question that your review addresses.

    B   The importance of the topic.

    C   Historical background of the topic (theory, methodological issues, previous reviews, etc.).

    D   The goal of your review: How you plan to add to the theory and information already available.

II Method section: Details regarding the makeup of the review.

    A   What years are covered?

    B   What preliminary sources were used to locate the studies?

    C   What key words guided your search?

    D   Criteria for deciding which studies to review.

        1   Description of the constraints that limited your selection.

        2   Rationale for choosing these constraints.

    E   What studies were excluded and why?

III The Results section: Studies summarized.

    A   An overview of what studies will be discussed and their relation to one another and the review as a whole.

    B   At least a paragraph for each study containing a summary of the following:

        1   The main point of the study.

        2   The question(s)/hypothesis being studied.

        3   Samples used and how they were chosen.

        4   Procedure(s) used.

        5   General findings (results).

        6   Author's interpretations/applications of the findings.

        7   Any concerns to which you might want to alert the reader.

IV Discussion section.

    A   Give an overview of major results of your review.

    B   Compare/contrast the results between studies.

    C   Provide possible reasons for any differences.

    D   Relate results to any theoretical issues you mentioned in the introduction.

    E   Compare with past reviews if any exist.

    F   Explain any difference in findings with past reviews.

    G   Application of findings toward future research.

When possible, construct tables to help summarize your findings. What you put in a table will depend on what you are trying to highlight in your review. The purpose of the table is to provide a visual aid that will work with your text in helping the reader understand all of the relationships that you are trying to point out.

Periathiruvadi and Rinn (2012) provided an excellent example of how to make good use of tables to summarize the information they extracted from 20 studies in their review. The question they addressed was stated in the title: "Technology in Gifted Education: A Review of Best Practices and Empirical Research." They captured in their table each study's reference, the samples used, the methodology, and the focus of the project. In a two-page table, they summarized the issues they wanted to draw the reader's attention to for the 20 studies. They listed multiple criteria that they used to select the studies in their review. In their discussion and conclusion sections, they related their findings to the previous literature reviews and the theoretical issues that they outlined in their introduction. We strongly recommend your perusal of this review as a model for you to follow. However, there are many other well-written literature reviews available that will vary in style, which you may also want to use as a prototype.

Meta-Analysis

Meta-analysis is different from the review of research discussed previously (see Cooper, Hedges, & Valentine, 2009, for a complete reference). It is not simply trying to make a mosaic out of all the research on a given topic. It is a research method on its own, that is, *primary* research. It involves sampling studies like you would sample participants for a normal primary research study. It involves doing statistics on these studies both descriptive and inferential. Only in this case you are looking at the effect size (see Appendix B) of each study.

It is unlikely that you will do a meta-analysis until you are much more familiar with the methodology for doing one. When you are ready, there are a number of good sources to guide you in the procedure (see Borenstein, Hedges, Higgins, & Rothstein, 2009; Lipsey & Wilson, 2001).

We leave you with a summary of an example of a meta-analysis done by Masgoret and Gardner (2003). They first wanted to do a meta-analysis on all the research that had been done on the relationships between attitude, motivation, and language learning. They quickly realized that there were too many studies to deal with, so they only looked at the research that had been done by Gardner and his associates. They ended with a sample of 75 studies—each study is equivalent to one participant in a normal study. They then performed a statistical analysis of the statistics that came from these 75 studies. The obtained results gave them a much clearer picture of the patterns that were latent in the pool of research studies that they analyzed. I urge you to read this study in its entirety to get a full appreciation for meta-analysis.

Maybe you are not ready to do a meta-analysis, but you are ready to do a review of research. You should be equipped to go into the world of research and approach any study unabashed. It is your time to decide on a research question based on your own interest and search for a number of studies that address your question. The following exercise will guide you in the experience.

EXERCISE A.1

The purpose of this exercise is for you to produce a review of research in an area of your own interest. You are to review whatever number of studies you find relevant in the space allowed. You are to develop an overall picture of what is being studied in your chosen area.

    Criteria for the main body of the text:

1   Introduction: Conceptual presentation.

    A   What is your research question(s) that motivates your review?
    B   Why is the answer to your question(s) important to applied linguistics?
    C   What is the historical perspective behind your question?
    D   What is the main aim of your review?

2   Method section.

    A   Details of the nature of your search.

        1   What years did you cover in your search?
        2   What preliminary sources did you use?
        3   What keywords guided your search?

    B   Criteria for deciding which studies to review.

        1   What criteria did you use for including a study?
        2   Why did you select these criteria?
        3   What studies did you exclude and why?

(Continued)

(Continued)

3   The Results section.

   A   An organized summary of the studies: Each study should include
        the following in your own words:
        1   The main point of the study.
        2   The question(s)/hypothesis being studied.
        3   The sample used and how and why it was selected.
        4   The procedure(s) used for implementing the study.
        5   The general findings (results) in words not statistics.
        6   The researcher's interpretations/applications of the findings.

4   Discussion section.

   A   Summarize the major results of your review. (Use Tables to provide
        visual aids in your summary if possible.)

        1   Compare/contrast the results between studies.
        2   Provide possible reasons for any differences.

   B   Compare with past reviews, if any exist.
   C   Explain any difference in your findings compared with past reviews.
   D   Apply your findings toward answering your future research.

BEST WISHES ON YOUR ADVENTURE IN RESEARCH!!!

References

Borenstein, M., Hedges, L. V., Higgins, J. P. T., & Rothstein, H. R. (2009). *Introduction to meta-analysis*. New York: Wiley.

Cooper, H. M., (1998). *Synthesizing research: A guide for literature reviews* (3rd ed.). Thousand Oaks, CA: Sage.

Cooper, H., Hedges, L. V., & Valentine, J. C. (Eds.). (2009). *The handbook of research synthesis and meta-analysis* (2nd ed.). Thousand Oaks, CA: Sage.

Lipsey, M. W., & Wilson, D. B. (2001). *Practical meta-analysis: Applied social research methods series* (Vol. 49). Thousand Oaks, CA: Sage.

Masgoret, A. M., & Gardner, R. C. (2003). Attitudes, motivation, and second language learning: A meta-analysis of studies conducted by Gardner and associates. *Language Learning, 53*, 167–210.

Periathiruvadi, S., & Rinn, A. N. (2012). Technology in gifted education: A review of best practices and empirical research. *Journal of Research on Technology Education, 45*(2), 153–169.

APPENDIX B

Going to the Next Level of Statistics

More About Descriptive Statistics

Types of Scales

Before looking at statistics in greater detail, you need to understand something about the type of numbers that are used as data. This is important because the type of descriptive or inferential statistic used is dependent on the nature of the data. Numerical data come in one of four forms, referred to as *scales*: *nominal, ordinal, interval,* and *ratio.* The word *nominal* means that the levels of a variable are categories. The categories can be identified with words (e.g., female, male,) or numbers (e.g., 1, 2). The numbers assigned would only be used to identify each level, without having any other meaning. That is, the value 2 for one of the sexes does not mean that sex had twice as much of gender than the other sex. It is just a numerical name. The frequency of individuals in each category is the data. The frequencies are sometimes converted to relative frequencies (i.e., percentages), but the results are the same. For example, a study may have 60 males and 80 females, or 43% males and 57% females.

Another example of the use of a nominal scale would be when a researcher is interested in knowing whether there are differences in the number of people representing three different nationalities. Nationality is the variable of the study, and the data are the frequency of people for each of the nationalities.

Data for the *ordinal scale* represents some type of ranking. As with the nominal scale, words, or numbers can be used. However, in contrast with the nominal scale the words or numbers have quantitative meaning. For example, the variable of writing proficiency might be expressed verbally as low, average, or high ability. It could also be in the form of numbers: 3 = high, 2 = average, or 1 = low ability.

A commonly used ordinal scale in education is known as the *Likert-scale*. One use is with measurements of attitude with the rankings: 5 = Strongly Agree, 4 = Agree, 3 = Neutral, 2 = Disagree, and 1 = Strongly Disagree. This scale has two important qualities: unequal distance between values, and *no true zero*. What is meant by the first quality is that the distance between a 2 and a 3 on a rating scale, for example, may not represent the same amount of difference in the trait (the attribute) being measured as the distance between the 1 and the 2. What is meant by *no true zero* is that if a 0 were used, it would only represent a level of ability that was lower than a 1. It would not mean that subjects at level 0 were absolutely devoid of the trait being measured.

To illustrate, the following graph shows what the real distances are between the numbers in the amount of a trait being measured—which in reality we do not know. Note the unequal distances between the numbers. The amount of trait measured (or distance) between 1 and 2 differs from that between 2 and 3. The problem is, we do not usually know how much of the trait is being represented by the numbers.

Many ordinal scales are used in applied linguistic research. In fact, any rating scale is almost always an ordinal scale. Besides attitude scales mentioned previously, there are rating scales for writing and oral proficiency, anxiety, and so on. A study that used a number of rating scales (all ordinal) was done by Sevinc, Ozmen, and Yigit (2011). They measured six factors, each using an ordinal scale to examine such traits as self-efficacy, use of active learning strategies, science-learning value, performance goals, achievement goals, and learning environment stimulation.

Measurement of a variable can also be in the form of an *interval scale*. Whereas the values used in the ordinal scale might represent unequal amounts of the variable being measured, the intervals between the values in an interval scale represent an *equal* amount, as illustrated below:

However, as with the ordinal scale, there is *no true zero*. A common example of an interval scale is the scale used to measure heat on a thermometer. The 1 degree difference between 20°C and a 21°C in amount of heat is the same as the 1 degree difference between 29°C and 30°C. In other words, the units of measurement mean the same in terms of the amount of the trait (heat, in this example) being measured no matter where it is on the scale. At the same time, there is no true zero. Zero degree Celsius (0°C) does not mean the total absence of heat. It is a *relative zero* in that it is used as a reference point determined by the freezing of water. And as we all know, 0°C is warmer than zero degrees Fahrenheit (i.e., 0°C = 32°F).

Scores on aptitude or achievement tests are usually treated as if they are on interval scales. Each correct item is considered as one unit of the trait being measured, so that a person scoring a 30 on the instrument is 10 units higher on the trait than one who scores 20. (In fact, in the measurement world, this is known to be not true, but that is for another book.) A zero on a test is not a true zero because it does not mean that the subject has absolutely no knowledge on what is being tested, even though some teachers might think so. It simply means that the examinee did not answer any of the items correctly. All data that consist of the total of summed scores are usually treated as interval scales.

Finally, there is the *ratio scale*, which is seldom used in educational research. As you might expect, this scale has it all. The units of measurement are equal in amount of trait being measured, and there is a true zero. A good example is using a ruler to measure length. One inch or centimeter means the same thing no matter where it is on the scale. In addition, a zero means that there is no length, which of course means that whatever we are measuring does not exist.

The one ratio scale measurement that we can think of that has been used in education is *reaction time*. This is the time it takes for participants to react to some form of stimulus by pressing a button or speaking out. Reaction time is measured in units as small as milliseconds. The millisecond units are equal; if the measurement is zero, there was no reaction to whatever was presented to the subject. Szyfman, Wanner, and Spencer (2003), for example, used reaction time to study the relationship of cellular phone use, performance, and reaction time among college students while driving an automobile. The researchers determined that mean reaction times were significantly higher when participants were talking on a cellular phone, either handheld or on a headset when compared with their baseline reaction time without distractions. The response time (also known as response latency) measured in milliseconds constituted the dependent variable.

At this point, you might want to digest what you have just read by doing the following exercise, not to mention taking a break.

EXERCISE B.1

1 Take any study and identify the variables under consideration.
2 Identify the type of scale that each variable is on: nominal, ordinal, interval, or ratio.

Shape of the Data Distribution

The shape of the distribution of the data is seldom discussed in Results sections of published research, but it is very important. On the basis of the shape of the distribution of the data, researchers should choose which estimates of average and variation they will report in their studies. In addition, some inferential statistical procedures require the data to be distributed in certain patterns before they can be used appropriately.

The distribution of data is best illustrated by a graphical display of how many (the frequency) participants/objects obtained certain measures beginning from the lowest measure to the highest. To illustrate, Figure B.1 is a bar chart representing a subsection of data based on the total scores taken from a classroom test. The graph shows the frequency of the scores ranging from 70 to 80. The height of each bar corresponds to the frequency (i.e., the number on top of each bar). Note that five people scored 70, eight people scored 71, 16 scored 77, and so on. The shape of the distribution is noted by mentally drawing a line connecting the tops of the bars. These data show that there is a tendency for the frequency of people to increase as the total scores increase.

When referring to the shape of the data (see Table 7.3), three issues are of concern: symmetricality, skewness, and number of modals.[1] All of these terms are concerned with how well the shape of the data conforms to a normal distribution. An example is presented in Figure B.2. A *normal distribution* has specific properties and is used as a reference point for comparing the shapes of data distributions. The reason it is used as the reference for other curves is because many traits that we study are considered by many to be normally distributed in the population.

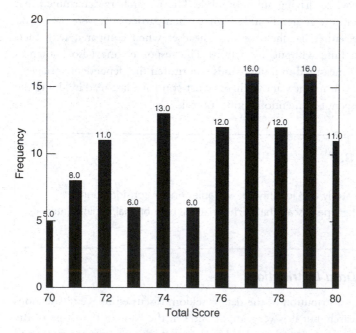

FIGURE B.1 Bar Graph of a Distribution of Data

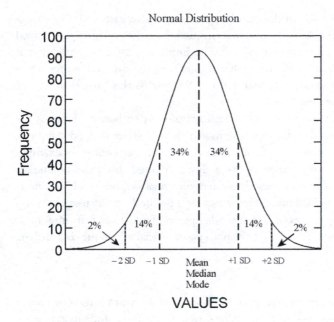

FIGURE B.2 The Normal Distribution

The distribution of the normal curve is perfectly *symmetrical* and has only one cluster of data in the middle. That is, by drawing a vertical line dividing the graph in half as seen in Figure B.2, the shape of the curve on the right side is the exact mirror image of the left half. In addition, notice that the distribution has certain properties. Approximately 34% of the subjects are found from the middle (i.e., the mean, median, and mode) to either the first dotted line on the right (i.e., +1 *SD* above the mean) of the middle or the dotted line on the left side (i.e., ±1 *SD* below the mean) of the middle. (For reference, these off-centered dotted lines are designated by *SD*, i.e., standard deviation.) That is, 68% of the cases (e.g., people) are clustered in the middle between ±1 *SD* and +1 *SD*. From +1 *SD* to +2 *SD* and −1 *SD* to −2 *SD*, there are approximately 14% of the people being measured. The two ends of the distribution have roughly 2% on each side. To the degree that these distributions stray from being normal, these percentages change accordingly.

When a distribution of data is not symmetrical, the issue becomes one of skewness. The *skewness* of the distribution has to do with how much the distribution strays from being symmetrical in terms of lopsidedness. When not symmetrical, a distribution is either *positively* or *negatively skewed*. If it is *positively skewed*, as shown by the distribution on the right of Figure B.3, the distribution will lean to the left with the skewness index above zero. If the distribution is *negatively skewed*, as illustrated by the left distribution in Figure B.3, it will be lopsided to the right side of the graph, and the skewness index will be less than zero depicted by a minus sign. A good way to remember is to look for the *long* tail. If it is on the right side of the distribution, it is positively skewed (i.e., strung out toward the higher values). If the tail is on the left side, it is negatively skewed (i.e., strung out toward the lower values). The important thing to remember is that if the data are lopsided, the researcher should treat the data differently when using either descriptive or inferential statistics. We discuss this further when we come to topics affected by skewness.

One other component important to the shape of the distribution of data is the numbers of *data clusters*. When the data have more than one cluster in the distribution, it means that there are subgroups of data in the data set. This is possible, for example, if the sample of participants consists of two ability groupings. This might be fine for some purposes, but certain other descriptive and inferential statistics would be drastically affected by such a distribution. How this works practically is discussed below.

Beside the shape of the distribution, two other pieces of information are important: average and variation (see Table 7.3). They both play a crucial role in the data analysis.

The Average

To understand the concept of *average*, think about how the word is used by almost everyone in everyday discussion. Teachers refer to their classes or students as average

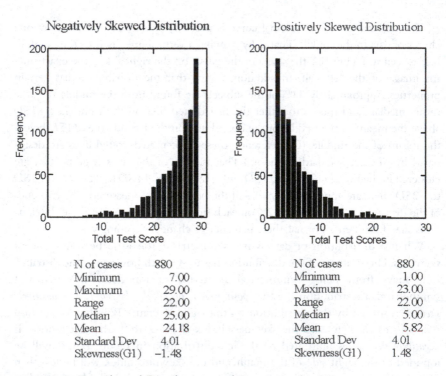

FIGURE B.3 Two Skewed Distributions and Descriptive Statistics

or above/below average. What do they mean? Are not they saying that they are like the majority of individuals in a group? *Above average* refers to those who are above the majority, and those *below average* measure below the majority. In other words, *average* is used to mean the usual (or normal), and *above* or *below* average is used to mean the unusual or not normal. In this sense, average should be thought of as an area or zone that encompasses the usual. Figure B.4 illustrates this point. Note the large box in the middle, which represents the average or what people are normally like. The smaller boxes on each side represent people who are above average and below average. The tiny boxes represent people who are exceptionally above (AA+) and below (BA–) average. Note that the boxes overlap to illustrate that the lines between average, above or below average and exceptionally above or below average overlap. In other words, there is not a clear border between being classified as average or above or below average at these points on the distribution.

Among educators, *the average* is often thought of as a single score on some measures. Those who achieve that score are average and those who score above or below it are above or below average, respectively. However, this interpretation can be somewhat misleading. As stated in the previous paragraph, average represents an area of scores that are considered *usual*, which means that there are a spread of scores that would fit into the *average zone*. The single value that is referred to as the average is only an indicator of where this average zone might be. Because this zone can change with the shape of the distribution, there are three indicators used to mark this zone: *mean, median,* and *mode* (see Table 7.3). These three descriptive statistics are used to represent the average zone, but they should never be thought of as the zone itself. Statistics books refer to these as measures of *central tendency* for this reason.

Of the three, the *mean* is the most commonly used indicator of the average zone. As you may well know, all the scores are added up and divided by the total number of scores. Many studies that you read will report means in their descriptive data.

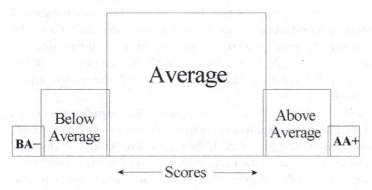

FIGURE B.4 The Concept of Average

The *median* might also appear in some Results sections of studies, although less often. The median is simply the value that splits the distribution of values in half. It is a point in the distribution of data where 50% of the scores fall above it and 50% below. For example, if you have nine measurements, such as:

$$3\ 5\ 6\ 6\ \textbf{7}\ 9\ 10\ 11\ 13$$

The value that would divide this distribution in half would be **7**, with four scores below and four scores above. The values of the numbers are not added up. We only look for the point that splits the number of scores in half.

So what is the difference between the mean and the median? Often they are equal, in which case the mean is always reported. However, they are not always equal. For instance, if you compute the mean by adding up all of the above values and divide by nine, you get 7.78, which is greater than the median of 7.00. The difference is due to the fact that the above list of values is not distributed symmetrically. It is slightly skewed to the right (i.e., positively skewed). If the shape of the distribution of data deviates from a symmetrical distribution to a large extent, the median would be the better indicator of averageness.

The third indicator of the average zone is the *mode*, which is the easiest one to understand, but the rarest one used in research. It is simply the most frequent score in the distribution. In the above list of values, the mode is 6 because it is the most frequent score, occurring twice. Sometimes there can be more than one mode, as when two different scores tie for most frequent. The shape of this distribution would be referred to as *bimodal*, where there might be two clusters of data. When there is only one mode, the distribution of values is referred to as *unimodal* (i.e., one cluster of data) as illustrated in Figure B.2.

Why have three measures of averageness? The answer is based on the shape of the distribution of the data. When the data are perfectly symmetrical and unimodal, the mean, median, and mode are the same value (see Figure B.2). For example, if a distribution is normally distributed and had a mean of 25, then the median and mode would also be 25. In such instances, the mean is always the best indicator of average to report. However, if the distribution is skewed there will be three different values for the three indicators. You can see from the information under the graph for the negatively skewed distributions in Figure B.3 that the mean is 24.18, the median is 25, and the mode is 29. For the positively skewed distribution, the mean equals 5.82, the median equals 5.00, and the mode is 2.

You may still be asking, why is this important? The significance of this becomes clearer when a researcher makes comparisons between groups of people using some form of inferential procedure. If the means of the groups are distorted due to skewness, then comparing the means may lead to false conclusions. More is said about this when we discuss inferential statistics. Suffice it to state here that journals should require researchers to include information regarding the shape of any data distributions used to help the consumer judge whether proper statistical procedures were used.

Data Variance

Not only are researchers in some studies interested in averages, they are also interested in how much people vary between one another in relation to the average. In fact, understanding variance is at the heart of every research question. Questions such as, On what traits do people vary? How much do they vary? And/or Why do they vary? are the main foci of most research.

As with the average, there are also three measures of variation (see Table 7.3): *standard deviation, interquartile range*, and *range*. As Table 7.3 shows, each one corresponds to one of the measures of average. The standard deviation corresponds to the mean, the interquartile range with the median, and the range with the mode. When reporting one type of average, the corresponding measure of variation should be reported as well.

The *standard deviation*, commonly reported as *SD*, can be thought of as the average deviation from the mean. (Note: Whenever you see the word *standard* in a statistical term, think *average*.) As with the mean, the *SD* is the most common measure of variation reported in published research for describing data. The *SD*s in Figure B.2 shows plus and minus 1 and 2 standard deviations above and below the mean.

The less used measure of variance is the *interquartile range*. In essence, it is used to estimate the central 50% of the subjects in the distribution. Although seldom used, there are studies that report this statistic. Franklin (2011), for instance, realized that his data did not approach a normal distribution, in addition to having a small sample. Instead of using means and *SD*s to describe his data, he used medians and interquartile ranges. Many who use nonparametric inferential statistics should follow Franklin's example.

The last measure of variance is *the range*. This is simply the distance between the lowest value and the highest value in the distribution. In Figure B.3, you will find that the range for both of the distributions is 22. For the data on the left, the minimum score was 7.00 and the maximum score was 29.00. The difference between the two is 22, the range. The principal use of the range is to get a quick idea of how far the distribution stretches and how many *SD*s fit inside the range.

Why is it important for the consumer of research to know anything about the variation of scores? Returning to our first comments in this section on the importance of variance, both the range and the standard deviation are distorted by data that are highly skewed or that contain unusual patterns of values. If those measures are used in such circumstances, the results of the study will be misleading. A well-written research article will alert the reader to any anomalies in the data and will explain how these are taken into consideration.

To digest the above discussion, this might be a good time to take a break by doing the following exercise before moving on to other topics.

EXERCISE B.2

Locate several research studies and do the following:

1   Determine what types of data are being used in each study.
2   Describe how the data are reported.

    a   What was reported about the shape of the data distribution?
    b   What measure of average was reported?
    c   What measure of variance was reported?

3   In your estimation, were the correct descriptive statistics used?

More About Inferential Statistics

Univariate Versus Multivariate Procedures

Different inferential statistical procedures are determined by the configuration of the independent variables (IVs) and the dependent variables (DVs). A study can have one or more IVs and one or more DVs. If there is only one DV then the statistical procedures are labeled *univariate,* regardless of how many independent variables there are. However, if a study has more than one DV, then the procedures are referred to as *multivariate.* In other words, the labels, *univariate* and *multivariate,* are only concerned with the number of DVs without reference to the number of IVs. Recall that independent variables can have two or more *levels.* For instance, Gender has two levels: male and female. Levels of language ability may have three levels: low, intermediate, advanced.

Based on the above, the following inferential statistical procedures are *univariate:* regression (simple and multiple), *t* test (dependent and independent), all forms of ANOVA and ANCOVA. *Multivariate* procedures commonly used in educational research having more than one dependent variable are factor analysis, multivariate analysis of variance (MANOVA), and multivariate analysis of covariance (MANCOVA). The following describes these procedures in addition to what was presented in Chapter 7.

More on Univariate ANOVAs

Multiway ANOVAs

In Chapter 7, we left off with 2 × 2 ANOVAs that had two independent variables with two levels each and one dependent variable. The following presents more complex configurations of ANOVA that you will encounter in educational research. For example, you might see a three-way or a four-way ANOVA. Again, remember that the number in front of the *-way* simply tells you the number of independent variables in the study. To illustrate, Dehaene-Lambertz and Houston (1997) used a three-way ANOVA to study infants' ability to discriminate between native and foreign languages. They used a $2 \times 2 \times 2$ ANOVA, meaning that there were two levels for each of the three factors (i.e., IVs): nationality (2), language of presentation (2), and presence of filtering (2). Note that they had to test for three main effects, three interactions between pairs of variables (i.e., N × LP, N × PF, and LP × PF), and one interaction between all three (i.e., N × LP × PF). So, all together, there were seven things that they had to test for statistical significance. As you can imagine, the more complex the configuration, the more complex is the statistical analysis.

Repeated Measures ANOVA

Another type of ANOVA is one that uses repeated measures. This is similar to the dependent *t* test in that there are multiple measurements of the same instrument administered repeatedly to the participants. However, if there are two or more administrations, a repeated measure ANOVA must be done. An example of this was completed by Powell and Newgent (2008) where they examined the use of disc golf as a creative, recreational play intervention for improving classroom behaviors in disruptive children. Twenty-two elementary students were randomly selected for either a treatment or control group and rated at pre- and post- by their teachers on the use of nine positive classroom behaviors (e.g., sharing, raising hand, and compliance) using the Brief Classroom Behavior Checklist (BCBC). Results of a two-way ANOVA with one between-subjects factor and one repeated measures revealed a significant difference $F = 48.25$, ($p < .0001$) between both groups over time.

Between-Subjects and Within-Subjects ANOVA

Related to the above, some studies use an ANOVA design that has one IV where the levels contain independent groups of participants and another IV that is *within* the participants. For example, if the first IV is gender, there are two separate groups of participants: males versus females. However, the second IV might be *time of testing* which could mean that each participant is given a pretest and a posttest. The result is a 2×2 ANOVA, where the first IV is a between-subjects factor and the second IV is a within-subjects factor. In essence, the second variable is a *repeated measure*. Some researchers refer this as a within-subjects factor. Others refer to it as a *nested* variable.

Analysis of Covariance

Recall back in Chapter 7 where researchers matched participants on some variable (e.g., intelligence) to eliminate its effect? There is a way to do this using a form of ANOVA as well—it is called *analysis of covariance* (ANCOVA). This procedure extracts the variance in the dependent variable that is due to some extraneous variable(s) and then looks at the relation of the independent variable to the remaining variance left in the dependent variable. No, this is not double talk; let us illustrate. Wyss, Heulskamp, and Siebert (2012) studied whether there were any differences in interest in science, technology, engineering, and mathematics (STEM) careers in middle school students after a treatment group of students were shown a series of video interviews from STEM professionals. Forty-one students were in the treatment group (watching the videos), and 43 were in the comparison control group. Students' interest in pursing STEM careers before, at midpoint, and after viewing the videos were compared. The researchers looked for changes after viewing just four videos, and again after viewing eight videos to observe any accumulated impact as the number of videos increased. Students who viewed videos compared with students who did not view the videos at each interval. Gender was controlled for with the ANCOVA design.

A chi-square analysis was initially used to determine whether gender and grade-level distributions were similar for the treatment and control group. Their results showed no significant initial differences between students in these two groups. Using the ANCOVA design, the researchers tested for any differences between groups prior to the treatment. An interaction between groups and the pretest versus midpoint scores revealed no significant interaction, $F = 1.06$, $p = .31$. The group (treatment vs. control) was a statistically significant predictor of midpoint test scores ($F = 4.41$, $p < .04$). Therefore, it was concluded that there was a significant difference in the average midtest score between the treatment and control groups when adjusting for the pretest score. In addition, the results of the ANCOVA test showed that the group in which the students were placed was a statistically significant predictor of the posttest score $F = 5.81$, $p = .019$ when also adjusting for the pretest score. Gender did not play a factor in this sample of students but in their discussion section, the researchers make note that this study represents a small subset of the population and that effort was made to represent women in STEM fields in the video development. Using ANCOVA, Wyss et al. (2012) were able to eliminate any competing explanations for their results. This procedure is also very useful for controlling variables that creep into a study because of the lack of random sampling.

Multivariate ANOVAs

Univariate statistics has only one dependent variable, whereas multivariate statistical procedures have more than one DV. In cases where a study has one or more IVs and more than one DV, the researcher can perform a separate *univariate* ANOVA on each DV or analyze everything all at once using a *multivariate* approach. The purpose of doing the latter is to control for the Type I error, as with the rationale behind using ANOVA rather than a number of *t* tests. That is, for every ANOVA, there is an overall probability of making a Type I error.

The most common form found in the literature is the MANOVA. This procedure basically uses any one of the independent variable configurations we have discussed regarding ANOVA, only with more than one dependent variable, all at the same time. For example, if we wanted to look at whether people from different cultural backgrounds (IV.1) varied on reading (DV.1) and writing (DV.2) ability, we could do two separate ANOVAs for each DV or we could do one MANOVA that does both at once. The rationale is that the two DVs in this case are related in that they are both reflective of verbal ability. In actual fact, when using MANOVA, the common factor shared by the DVs is what is being compared in the independent variable. If an overall finding is statistically significant, it would suggest that somewhere in the analysis there is a significant difference. You will sometimes see values for *Wilke's lambda* or *Pillai's trace* reported for a statistically significant MANOVA, but they are converted into *F* ratios and interpreted as any *F* ratio would be. If a MANOVA is found to be statistically significant; typically, separate ANOVAs would then be done on each of the DVs, followed by post hoc pairwise comparisons to tease out the differences as we have already discussed in Chapter 7.

Tyler, Love, Brown, and Roan-Belle (2010), for example, used MANOVA to investigate the differences in self-esteem, self-efficacy, identified motivation, motivation to know, and amotivation scores on the Home Communalism Measure subscales as a function of race and other demographic variables. The participants in the study were 165 Black and 125 White undergraduates from multiple universities. The research design called for one level (race/ethnicity), and four different constructs of belief and achievement: home communalism, self-esteem, general self-efficacy, and academic motivation (four dependent variables). Because these four measures were highly related, Tyler et al. used the MANOVA procedure. They found no significant differences in each of the three communalism subscales as a function of race or ethnicity. They also found that there were no significant main or interaction effects of these demographic variables on the four subscales. These findings helped them to eliminate these variables for the second phase of their study to explore the predictive nature of the communalism subscales via multiple regression analysis.

Finally, we close this section with MANCOVA, which is a MANOVA with one or more *covariates*. This is the same as ANCOVA except it has more than one DV, thus MANCOVA. An example of this technique is the study done by Katz and Porath (2011). They explored the emotional and behavioral outcomes of the Respecting Diversity program, a social and emotional learning intervention to develop self-awareness, self-respect, and respect for divers others. Intervention and control groups were assessed pre- and postintervention for each of the dependent variables listed above. The pretest was used as the covariate to control for pretreatment differences. A main effect was discovered using MANCOVA controlling for grade, with treatment group, gender, and English as a Second Language (ESL) status. They followed correct procedures by first looking at the overall MANCOVA.

Upon finding it statistically significant, they moved to more specific analysis to determine where the exact differences lie as outlined previously.

As with the other categories of statistics discussed above, there are a number of other multivariate procedures available. We have not included them here. However, when you come across some type of statistical procedure that we have not touched on, remember that the same principles apply. You can Google them, and you will find more than you will have time to read.

Degrees of Freedom

When you see various inferential statistics reported in Results sections, you might wonder what the numbers in brackets mean. For example what does (3, 76) mean in the ANOVA results of $F (3, 76) = 20.64, p < .0001$. (We have deliberately left this out of previous reporting of F values to avoid overload.) These are known as *degrees of freedom* (*df*) that you will see with various statistical results. One way that might help you to understand this is that it works like Sudoku. If you know eight of the numbers on a row or column, you automatically know the ninth. In other words, it has eight cells free to vary (i.e., 8 df). For a one-way ANOVA, the first number is the number of *levels* of the *one* independent variable being tested minus one, and the second number is number of participants being used minus the number of levels in the IV. In the example above, there are four levels and 80 participants, therefore, $df = 3, 76$. It has nothing to do with how many dependent variables there are. The *df*s are used by statisticians to determine whether the F ratio, or whatever statistic being used, is large enough to be statistically significant. If you want to know more about this, consult any elementary applied statistics text or enter the term *degrees of freedom* into your favorite Internet search engine along with the word *statistics*.

EXERCISE B.3

Find a study that looked for differences between variables but that has more than one dependent variable.

1   Identify the independent variables? The dependent variables?
2   What type of data is being used?
3   What is the null hypothesis being tested (explicit or implicit)?
4   What statistical procedure(s) is used (MANOVA, MANCOVA, etc.)?
5   What followup statistics are used?
6   Are the results statistically significant? At what level? What does this mean regarding making inferences?
7   Are the interpretations given by the researcher(s) consistent with the findings?

Type II Error and Power

Recall in Chapter 7 that a Type II error is made when the null hypothesis is falsely accepted. That is, a study that fails to find a statistically significant relationship between variables or a difference between groups at the $p < .05$ may have made a mistake (i.e., a Type II error—there is an actual relationship or difference in the population, but the study missed it). The probability of making this mistake is indicated by beta (β) (see Figure 7.2). However, the probability of not making a Type II error is $1 - \beta$, referred to as the *power* of the test. That is, the probability of correctly rejecting the null hypothesis increases. Obviously, a researcher wants to have the most power in trying to support their hypothesis—usually the opposite of the null hypothesis.

There are three things that affect the power of statistical procedures. One is the stringency of the probability of making a Type I error (i.e., the α level). The rule is that the lower the α level, the greater the β and, thus, the lower the power $(1 - \beta)$. Ok, enough of the Greek. In plain English, this means that as the probability of falsely rejecting the null hypothesis decreases (e.g., $p < .05$ to $p < .001$), the probability of falsely accepting it increases. Logically, this means that as the probability of falsely accepting the null hypothesis increases, the power of the test decreases (i.e., there is less chance of discovering a relationship or difference). In practice, this works out to mean that the researcher should choose the largest α level permissible to increase the chances of a statistically significant finding, although this increases the chance of making a Type I error. Remember, however, that $p = .05$ is as high as one can go for statistical significance.

The other two things that can influence ability of a statistical procedure to detect either a relationship or a difference are *sample size* and *direction of the prediction*. Sample size is positively related to power. That is, as sample size increases so does the power of the procedure and vice versa. Studies that do not find statistical significance, and have small sample sizes, have low power. Had there been larger samples, the findings may have been different. Studies with large sample sizes may find statistical significance even with small correlations or small differences between groups of participants. For example, a correlation coefficient of 0.37 is not statistically significant for a study with a sample size of 15, but is for one that has 30 participants.

Direction of prediction is a third factor that can influence the statistical power of a procedure. Studies that test directional predictions have more power than those that do not. What is a directional prediction? If researchers predict that there will be a positive relationship between variables (or negative ones), they have proposed a directional hypothesis. On the basis of theory or previous research, they may state that as one variable increases so will the other (i.e., positive), or, as one increases the other decreases (i.e., negative). However, researchers may not be able to make predictions of a directional relationship but only predictions of nondirectional relationships (e.g., one variable relates in some way to the other). If directional relationships are predicted, then the power of finding these predictions statistically significantly increases over those that have no direction in their predictions. The reason is that the critical value[2] of the correlation coefficient is lower for a directional prediction than for a nondirectional prediction. For example, for a study with sample size = 30 that predicts there will be a positive relationship between two variables, any correlation equal to or greater than 0.31 is statistically significant. However, if there is a nondirectional prediction, then the study must find a correlation equal to or greater than .36 to be statistically significant.

The same principle as the above holds for differences between groups as well. Researchers may predict that the treatment group will do better than the control group (i.e., a directional hypothesis), or they may only predict that there will be a difference without any direction. The former will have more power in predicting a significant difference than the latter—not because the former is a stronger prediction but because the critical t test value used to test the difference between the means of the two groups does not have to be as great as that of the latter.

Connected to the direction of prediction issue above, there are two expressions that you will encounter: *one-tailed* versus *two-tailed* tests of significance. Without going into probability theory, the following should be sufficient. If there is a directional hypothesis, you should see the term *one-tailed* test of significance. If there is no direction in the prediction or no prediction at all, then you should find a *two-tailed* test. If there is no statement about a one-tail test, then assume that the procedures are using two-tailed tests. These two terms relate to the issue discussed above about how the critical value is chosen for determining statistical significance. It is enough to know that the one-tailed test uses the lower critical value and the two-tailed test uses the higher critical value as illustrated above.

Effect Size

Many journals require researchers to include *effect size* with their inferential statistics (e.g., *reading or math achievement*). As the term suggests, it is an estimate of the extent to which one group differs from another, one variable correlates with another, and so on. This statistic directly relates to the *power* of a statistical procedure and the practical significance of the findings. It relates to power in that the greater the effect size, the greater the power of the statistical test. It relates to practical application in that the greater the effect size, the greater the implications for practical use. Do not think that effect size only relates to quantitative research. Onwuegbuzie (2003) provided typologies of a number of effect sizes for qualitative data analysis. Though these are not commonly reported in qualitative research, it is only a matter of time before some form of these will be required.

There are a number of statistics used to indicate effect size. The reason is that for every type of statistical procedure used, there is a separate formula to compute effect size. In addition, there may be several ways to compute effect size, depending on one's preference. Google *effect size calculator* and see all the different methods.

For example, in their study of the relearning of second language vocabulary, Hansen, Umedo, and McKinney (2002) used squared point-biserial correlations (r^2_{pb}) to show the effect size of their t test findings (e.g., $t = 24.19$, $p < .001$, $r^2_{pb} = .862$). The r^2_{pb} of .862 indicated "a massive effect size" showing that forgotten words were much better learned than psuedowords. Later in the same study Hansen et al. used another statistic η^2 to show effect size for a one-way ANOVA, which also provided evidence for a strong effect size. For more about this, Google *effect size* if you dare.

Key Terms and Concepts

univariate ANOVAs

analysis of covariance (ANCOVA)
between subjects and within subjects ANOVA
repeated measures ANOVA

multivariate ANOVAs

multiple analysis of covariance (MANCOVA)
multivariate analysis of variance (MANOVA)

Miscellaneous statistical terms
central tendency
covariate
degrees of freedom (df)
effect size
nested variable
normal distribution
one-tailed versus two-tailed test of significance
positively or negatively skewed distributions
Pillais' trace
Power
scales: nominal, ordinal, interval, and ratio
Wilkes' lambda

Notes

1 Usually there is only one mode (i.e., most frequent score). However, if there are more modes in a data set, then there are more clusters of data.
2 The critical value is the value that determines whether it is statistically significant.

References

Dehaene-Lambertz, G., & Houston, D. (1997). Faster orientation latencies toward native language in two-month-old infants. *Language and Speech, 41*, 21–43. doi:10.1177/002383099804100102

Franklin, E. A. (2011). Greenhouse facility management experts indemnification of competencies and teaching methods to support secondary agricultural education instructors: A modified Delphi study. *Journal of Agricultural Education, 52*(4), 150–161.

Hansen, L., Umedo, Y., & McKinney, M. (2002). Savings in the relearning of second language vocabulary: The effects of time and proficiency. *Language Learning, 52*, 653–678.

Katz, J., & Porath, M. (2011). Teaching to diversity: Creating compassionate learning communities for diverse elementary school students. *International Journal of Special Education, 26*(2), 29–41.

Onwuegbuzie, A. J. (2003). Effect sizes in qualitative research: A prolegomenon. *Quality & Quantity, 37*, 393–409.

Powell. M. L., & Newgent, R. A. (2008). Disc golf play: Using recreation to improve disruptive classroom behaviors. *Journal of School Counseling, 6*(2), 1–17.

Sevinc, B., Ozmen, H., & Yigit, N. (2011). Investigation of primary students' motivation levels towards science. *Science Education International, 22*(3), 218–232.

Szyfman, A., Wanner, G., & Spencer, L. (2003). The relationship between cellular phone use, performance, and reaction time among college students: Implications for cellular phone use while driving. *American Journal of Health Education, 34*(2), 81–83.

Tyler, K., Love, K., Brown, C., & Roan-Belle, C. (2010). Linking communalism to achievement correlates for black and white undergraduates. *International Journal of Teaching and Learning in Higher Education, 22*(1), 23–31.

Wyss, V. L., Heulskamp, D., & Siebert, C. J. (2012). Increasing middle school student interest in STEM careers with videos of scientists. *International Journal of Environmental & Science Education, 7*(4), 501–522.

GLOSSARY

Accumulative treatment effect   The result of the accumulative effect due to the particular order in which treatments are presented. Also known as the multiple-treatment interference or order effect.

Alternate-form reliability   The degree to which different forms of a test measure the same general attribute.

Analysis of covariance (ANCOVA)   A parametric statistical procedure that removes differences between groups prior to treatment.

Analysis of variance (ANOVA)   An inferential statistic used to compare the difference among three or more sets of data.

Applied linguistics   A discipline that focuses on practical issues involving the learning and teaching of foreign/second languages.

Applied research   Research that is directly applicable to practical problems in teaching and learning.

Automatic response   Occurs when a respondent selects only one choice throughout the questionnaire without thinking.

Average   A measure that best represents the central core in a distribution of data, that is, mean, median, and mode.

Basic research   Research dealing mainly with highly abstract constructs and theory which has little apparent practical use.

Case   One participant or record in a data set.

Case study   An in-depth study of an example(s) that represents a phenomenon in its natural setting.

Causal-comparative design   Characterized by variation in the independent variable found in nature rather than a result of experimenter manipulations, thus making the findings suggestive of cause/effect at most.

Central tendency   The term used by statisticians for average.

Chi-square   An inferential statistical procedure for comparing observed frequencies with expected frequencies.

Closed-form questionnaire   These items provide a set of alternative items answers from which the respondent must select at least one.

Coefficient   A number that represents the amount of some attribute, such as a correlation coefficient.

Compensatory equalization of treatments   Occurs when attempts are made to give the control group extra material or special treatment to make up for not receiving the experimental treatment.

Confirmatory research   A study that is designed to test an explicitly stated hypothesis.

Construct   A concept that a given discipline (e.g., applied linguistics) has constructed to identify some quality that is thought to exist (i.e., language proficiency).

Construct validity   The global concept that encompasses all the facets of validity.

Constructed response items   Test items that require participants to recall and integrate information, such as a test of writing ability where they must compose an essay.

Content coverage   The facet of validity that indicates how well the "content" of the measurement procedure aligns with the treatment objectives.

Control group contamination   A result of anything that might cause the control group to behave differently than normal.

Convenience sampling   Using participants who are chosen because they are conveniently available for use in a study.

Conversational analysis   A research technique that analyzes verbal output from a totally inductive perspective without any prior knowledge about the context of the participants. Resulting verbal data is seldom coded or transformed into numerical data.

Correlational study   One that investigates relationships between variables.

Covariate   An unwanted variable that is controlled by statistical procedures.

Criterion related   The facet of validity which indicates how well a measurement procedure corresponds to some external criterion, such as predicting the capacity to succeed or identifying current characteristics.

Criterion-referenced tests   Interpretation of the results of such test is based on one or more criteria for deciding the status of examinees.

Cronbach's alpha   An estimate of the reliability of a Likert-type questionnaire (i.e., degree of internal consistency of the items).

Degrees of freedom (df)   Numbers that are used for identifying the criterion the determination of statistical significance—usually associated with number of groups and sample size.

Demoralization (boycott)   This potential contaminator occurs when participants in the control group resent the special treatment given to the treatment group and lowers their performance.

Dependent _t_ tests An inferential statistic that assesses the difference between the means of two sets of scores for either the same group of participants or two groups whose participants have been matched (also called correlated _t_ test or paired _t_ test).

Dependent variable The variable that is analyzed for change as a result of change in another variable (i.e., the independent variable).

Descriptive statistics Estimates of parameters that describe a population such as means and standard deviations.

Differential selection The selection procedure results in groups of participants who possess preexisting differences that may affect the variable being investigated.

Discrete-point item This test item measures only one thing and is scored correct or incorrect.

Effect size An estimate of the extent to which one group differs from another, one variable correlates with another, and so forth. Used for determining practical significance.

Ethnography A procedure whereby data are gathered from a number of sources in a natural setting resulting in large quantities of verbal data.

Experimental design A research design that involves manipulating the independent variable(s) and observing the change in the dependent variable(s) on a randomly chosen sample.

Experimental treatment diffusion (compromise) Occurs when the control group gains knowledge of the factor(s) making up the treatment condition(s) and employs this factor(s) in its own situation which distorts the results.

Experimentally accessible population A population that is a subset of a larger population but more accessible for obtaining a sample.

Exploratory research A study that seeks to answer research questions without testing any hypothesis.

External validity The degree to which the findings of a study can be generalized to a target population.

Extraneous variable A variable that can adversely affect the dependent variable other than the independent variable(s).

F ratio A value used to indicate statistical significance of differences between groups of data in such inferential statistics such as ANOVA.

Face appearance The facet of validity that indicates the degree to which a measurement procedure appears to measure what it is supposed to measure.

Friedman test A nonparametric procedure for testing the difference between three or more sets of data gathered on the same people.

Full-participant observer An observer who is, or becomes, a full member of the group being observed.

Grounded theory A theoretical hypothesis that develops as the data accumulates in a study.

Halo-effect The biasing effect of judging the work of one participant on the work of a following participant.

Hawthorne effect   Occurs when participants behave unnaturally because they know they are in a research study.

Highly structured interview   One that follows a predetermined set of questions with no allowance for variation.

History   Effects due to the influence of events that take place at different points in time on the dependent variable other than the independent variable.

Homogeneity of variance   The degree to which the variances of different groups of data are similar.

Hypothesis   A theoretical statement that proposes how several constructs relate to one another.

Independent *t* test   An inferential statistic that analyzes the difference between the averages (i.e., means) on one dependent variable for two independent groups of data.

Independent variable   The principal variable(s) being investigated regarding its influence on some dependent variable.

Inferential statistics   Statistics used to make inferences from samples to populations.

Informant   A person from the group being observed who gives verbal information to the researcher.

Information-rich paradigm   A sampling strategy for selecting the best participants for providing the information needed for a particular study.

Instrumental procedures   Procedures that use some form of impersonal instrument for obtaining research data.

Internal consistency   The degree to which all the items in an instrument measure the same general attribute.

Internal validity   The degree to which the results of the study are due to the independent variable(s) under consideration and not due to anything else.

Interquartile range   An estimate of where the middle 50% of the scores are located in the data distribution—half the distance between the first quartile and the third quartile of the frequency of scores.

Inter-rater reliability   The degree to which different observers/raters agree in their observations/ratings of the behavior of participants.

Interval scale   The values represent equal amounts of the variable being measured but have a relative zero, such as, temperature on a thermometer.

Intra-rater reliability   The degree to which observers/raters give the same results given the opportunity to observe/rate participants on more than one occasion.

Introspection   A procedure which requires participants to observe their own internal cognitive (or emotional) states and/or processing strategies during an ongoing task such as reading.

Item quality   The degree to which an item in a test or questionnaire is understood by the respondents due to the manner in which it is written.

John Henry effect   Occurs when the difference between the control group and the treatment group is due to competition rather than the treatment.

Kruskal–Wallis test   A nonparametric statistical procedure that analyzes the differences between three or more independent groups of participants.

Kuder-Richardson K20 and K21   Two related formulas for calculating the reliability for tests consisting of items that are scored dichotomously, that is, correct/incorrect, true/false, yes/no, etc.

Longitudinal study   A study designed to collect data over a period of time.

Mann–Whitney *U* test   A nonparametric statistical procedure used to analyze the difference between two independent groups of participants.

Maturation   Effects due to natural changes in the participants that take place over time other than due to the variables being studied.

Mean   The most common index of average: the sum of all the scores divided by the number of scores.

Measurement–treatment interaction   Occurs when the results are only found when using a particular type of measuring procedure.

Median   A measure of average: the point that divides the number of scores in half.

Mode   The least used index of average: the most frequent score.

Moderating variable   A variable that moderates the effect(s) of the independent variable on the dependent variable.

Multiple analysis of covariance (MANCOVA)   ANCOVA with more than one dependent variable.

Multiple regressions   An inferential statistical procedure used to determine which combination of independent variables best predicts or explains the variation in one dependent variable.

Multivariate analysis of variance (MANOVA)   ANOVA with more than one dependent variable—all at the same time.

Multivariate statistics   Procedures that analyze more than one dependent variable at the same time.

Multiway ANOVAs   ANOVA procedures with more than two independent variables.

Negatively skewed distribution   Data that are lopsided to the right side.

Nested variable   One where the levels are within the participants rather than between them, such as a repeated measurement on the same subjects.

Nominal scale   One where the values of a variable represent categories, such as, 1 = male, 2 = female. Other than identifiers, they have no quantitative value.

Nonparametric statistics   Inferential statistical procedures used for analyzing data in the form of frequencies, ranked data, and other data that do not meet the assumptions for parametric procedures.

Nonparticipant observer   One who does not personally interact with the participants in any manner while making observations.

Nonproportional stratified random sample   A sample of equal numbers of participants randomly sampled from each strata in the target population.

Normal distribution   A symmetrical, bell-shaped distribution of data that has specific properties and is used as a reference point for comparing the shapes of data distributions.

Norm-referenced test   One where scores are interpreted by comparing them with scores from a body of people that represent the population.

Null hypothesis   One which states that there is no true relationship between variables in a population.

Objectivity   The degree to which the data are not influenced by bias due to attitude, temporary emotional states, and so forth, of the data collector.

Objects   Inanimate sources of data, such as a corpus of text.

Observational procedure   Any procedure that captures data through visual observation.

Observational variable   A variable that consists of data in the form of observations and descriptions.

One-tailed test of statistical significance   A method for testing statistical significance that is based on one end of the probability distribution. It is used for testing directional hypotheses.

One-way ANOVA   The simplest form of ANOVA involving the use of one independent variable and one dependent variable.

Open-form questionnaire items   Questions that allow respondents to give their own answers without restrictions.

Open-structured interview   One that follows a general plan but is not restricted to predetermined questions.

Operational definition   One that defines a construct in terms of observable behavior.

Ordinal scale   One where the values represent some type of rank order, such as, first, second, third, and so forth. It represents relative amounts of a variable, for example, small, large, and largest.

Pair-wise comparisons   Procedures that compare the differences between groups of data, two at a time.

Parameters   Measurements on an entire population.

Parametric statistical procedures   Inferential procedures used on data that meet the assumptions of normalcy of distribution and homogeneity of variance.

Partial-participant observer   One who has developed a personal relationship with the group being observed but is not a full member of the group.

Participant observer   One who has a personal relationship with those being observed by being a member of the group.

Participants   People from whom data are gathered—synonymous with "subjects."

Pearson product moment correlation   A parametric statistical procedure that measures the linear relationship between two sets of data, also known as the Pearson r, or simply r.

Position paper   A document in which a writer argues his/her particular viewpoint, or position, on some issues without doing a research study for support.

Positively skewed distribution   A data distribution lopsided to the left side.

Power   The probability of not making a Type II error.

Predictive utility   The aspect of the criterion-related facet of validity that indicates how well an instrument predicts performance.

Preliminary sources   Publications designed to reference and catalogue documents in various disciplines. These are extremely useful for locating primary research.

Pretest effect   Occurs when a test given before the administration of the treatment interacts with the treatment by heightening participants' awareness of importance of certain material.

Primary research   Research performed and reported first-hand by the researcher(s).

Proportional stratified random sampling   A technique that randomly selects cases that represent the proportion of each strata of the population.

Purposeful sampling   A technique that selects samples based on how information-rich they are for addressing the research question.

Pygmalion effect   A type of researcher effect caused by the bias in the researcher's perception of the behavior of the participants due to preexisting expectations of the participant's performance.

Qualitative research   Research that is done in a natural setting, involving intensive holistic data collection through observation at a very close personal level without the influence of prior theory and contains mostly verbal analysis.

Quantitative research   Any study using numerical data with emphasis on statistics to answer the research questions.

Quasi-experimental design   Ones that look at the effects of independent variables on dependent variables, similar to experimental designs, only the samples are not randomly chosen.

Range   A measure of how much data varies based on the distance from the lowest to the highest scores in the distribution.

Ratio scale   One where the values represent equal amounts of the variable being measured and has a real zero, such as, response time.

Regression analysis   A parametric procedure used to identify variables (i.e., independent variables) that either predict or explain another variable (i.e., the dependent variable).

Reliability   The degree to which a data-gathering procedure produces consistent results.

Reliability coefficient   A correlation coefficient that indicates the reliability of a data-gathering procedure.

Replication of research   The repetition of a study typically using a different sample.

Representative sampling paradigm   A strategy for obtaining a sample that represents a target population.

Researcher effect   Occurs when data are distorted by some characteristic of the researcher either in administering the treatment or collecting the data.

Retrospection   A technique that requires participants to wait until after the task before reflecting on what they had done cognitively.

Rubric   A detailed definition of each level of a rating scale.

Sample   A portion of a larger population.

Secondary sources   These summarize other people's research rather than provide firsthand reports by the original researchers.

Semi-structured interview   One that has a set of predetermined questions, but the interviewer is free to follow up a question with additional questions that probe further.

Simple random sampling   Occurs when everyone in the population has an equal chance of being chosen for the sample.

Skewed distribution   One that is lopsided—more scores on one side of the distribution than the other.

Spearman rank-order correlation (rho)   A nonparametric correlation that indicates the relationship between sets of data are in the form of ranked data.

Spearman–Brown prophecy formula   A method for estimating the reliability of a test if the number of test items increase.

Split-half (odd/even) reliability   A measure of the internal consistency of a test by correlating one half of the test with the other, usually the odd items with the even ones.

Standard error of measurement (SEM)   An estimate of the average amount of error made by a measurement instrument.

Standardized test   A test which has been designed to be given under strict guidelines for administration and scoring across each occasion.

Statistical regression   An effect where the difference between scores on the pretest and posttest is due to the natural tendency for initial extreme scores to move toward the average on subsequent testing.

Statistical significance   Determined when the chances of making a Type I error is equal to or less than 5%.

Stratified random sample   One where a random sample is chosen from each strata in a population.

Subject attrition (also experimental mortality)   Occurs when there is a loss of participants during a research study.

Subjectivity   The degree to which the data are influenced by bias due to attitude, temporary emotional states, and so forth, of the data collector.

Subjects   People from whom data are gathered (synonymous with participants).

Target population   All the members of a group of people/objects to whom the researcher wants to generalize his or her research findings.

Test–retest reliability   An estimate of the stability of measurement results for the same instrument repeated over time.

Theory   An explanation attempting to interrelate large sets of observed phenomena or constructs into a meaningful holistic framework.

Think-aloud technique   A procedure where participants are required to talk about what they are thinking. Usually they are audio-recorded while talking.

Time of measurement   Occurs when the results of a study are not stable over different times of measurement.

Trait accuracy   The facet of validity which indicates how accurately a procedure measures the trait (i.e., construct) under investigation.

Transferability   The extent to which the findings of a study can be transferred to other similar situations.

Treatment fidelity   The degree to which a treatment is correctly administered.

Treatment intervention   Occurs when the results of a study are distorted due to the novelty or disruption of a treatment.

Treatment strength–time interaction   Occurs when the time needed for the treatment to have any noticeable effect is not sufficient.

Triangulation   A procedure using multiple sources of data to see if they converge to provide evidence for validating interpretations of results.

Two-tailed test of statistical significance   A method for testing statistical significance that is based on both ends of the probability distribution. It is used for testing nondirectional hypotheses.

Type I error   Occurs when the null hypothesis is rejected in a sample while it is true in the population.

Type II error   Occurs when the null hypothesis is not rejected in a sample while it is false in the population.

Utility   The facet of validity which is concerned with whether measurement/observational procedures are used for the correct purpose.

Validity   The degree to which a measurement/observational procedure accurately captures data and is used correctly.

Volunteers   Participants who have been solicited and have agreed to participate in a study.

Wilcoxon matched-pairs signed rank test (or the Wilcoxon *T* test)   A nonparametric procedure for analyzing the difference between two sets of data that are related in some fashion.

Wilke's lambda   A statistic used in multivariate statistical procedures for indicating overall statistical significance.

INDEX

accumulative treatment effect 104
action research 78
Aeen, L. 169
Afflerbach, P. 115
Ahadi, H. 63
Ahghar, G. 63
Ajayi, L. 48
Akbas, O. 66
Alameda-Lawson, T. 56
Alivernini, F. 49
Allsop, Y. 120
Al-Seghayer, K. 181
analysis of covariance (ANCOVA)
    218-220
analysis of variance (ANOVA) 184;
    between-subjects 219; multi-way 218;
    one-way 184; repeated measures 219;
    two-way 185; within-subjects 219
Anderson, R.C. 77
Anderson, S. 15
Andrews, M. 172
Asadzadeh, H, 63
average 165, 166; see also mean;
    median; mode

Bachman, L. F. 143
Bagheri, M. 169
Bailey, J. 67
Bailey, P. 176

Baker, J. C. 40
Bang, E. 184
Bhaskar, R. 16
Biklen, S. K. 154
Binyan, X. 25
Birgin, O. 182
Blakesley, S. 85
Blumberg, F. C. 81, 83
Bogdan, R. C. 154
Bon, S. C. 91
Bond, J. 157, 160
Bong, M. 15
Bonner, J. M. 173
Books, S. 41
Boon, J. 82, 83, 109
Boraie, D. 114
Bordelon, T. D. 159
Borenstein, M. 206
Borg, W. R. 13, 59, 79, 84
Bornsheuer, J. N. 172
Boshuizen, H. P. A. 35
Bracht, G. H. 93
Brand-Gruwel, S. 35
Bronfenbrenner, U. 12
Brooks, M. 40
Browder, D. M. 12
Brown, C. 134, 221
Brown, F. 12
Brown, J. R. 134

Brown, L. J. 134
Brown, M. 101
Burns, A. 76
Burns, A. B. 89
Bursuck, W. D. 10

Cai, W. 115, 116
Campbell, D. T. 93
Canfield-Davis, K. 119, 150, 160, 189,
   195, 199
Caranikas-Walker, F. 91, 110
Cardona, B. 119, 121, 124, 125, 126, 160,
   161, 162, 189, 195, 196
Carrier, S. J. 160
case 55, 56
case study 79, 80
Catlioglu, H. 182
causal hypothesis 15
causal-comparative design 89
Cavenaugh, B. S. 94
Celikten, O. 97, 98, 99, 100, 101
central tendency 215; *see also* average
Chaapel, H. 67
Chan, C-K. 49
Chang, C-C. 183
Chang, M. 32,
Charles, C. A. 84, 92
Chavez, A. F. 67
Chen, W-P. 183
chi-square 78, 171, 172
Choi, E. 156
Chou, M. 103, 104
Christensen, L. B. 108
Chudowsky, N. 12
Chun, E. 104
Chung, C-G. 86
Clarke, R. C. 78
closed-form questionnaire items 130
Cobb, C. D. 78
Coladarci, T. 78
Coleman, L. J. 78, 83
Columna, L. 67
compensatory equalization of treatments
   98, 99
competing group contamination
   97, 98
Compton, D. L. 61
construct 10, 12; as constitutively defined
   13; as operationally defined 13, 16

construct validity 143; *see also* facets
constructed response items 131
content coverage 144, 146
continuous vigilance 122
conversational analysis 80
Cook, T. D. 93
Cooper, H. 9, 206
Cooper, H. M. 205
Cordray, S. S. 61
Cornell, D. 14, 174
Corpus, J. H. 16
correlation 86
correlation coefficient 87, 136
correlational studies 87
Coulter, G. A. 179
covariate 221
credibility 93; *see also* internal validity
Creswell, J. W. 82, 84, 153, 154, 155, 158,
   160, 162
criterion related 144, 145; *see also* capacity
   to succeed 144; *see also* current
   characteristics 145
criterion-referenced tests 135
Cronbach alpha coefficient 137, 139,
   140, 164
Curran, M. 10
Cutuli, J. J. 49

Daley, C. E. 176
Daniel, C. 150
Darvin, J. 160
Davis, A. 56
degrees of freedom (*df*) 222
Dehaene-Lambertz, G. 219
Delice, A. 69
Delpit, L. 44
DeLuca, S. 41
demoralization of competing group 99
Denzin, N. K. 79
Derous, E. 13
descriptive statistics 165
differential selection 95, 106
directional hypothesis 223, 224
discerning consumer i, xi, 4
discrete-point items 140
Distefano, C. 150
Dolan, R. P. 104
Dörnyei, Z. 67
Dowden, A. R. 76, 83

Drechsler, R. 151
Dupoux, E. 141, 196, 197
Durlak, J. A. 14
Dweck, C. S. 13
Dyb, G. 41
Dymnicki, A. B. 14

Edens, K. M. 51
Edwards, M. C. 167
effect size 170, 224
Elbert, C. D. 62
Elias, M. J. 14
Elliot, A. J. 13
Erdem, E. 182
Ertepinar, H. 97
Espin, C. 9
Estacion, A. 41
ethnography 80, 85
experimental design 91, 175; *see also*
    quasi-experimental design
experimental treatment diffusion 98
experimentally accessible population 59
external audits 155, 60
external validity 60
extreme cases 156

F ratio 184, 186, 187, 221, 222
face appearance 144, 146, 147
facets 143; *see also* trait accuracy; utility
Fan, X. 14, 174
Feggins-Azziz, R. 86
Fore, B. 172
Franklin, E. A. 217
Freeman, J. D. 149
Friedman test 180, 184
Fuchs, D. 61
Fuchs, L. S. 61
Fugate, C. M. 68

Gall, J. P. 13, 59, 62, 64, 68, 71, 79, 81, 84,
    92, 93, 104
Gall, M. D. 13, 59, 62, 64, 68, 71, 79, 81,
    84, 92, 93, 104
Garbati, J. 117
Gardner, R. C. 206, 207
Garvis, S. 159
Gasper, J. 41
Geban, O. 97
Geis, I. 189

Gentry, M. 68
Georgas, H. 35
Giere, R. N. 27, 43
Giesen, J. M. 94, 95
Gkouvatzi, A. N. 187
Glaser, R. 12
Glass, G.V. 93
Glenberg, A. M. 101
Goh, C. C. M. 137
Gökalp, M. S. 130, 131, 139
Goldman, S. R. 35
Gonick, L. 189
Greenberg, M. T. 14
Gregory, A. 14, 174, 175
Greiner, K. P. 65
Grissom J. A. 15
grounded theory 78, 85
Guil, R. 55
Guilloteaux, M. J. 67
Gummer, E. S. 26, 27
Gurbuz, R. 182

Hall, M. B. 104
halo-effect 129
Hamamci, Z. 138, 145
Hammond, H. 141, 196
Hansen, L. 225
Hatcher, B. 159
Hawthorne effect 103
Haynes, J. C. 109
Hedges, L. V. 206
Heistad, D. 49
Hendershot, J. 41
Herbers, J. E. 49
Herrera, F. A. 67
Heulskamp, D. 220
Hickey, M. G. 80, 83
Higgins, J. P. T. 206
Hinson, J. 139
Hinz, E. 49
history 93
Hock, R. 35
Holmes, R. M. 89, 102, 118, 119
homogeneity of variance 182
Hong-Nam, K. 60
Hossein, M. 63
Houston, D. 219
Huberman, A. M. 60, 77, 79, 89, 93, 96,
    110, 123, 153, 154, 155, 158, 162, 189

Huff, D. 189
Hughes, A. 142
hypotheses: causal 15; directional 15, 223, 224; nondirectional 15, 16; simple-predictive-relational 15; simple relational 14; theoretical 13, 78

if–then tests 158
Inan, Z. H. 64
inferential statistics 165, 166, 171, 194, 214, 218
informant 117, 123
informant feedback 162
informants access 126
information-rich 66, 157
Ingalls, L. 141, 196
instrumental procedures 129
instrumentation 100, 131
intact groups 92
internal consistency 139, 140; *see also* reliability
internal validity 92
interquartile range 165, 166, 217
interviews: highly structured 120; loosely structured 121; open-structured 121; semi-structured 121
introspection 114
Ipekcioglu, O. 97
Isik-Ercan, Z. 64
item quality 141
Iyengar, S. S. 16

Jadallah, M. 77
Jain, S. 119, 160, 195
Jaisingh, L. J. 189
Jessen, C. M. 65
John Henry effect 98
Johnson, B. 108
Johnson, D. W. 13
Johnson, R. T. 13
Jones, W. A. 62
judge/rater 127

Kablan, Z. 140
Kambas, A. 187
Kao, G. 81, 83, 85, 86
Karabay, A. 146
Kassabgy, N. 114
Kassabgy, O. 114

Katz, J. 221
Kaufman, J. H. 49
Kaya, I. 138, 145
Kayiran, B. K. 146
Ke, F. 67
Kelly, S. 48
Kennedy, T. D. 179
Kevorkian, M. M. 179
Kim, B. 64
Kim, I-H. 133,
Kim, J. K. 180
Kleinert, H. L. 12
Kobayashi, M. 134
Kong, S. C. 51
Koyoma, C. 178
Kremenitzer, J. P. 55
Kuhn, D. 49
Kupczynski, L. 66

Ladson-Billings, G. 44
Lane, D. M. 71
Larke, A. 62
LaVergne, D. D. 62
Lawson, M. A. 56
Leavell, A. G. 60
Lee, B. P. H. 115, 116
Lee, J. 40,
Leech, N. L. 71
Leedy, P. D. 71
Leising, J. G. 167
Lepper, M. R. 16
Leston, J. D. 65
Leung, C-H. 156
Levin, J. R. 101
Levitt, R. 43
Lewis, R. L. 47
Lincoln, Y. S. 79
Lipsey, M. W. 206
longitudinal study 95
Lopes, P. N. 55
Lou, S. J. 183
Loyens, S. M. M. 13
Lucidi, F. 49
Luft, J. A. 184
Lundervold, D. A. 138
Lytle, R. 67

Mackintosh, N. J. 149
Maden, S. 105

Maher, M. J. 60
Mahoney, M. P. 140
Maloney, C. 91
Mandinach, E. B. 26, 27
Mann-Whitney U test 179, 180
Mantis, K. 187
Margiotta, M. 80
Martins, M. A. 128, 129, 137
Masgoret, A. M. 206
Masten, A. S. 49
maturation 95
Maxwell, G. 66
McCormick, C. B. 51
McCrudden, M. T. 82
McDonnall, M. C. 94
McDougall, W. 13
McGrail, E. 56
McKenna, M. K. 158
McKinney, M. 225
McLeskey, J. 40
McMaster, K. 9
McMillan, J. H. 84, 92, 143
McNeil, N. M. 95
mean 96, 165, 166
measurement–treatment interaction 100
median 165, 166
Menhil, V. C. 71
Mertler, C. A. 84, 92
Messick, S. 143
Mestre, J. M. 55
meta-analysis 194, 206
Midgley, C. 13
Miles, M. B. 60, 77, 79, 89, 93, 96, 123,
   153, 154, 155, 158, 162, 189
Millen, J. 158
Minium, E. W. 78
mode 165, 166
Morgan, P. L. 61
Moss, B. 41
Moss, G. 66
Mueller, J. 47
multiple analysis of covariance
   (MANCOVA) 187, 218, 221
multiple regression 176
multiple-treatment interference 104
multivariate analysis of variance
   (MANOVA) 187, 218, 221
multivariate statistics 218, 220

Mundy, M. 66
Munk, D. D. 10

Nash-Ditzel, S. 114, 115
Ndlalane, T. 41
negative evidence 155, 157
negatively skewed distribution 213, 214
Nelson, C. 10
Newgent, 219, 226
Nguyen-Jahiel, 110
Nichols, G. W. 133
Nichols, J. D. 66, 133
Niesz, T. 157
Nieto, S. 76
Nitko, A. J. 136, 141, 142, 145
normal distribution 166, 171, 178,
   212, 213
norm-referenced test 134
Nosek, B. A. 40, 44
Nowak, J. 64
null hypothesis 166–8; see also statistical
   significance , Type I and Type II errors
Numer, J. 159

O'Connor, C. 47
O'Dochartaigh, N. 35
objective 118
objects 46, 47
observational procedures 50, 113, 114
Odinko, M. 62
Ogden, H. 117
Olsen, C. B. 92
Onwuegbuzie, A. J. 71, 172, 176, 177, 224
Opatrny, M. 159
open-form questionnaire items 130
order effect 104
Ormrod, J. E. 71, 77, 95
outliers 156
Ozmen, H. 210

pairwise comparisons 180, 184
parameters 164
Parker, J. 32
participant observers: full-participant
   117, 118; non-participant 188;
   partial-participant 118
participants 56
Patall, E. SA. 9

Patton, M. Q. 64
Paulsel, J. 159
Pearson product moment correlation (PPMC) 174, 175; *see also* Pearson *r*
Pearson *r* 174
peer review 28, 158
Peine, L. J. 78, 83
Pellegrino, J. 12
Periathiruvadi, C. 206
Perry, F. L. 14, 114, 147
Piaget, J. 12, 95
Pillai's trace 221
Pinar, E. 149
Pitney, W. A. 32
Plash, S. 178
Poloni-Staudinger, L. 86
Polonyi, M. A. 172
Porath, M. 221
position paper 26, 27
positively skewed distribution 213, 214, 216
posttest effect 101
Powell, M. L. 219
power 223, 224
practical significance 169; *see also* statistical significance
preliminary sources 21
Pressley, M. 115
pretest effect 100
Price, H. 48
primary research 9, 16, 20
Prior, M. A. 157
prolonged engagement 122, 125
protocol analysis 79, 81
Pumpian, I. 33
Pygmalion effect 102

quasi-experimental design 91, 92; *see also* experimental design

Randall, J. D. 81, 83
random assignment 92
range 166
Ray, B. 179
Red Owl, R. H. 43
regression analysis 175
reliability 136–42, 148: alternate-form 138; inter-rater 137; intra-rater 137; split-half (odd/even) 139; test-retest 138; *see also* internal consistency
reliability coefficients 136, 137; *see also* reliability
replicating findings 159
research types: action 76; applied 76; basic 76; confirmatory 82–4; exploratory 82–4; qualitative 64, 78, 79; quantitative 60, 77, 78
researcher bias 122
researcher effect 102, 125
researcher on persons/events 125
retrospection 114, 115
rich/thick description 160
Rinn, A. N. 206
rival explanations 159, 162
Rivas-Drake, D. 47
Rizzo, O. 144, 145
Roan-Belle, C. 221
Robinson, J. C. 9
Rosenberg, S. 47
Rothstein, H. R. 206
Rott, S. 158
rubric 127, 128
Russom, A. G. 179

Salovey, P. 55
sampling methods: cluster 63; convenience 64, 65; criterion 66; extreme/deviant case 65; homogeneous 68; intensity (expert, critical case) 65; maximum variation 67; multistage 63; proportional/non-proportional stratified random 62; simple random 61; snowball/chain 66; stratified purposeful 65; stratified random 62; systematic random 62; typical case (modal) 67
sampling paradigms: purposeful (nonprobability) sampling paradigm 56; representative (probability) sample paradigm 56, 58; *see also* sampling methods
scale types: continuous 47, 209; discrete 47; interval 210, 211; nominal 209; ordinal 209, 210; ratio 211
Schellinger, K. B. 14
Scholfield, 149

Schumacher, S. 84, 92, 143
secondary sources 9, 25
Sevinc, B. 21
Shabani, H. 63
Shamir, A. S. 63
Shapley, K. 91
Shechtman, Z. 14
Sheehan, D. 91
shot-gun method 87, 180
Siebert, C. J. 220
Silverman, R. 48
Silverman, S. K. 43, 48, 54, 87
Simmons, A. B. 86
Simons, B. C. 65
Singh, L. 80
Skaalvik, E. M. 15
Skiba, R. J. 86, 87
Skinner, B. F. 12
Smith, W. 189
Smithrim, K. 117
Smyth, F. L. 40, 44
Snell, M. 12
Solorzano, R. W. 31
Sotiropoulou-Zormpala, M. 33
Sparks, P. C. 82
Spearman rank correlation (rho) 141;
    see also reliability
Spearman-Brown prophecy formula 148
Spencer, L. 211
spurious relationships 158
standard deviation 166, 217
standard error of measurement (SEM)
    142; see also reliability
standardized test 132, 134, 138, 140
Stanley, J. C. 93
statistical regression 96; a.k.a regression
    toward the mean
statistical significance 166–70; one-tailed
    test 224; two-tailed test 224
statistics: nonparametric statistics 171;
    parametric statistics 171, 182
Stein, M. K. 49
Steinhausen, H-C. 144
Strangman, N. 104
Strom, I. F. 41
Stuart, M. E. 32
subject attrition 61, 96
subjectivity 113, 114, 127, 128, 140

Sucuoglu, B. 149
Supkoff, L. M. 49
surprises 157
Szyfman, A. 211

t test 182: dependent 183, 184;
    independent 182, 184
target population 58–62
Tashakkori, A. 78, 82, 112
Taylor, R. D. 14
Teddlie, C. 71, 78, 82, 112, 149
Tekinarslan, C. 149
theory 16
think-aloud 81; see also protocol analysis
Thoresen, S. 41
time of measurement effect 101
Towles-Reeves, E. A. 12
trait accuracy 143-145
Tran, T. H. 31
transferability 60; see also external validity
treatment fidelity 104
treatment intervention 103
treatment strength–time interaction 105
triangulation 115, 155, 156
Trochim, W. M. 71
Tseng, K-H. 183
Turner, W. G. 159
Turney, K. 81, 83, 85, 86
Tyler, K. 221
Type I error 168, 169; see also statistical
    significance; null hypothesis
Type II error 168, 169, 223
Tze, P. 103, 104

Umedo, Y. 225
univariate statistics 185, 218
Upitis, R. 117, 118, 119, 121
Urdan, T. C. 13
utility 144: diagnostic 144; predictive
    145, 147
Uttal, D. H. 95

Valentine, J. C. 206
validity 142–8; as construct 143; as
    external 60, 92, 93; as internal 74, 92,
    93, 102, 106; see also credibility
variable types: correlational 48; dependent
    48, 49, 88–93; descriptive 48;

extraneous 50, 61; independent 48,
    88–91; moderating 49; nested 219
variance 166, 217; *see also* interquartile
    range; range; standard deviation
volunteers 68
Vurdien, R. 47
Vygotsky, L. S. 12, 77

Wallinger, L. M. 96, 97
Walraven, A. 35
Wanner, G. 211
weighting the evidence 123
Weissberg, R. P. 14
Weitzman, E. A. 189
Wentzel-Larsen, T. 41
West-Olatunji, C. 40
Wijnia, L. 13
Wilcoxon matched pairs signed
    rank test 179
Wilcoxon T test 179, 180, 182, 184
Wilke's lambda 221
Williams, J. 62

Williams, S. D. 159
Williamson, P. 40
Wilson, D. B. 206
Winter, G. 143, 144
Wirkala, C. 49
Wolcott, H. E. 79, 154
Wu, H. 88
Wyss, V. L. 220

Xu, J. 88

Yaman, M. A. 14
Yeung, A. S. W. 178
Yigit, N. 21
Young, R. B. 124, 167
Yu, F. 71, 149
Yu, J. H. 180

Zehr, H. 66
Zeichner, K. M. 44
Zentall, S. S. 68
Zins, J. E. 14